VOLUME 1

HOLY LOVE: A WESLEYAN SYSTEMATIC THEOLOGY

Christology as Theology

John N. Oswalt, senior editor
Christianne Albertson & Matt Ayars, associate editors

Francis Asbury Press
Wilmore, Kentucky

Copyright © 2024 Francis Asbury Society. All rights reserved. No part of this book may be photocopied, scanned, emailed, placed on the Internet, or otherwise reproduced or transmitted in any form or by any means, electronic or mechanical, or used in any information storage and retrieval system per United States copyright law unless expressly consented to by the copyright holder in writing.

Cover design by D. Curtis Hale.

Published by The Francis Asbury Society
ISBN 978-0-915143-59-7
Printed in the United States of America

To order this book, go to www.francisasburysociety.com or contact:

The Francis Asbury Society
PO Box 7
Wilmore, KY 40390–0007
859–858–4222
800–530–5673
fas@francisasburysociety.com

Unless otherwise indicated, all Scripture quotations are from the Holy Bible, New International Version®, NIV® Copyright ©1973, 1978, 1984, 2011 by Biblica, Inc.® Used by permission. All rights reserved worldwide.

Scripture quotations marked "ESV" are from The Holy Bible, English Standard Version. ESV® Text Edition: 2016. Copyright © 2001 by Crossway Bibles, a publishing ministry of Good News Publishers.

Scripture quotations marked "KJV" are taken from the Holy Bible, King James Version (Public Domain).

Scripture quotations marked "NLT" are taken from the Holy Bible, New Living Translation, copyright © 1996, 2004, 2015 by Tyndale House Foundation. Used by permission of Tyndale House Publishers, Inc., Carol Stream, Illinois 60188. All rights reserved.

VOLUME 1

HOLY LOVE: A WESLEYAN SYSTEMATIC THEOLOGY

Christology
as
Theology

John N. Oswalt, senior editor
Christianne Albertson & Matt Ayars, associate editors

Contents

Foreword

Ronald E. Smith, PhD

THE PURPOSE OF THIS foreword is to introduce its readers to this collaborative project in systematic theology, touching upon it origins and briefly characterizing its contributors.[1] The imagery of Isaiah 35 resonates in our hearts as the prophet portrays the covenant people as those participating on a journey traversing a road called the "highway of holiness." This work represents a journey of nearly a quarter century of collaboration and cooperation in order to bring forth this living document of systematic theology. What a journey! Tolkien was enthralled with the new dimensions of life that were possible if one was ready to engage. His well-known poem elucidated that life's greatest journey began from one's front door:

> *The Road goes ever on and on*
> *Down from the door where it began.*
> *Now far ahead the Road has gone,*
> *And I must follow, if I can,*

---

1. Besides Dr. Smith, who wrote this Foreword, others who were valued "coadjutors" in the process, though they did not write a chapter or section, were Dr. Paul Blair, Dr. Harold Burgess, Mr. Burt Luce, and Dr. Paul Vincent. It was through the generosity of Mr. Luce and others that the project was brought to completion. For those interested in our process, the author wrote a first draft, which was submitted to the entire group for written suggestions. The resulting second draft was discussed in an extended group meeting, which resulted in a third, and hopefully, final draft. In some cases, however, there were more than three drafts before the final version was complete.

Pursuing it with weary feet,
Until it joins some larger way
Where many paths and errands meet.
And whither then? I cannot say.

Tolkien wanted everyone to know the road that, when traveled, could lead to life's greatest enterprise. And that is the very same road Isaiah saw—the highway of holiness. We, the fellowship who have produced this series, can testify that our feet have been on a Kingdom road. We have attempted to use our mortal lips to articulate how the immortal God could be a Lamb who would rescue the souls of men. Underneath our "comings and goings" is the mark of a Gracious Redeemer who orders the steps of the righteous and directs their paths. The path of our initiative found its larger way in conversation with a variety of persons who wanted to see their most sacred beliefs regarding Christian holiness articulated so that another generation could also "taste and see" these great truths. To them we are eternally indebted. In the Providence of God, it was they who reached out to Dr. Dennis F. Kinlaw who in turn mobilized a group of scholars who sought to make a fresh statement about the Author and Finisher of our faith. The result is, understandably, that this collective work clearly bears the "fingerprint" of Kinlaw. We gladly own that and are honored to have been fellow sojourners on this road at his direction and leadership. Our deepest prayers are that, now in glory, Dr. Kinlaw will see the "travail of his soul and be satisfied."

To own Dr. Kinlaw as our leader in writing a systematic theology was to own his many predilections. As one theologically formed by the Wesleyan holiness tradition, Kinlaw felt that the tone of our work should reflect the highest commitment to the integrity of Scripture. The Scriptures are revered as trustworthy in all that pertains to matters of faith, practice, and revelation of God. Second, Dr. Kinlaw felt that orthodoxy and orthopraxy ought always to be held concomitantly. Our writers, while holding the highest academic credentials for higher education, are also practitioners. They have been preachers, pastors, evangelists, and missionaries in addition to being classroom professors. One of the many "Kinlaw-isms" we heard him often articulate was, "If you love Him, you find joy in walking by grace with Him for the redemption of the world." He taught that the sanctifying work of God's Spirit freed one from self-reference to live with a Kingdom agenda. Third, Dennis Kinlaw exuded a life commitment to the Asbury institutions in Wilmore, Kentucky—Asbury College (now University) and Asbury Theological Seminary where he taught Old Testament, later crossing the street and becoming president of Asbury College. All the writers in this series either have had or currently have a direct relationship with the Asbury institutions. Finally, Dr. Kinlaw founded the Francis Asbury Society as a group of believers committed to "receiving, modeling, and sharing the transforming love of God for the redemption of the world." This was to be pursued through evangelism, exponential discipleship, and education. It was Kinlaw's desire that all participants in this systematic theology initiative would be willing adherents to this Society in the body of Christ, with its major emphasis on the sanctifying work in the atonement. Kinlaw wrote:

> The purpose of the Francis Asbury Society is to spread the message of Scriptural holiness to the ends of the earth in accordance with the Great Commission. Jesus said that His disciples were to be the salt of the earth. They were, through His grace in them, to be the counterforce to the corruption that is perpetually at work in our fallen world. The Church is never stronger, no person is ever happier, and no Society ever healthier than they are holy. God in Christ is in the business of drawing to Himself a people whom He, through His Spirit, can renew in His own holy image. The members of this Society, committed to the inerrancy of the Scriptures of the Old and New Testaments and the power of the Spirit of God, through Christ, to regenerate and sanctify wholly the human heart, give themselves to do what they can that all come to know Christ, be confirmed in Christian discipleship that produces character

and integrity, and enjoy the freedom and power that comes to those who are fully sanctified by His cleansing Spirit. To this we commit ourselves.

Dr. Kinlaw expressed the convictions just articulated in his book *Let's Start with Jesus*. Those who are interested in pursuing further the foundational thinking underlying this series will find this book very helpful.[2] In his work, Dr. Kinlaw challenged those systematicians who habitually make redeemed Adam the picture of personhood in the Christian system. He strongly advocated that the Incarnate Christ, "perfect Adam," is the consummate picture and norm for persons. Kinlaw's analogy was that one doesn't go to the junkyard to understand what a car is supposed to be but rather the showroom. In the same sense, one should not go to Adam, especially fallen Adam, as the model for personhood but Jesus. Subtle though it may be, when Christ is the direct object as the norm for personhood rather than redeemed Adam, then Christ rightfully remains the exclusive exemplary norm for personhood. In his two-volume work on ethics and biblical theology, Dr. Ben Witherington supports Kinlaw's assertion):

> In a small and helpful theological study, Dennis Kinlaw suggests *Let's Start with Jesus*. I like this line of thinking . . . . The story of Jesus is the climax of the biblical narrative . . . . From a theological and ethical point of view. . . Kinlaw is quite right. If we are to understand God and the divine blueprint for humankind, we need to begin where the light is brightest and the insights into divine character are clearest.[3]

Nowhere are these ideas more exhaustively researched and reported than in Dr. M. William Ury's published dissertation *Trinitarian Personhood*. Ury's foundational work served as an epistemology for Kinlaw's anthropological deliberations. Derived from their work is the central axiom that the Social Trinity is the meta-

---

2. A summary of the book in provided in Appendix A on page.
3. Witherington, *The Indelible Image*, 1:25–26.

HOLY LOVE: A WESLEYAN THEOLOGY

physical reality for humanity's relational existence. No single truth raises a sharper polemic with post-modern existential realities than this. The all-too-common cultural adage, "follow the science," offered today reveals an existentialism that lacks the metaphysical foundations of thought offered in this work. Although in recent years there has been a swing away from the emphasis on the Social Trinity found in the works of Gunton and Torrance, that understanding must not be lost for our present day.

Also growing out of Ury's thesis is the premise that has been used in this work to define holiness: *Holiness is the self-giving love of God, the Holy One.* As the Holy One shares his love with us, we can be like him. This is the gracious reality that was embraced by John Wesley. He believed it to be the way we respond to God:

> Let the Spirit return to God who gave it, with the whole train of its affections. . . . Let it be *continually* offered up to God through Christ, in flames of holy love. . . . His throne will he not divide with another. He will reign without a rival. . . . Be no design, no desire admitted there but what has him for its ultimate object.[4]

We see here, through Wesley, that the self-giving love of God to humanity may, through grace, be reciprocated in our self-giving love to God, which because of him also will be holy. This establishes the norm for human relationships. As the Apostle Peter has said, we are to be holy as God is holy.

If the truth has been told that Dennis F. Kinlaw's fingerprint is on our work, then it is also true that in these last days, months, and years, the hand of Dr. John N. Oswalt marks the work. Oswalt, who wrote material on hamartiology and cosmology, assumed the reins as senior editor when the whole project was in "the wilderness" state. His strength, determination, and ultimately his discipline delivered this work to its day for publication. Oswalt's definitive work, *Called to be Holy*, has influenced this project. His Old Testament scholar-

---

4. Wesley, *BE Works*, 13:139.

ship over his fifty-plus-year illustrious career has certainly marked the landscape of biblical studies. Oswalt was especially helped by Dr. Kinlaw's granddaughter and trusted scribe, Mrs. Christiane "Cricket" Albertson. Albertson is Kinlaw's literary executor and has authored and edited several books relating to his work. She is especially influential through her work with Titus Women, a ministry of the Francis Asbury Society.

Dr. Gareth Lee Cockerill, author of an acclaimed commentary on Hebrews in the New International Bible Commentary series, spent his forty years at Wesley Biblical Seminary in Jackson, Mississippi, where he taught New Testament. He has indelibly marked the educational world by his extra-mile commitment to students, both in moving them to the highest levels of scholarship and, equally importantly, through shaping students in the best tenets of spiritual formation. Cockerill authored the section on bibliology.

Dr. Allan Coppedge, who authored the chapters on theology and soteriology, served his entire career at Asbury Theological Seminary, closing that career as Beeson Professor of Christian Theology. Throughout his tenure he was deeply committed to Wesleyan small-group discipleship. He founded the Barnabas Foundation as a group practicing his principles of discipleship. A major denominational leader recently shared that his life was most impacted in seminary by the spiritually formative experiences he shared with Coppedge in the Barnabas Foundation. Coppedge, in addition to his books, *John Wesley in Theological Debate*, *Portraits of God*, and *The God Who Is Triune*, authored *The Biblical Principles of Discipleship*.

Dr. Steve Blakemore is a PhD in philosophy from the University of Tennessee. He currently serves as professor of Christian Thought at Wesley Biblical Seminary. Blakemore is a gifted man in many ways, most especially as a philosophical theologian. He is a vocal recording artist, an athlete, a dynamic churchman, and a rare individual in the classroom. His students believe his ability to teach philosophy for understanding theology is incomparable. Blakemore's cutting-edge work on the seventeenth-century Dutch Sephardi Rationalist philosopher Baruch Spinoza will be a major contribution to the philosophical theological discipline, particularly as it relates to the work of Thomas Aquinas. In our work, Blakemore writes on ecclesiology, a subject on which he has thought profoundly.

Dr. Christopher T. Bounds, author of the chapter on eschatology, is a pastor, missiologist, and theologian. He is a graduate of the Casperson School for Graduate Studies and wrote his dissertation on the doctrine of Christian Perfection among the Apostolic Fathers under the supervision of the noted theologian, Dr. Thomas Oden. Bounds serves on the board of One Mission Society, has served on the board of trustees at Asbury University, and is the current chair of the board of directors of the Francis Asbury Society. Bounds has published works on Augustine and Pelagianism/Semi Pelagianism, and Tertullian, as well as on the Apostle's Creed and its use in the historic Church. Bounds also has written *unHoliness*, on the doctrine of holiness as it may be practically lived in everyday life.

Dr. Matt Ayars is an Old Testament scholar with a special interest in the Psalms. He is a past president of Wesley Biblical Seminary and currently serves as a pastor. Ayars and his wife, Stacie, served several years with One Mission Society as missionaries to Haiti. While serving in Haiti, Ayars was president of Emmaus Biblical Seminary. His prominent leadership in the evangelical world has made him a contributing author, a distinguished platform speaker, and a prolific lecturer across the spectrum of the Church. Ayars, who wrote the chapter on pneumatology, came lately to the group but has made a fine contribution as a result of his expertise as an exegete of God's Word and his practical experience in life.

Dr. Tom McCall, distinguished chair of systematic theology at Asbury Theological Seminary, and author of several important books, among which is *Forsaken*, a study of Jesus' cry of dereliction, wrote the material on perseverance. Then, near the end of the project Dr. McCall came forward to provide the introduction, which situates our effort in the contemporary world of trinitarian scholarship. He shows how, although the social trinitarianism which provided the initial foundation of our thinking has come to be sharply challenged, it still has a relevance that must not be lost.

Because the direct object of the work is the Ever Present "I AM," we bring our work to the table, trusting that it has a continuing relevance and offering it to him as our gift of love. Our prayer is that the self-giving love of God will be shed abroad in the hearts of all who read. Søren Kierkegaard speaks for us as we present this work: "When one has once fully entered the realm of love, the world—no matter how imperfect—becomes rich and beautiful, it consists solely of opportunities for love."

> Submitted with profound love and respect,
> Ronald E. Smith, PhD
> President, Ohio Christian University

A Trinitarian Theology of Holiness

Thomas McCall, PhD

EDITOR'S NOTE: When this project began, now some twenty years ago, the group was immediately captured by the idea that the work needed to have its center in the Trinity. Dr. Dennis F. Kinlaw stressed to us what was to become the thesis of his book, *Let's Start with Jesus*, namely, that the Christian concept of God is necessarily shaped by the way in which the Incarnation of Christ, and then the coming of the Holy Spirit which that Incarnation makes possible expands and interprets the Old Testament's Yahweh. In short, the Christian concept of God is distinctly characterized by multiplicity in unity, and unity in multiplicity. Beyond this, if we were to maintain—as we do—that the essence of God's otherness, his transcendence, is love, then we must continually hearken back to the Trinitarian understanding that the Father, Son, and Spirit exist together in a relationship of self-giving, self-denying love. But then it must be asked whether taking this approach weds us to one theory of the Trinity, namely, what is known as "Social Trinitarianism." Dr. Thomas McCall explains that this is not the case.

A VISION OF GOD AND HUMANITY

The doctrine of the Trinity is sometimes taken to be an irrelevant or even unbiblical and unnecessary add-on to Christian doctrine. It is true that there is no single biblical "proof-text" for the doctrine; there is no "Trinity verse" in Scripture. But the doctrine is grounded in the revelation of God in Jesus Christ, and it can be seen as the whole teaching of Scripture. To briefly summarize, it is what you get when you hold together the biblical commitment to monotheism along with the biblical witness to the fully personal distinction of the persons called "Father," "Son," and "Holy Spirit" and the scriptural witness to the full divinity of the Father, Son, and Holy Spirit. Taken together, the Trinitarian doctrine encapsulated in the ecumenical creeds of the Christian faith teaches us that there is only one God; that the Father, Son, and Holy Spirit are fully and equally divine; and that the Father, Son, and Holy Spirit are distinct persons. While this is certainly mysterious, it is not (on closer analysis) logically contradictory.[1]

What does this doctrine have to do with holy love? In a word, everything. For the Christian doctrine of God, the inner life of the triune God is a life of holy love shared between the divine persons; Father, Son, and Holy Spirit love one another with the purest and strongest love. Love is *essential* to God; God could not be God without it; God could not so much as exist without it. God does not *need* the creation of an external cosmos to be love, for God as Trinity just *is* love. God is primordially loving, necessarily love, completely and utterly and holy loving. Indeed, we can say with the Apostle John that God simply *is* love, for the life of the triune God is a life of holy love given and received among the three divine persons.

---

1. For a sampling of such closer analysis, see McCall and Rea, eds., *Philosophical and Theological Essays on the Trinity* (2009).

As C. S. Lewis notes, when we think about the Trinity, "the most important thing to know is that it is a relationship of love."[2] Lewis observes that many people are very quick to say that "God is love," but he also points out that "they seem not to notice that the words 'God is love' have no real meaning unless God contains at least two persons," for "love is something that one person has for another person."[3] What Christians mean is markedly different than the common cliché, for what Christian theology means by the claim is that "the living, dynamic activity is not a static thing—not even a person—but a dynamic, pulsating activity, a life, almost a kind of drama... if you will not think me irreverent, a kind of dance."[4] The love of God is, as the medieval theologian Richard of St. Victor put it, entirely pure and perfect, and it is essential to God. It just is God's life, and there is "nothing better" and "nothing greater." Within the simplicity of the divine life, being is identical to loving, and the love that just *is* the divine life is "so great that there cannot be a greater love and so excellent that there cannot be a better love."[5]

The triune God has made humans so that they might know that holy love. They are made so that they might be drawn into the very life of the triune God—so that they too might take their place within the mutual love of the Father, Son, and Holy Spirit. How does that happen? How do finite creatures enjoy communion with the triune God—how do perverted and twisted sinners come to give and receive the holy love of the Trinity? That is the question that motivates this project in systematic theology, and the answer to that question is what fills these volumes.

---

2. Lewis, *Mere Christianity*, 135.

3. Lewis, *Mere Christianity*, 135–36.

4. Lewis, *Mere Christianity*, 136. Those tempted to think that Lewis indeed is being irreverent should be reminded that historic Christian theology has affirmed the doctrine of "perichoresis."

5. Richard of St. Victor, *De Trinitate* in *Trinity and Creation*, 313; 310.

PROBLEMS AND PROSPECTS
FOR OUR PROJECT

Some theologians might immediately raise objections and protest that we are working from a very flawed presumption. They might argue that we are starting from a set of convictions about Trinitarian theology that are deeply mistaken and perhaps even heretical. For we are convinced that mutual holy love is essential to the intra-Trinitarian life of God.

Not long ago, something called "Social Trinitarianism" was popular in theology. While not always clearly defined or sharply demarcated, in general it emphasized the intra-Trinitarian love and relationality of God and sought to apply that Trinitarian theology to all areas of Christian life and thought. Often, its proponents rejected "Latin" or "Western" theology as tending toward unitarianism rather than being sufficiently Trinitarian; accordingly, the defenders of the "Social" doctrine worked to retrieve "Greek" and especially "Cappadocian" theology for contemporary theology. In addition, the defenders of Social Trinitarianism were energized about "applying" the doctrine to such areas as theological anthropology, ecclesiology, and ethics. It was a popular and powerful movement, and many leading theologians were committed to it.[6]

Today things are very different. Indeed, there is a massive backlash against not only Social Trinitarianism but also everything that resembles it. Thus Stephen R. Holmes likens love shared between and among the divine persons to "'whispering sweet nothings' between lovers," as in a "cliche of poorly written romance novels."[7] Katherine Sonderegger denies that divine love is relational or directed at other persons; to the contrary, it is actually "object-less."[8] Craig Carter says that doctrines of the Trinity that

---

6. E.g., Moltmann, Gunton, the Torrances, et al.
7. Holmes, "Response to McCall," 139.
8. Sonderegger, *Systematic Theology*, 1:469–90.

affirm divine love between the persons are "deviating from Nicene orthodoxy."[9] Vincent Brummer denounces mutual love between the persons on the grounds that such doctrines "cannot do justice to the unity between the persons of the Trinity."[10] The criticisms of the Social Trinitarian movement are centered around three basic charges, all of which are very serious. First, Social Trinitarianism is said to be deeply and fatally flawed from the perspective of historical theology. Critics who are specialists in patristic studies argue that the neat and easy stereotype of "East vs. West" is mistaken; Gregory of Nazianzus and Basil of Caesarea believe in divine simplicity as much as Augustine, and it simply is not right to say that "the West" (or "the Latin tradition") is really unitarian rather than Trinitarian.[11] Second, Social Trinitarianism is said to be a version of tritheism rather than truly monotheistic.[12] Third, Social Trinitarianism is charged with importing human notions of "community" into the divine life and is thus a particularly wrongheaded example of "projectionism."[13] In other words, the worry is that Ludwig Feuerbach might have been right after all when he said that belief in God was mere projection of human ideals onto a "being" who would then license those human ideals.

So what do we say in response to such criticisms? How does our project stand in relation to Social Trinitarianism? Is ours a "social" doctrine—and subject to the criticisms that are commonly taken to be so devastating? While a full response is beyond the scope of this introduction (and in some sense is contained in the overall project— the proof is in the pudding), we can make the following points at the outset. First, while we readily admit that some statements of Social Trinitarianism have been built upon problematic readings of the Christian tradition, nothing in our account presupposes or

---

9. Carter, *Contemplating God with the Great Tradition*, 2.
10. Brummer, *The Model of Love*, 238.
11. E.g. Ayres, Barnes, et al.
12. E.g., Leftow, Ward.
13. e.g., Kilby.

relies upon such historiography. We do not need to pit the "East" against the "West" or "the Cappadocians" against Augustine—nor do we wish to do so. But commitment to an improved understanding of the history of doctrine does nothing to undermine our project. To the contrary, it turns out that a better understanding of the history of doctrine actually supports our position: affirmations of mutual holy love within the Trinity are to be found throughout the mainstream Latin tradition. Second, we are alert to the concerns about projectionism, and we take the criticisms to be timely and helpful. At the same time, however, we are committed to following the full biblical teaching where it does connect the doctrine of the Trinity to broader areas of Christian life and thought, and we are willing to explore the implications of the doctrine. Third, we note again the ambiguity surrounding the term "Social Trinitarianism," and we note further that we have no commitments to the term as a label.[14] We *are* committed to the belief that mutual holy love is shared between and among the Father, Son, and Holy Spirit, for we are convinced that the life of the Trinity is a life of holy love. And we are committed to this belief for good reason: the love of the eternal Father for the eternal Son is revealed explicitly in Holy Scripture and affirmed all across the historic theological tradition. Indeed, this core conviction is shared across traditional lines—it is not merely an "Eastern" or "Cappadocian" anomaly but instead is held by such eminent "Latin" or "Western" as Augustine, Anselm, Alexander of Hales, Richard of St. Victor, Thomas Aquinas, Bonaventure, Henry of Ghent, John Duns Scotus, Johann Gerhard, Francis Turretin, Petrus van Mastricht, and Amandus Polanus. If this is tritheism, then a vast host of theologians in the Orthodox, Roman Catholic, and Protestant traditions alike will qualify as tritheists.[15]

---

14. For discussion and analysis of various ways that the term "Social Trinitarianism" is used (and misused), see McCall, *Analytic Christology and the Theological Interpretation of the New Testament*, 137–76.

15. For substantiation of this claim, see McCall, "What's Not to Love?" *International Journal of Systematic Theology*, 610–30.

But we do not think that there is good reason to think of such theology as tritheism anyway; to the contrary, it is simply Trinitarian monotheism.

MOVING FORWARD

The God of the Christian faith—the God revealed by Jesus Christ—is the triune God. The God of the Christian faith is the God whose own life is a life of holy love, the God whose very essence is the holy love given and received among the Father, the Son, and the Holy Spirit. This triune God has made creatures in his image, and he has made these creatures so that they may know and share that holy love. When these creatures reject that love in rebellion and bring ruin upon themselves, this God does not stand aloof but instead becomes incarnate as Jesus Christ and gives himself away for his enemies. This God brings salvation—he brings not only hope but healing, not only a change of legal status but a radical renovation of perverted human nature, not only justification but sanctification and glorification.

This is the theological vision that motivates the current project. The respective contributors are not unanimously agreed on every statement, but the grand theological vision is shared by all. And it is one that is grand indeed—breathtaking in scope and astounding in depth. God so loved the world—because God *is* love.

The Implications of the Personhood of Christ

Dennis F. Kinlaw, PhD

THERE IS A CERTAIN presumption among humans when it comes to the field of religion. We cannot seem to leave the subject alone and feel we must speak on it regardless of competence or experience; witness the near universality of religion as a human expression across the millennia of human existence. That is why some have described humanity as the religious animal. Even when one finds that small minority in the course of human history who want to deny it all, one finds a certain religious fervor in the very denial. Other possible nonentities do not seem to produce such vigorous protestations. Yet, even the irreligious among us often seem religious in their inability to leave it alone. Truth in this area seems so important that we, even if we believe no truth exists here, seem to feel a moral obligation in this supposedly amoral world to prove the truth of the fact that there is no truth here.

The presumptuousness seems even more obvious when we stop to think of the nature of the subject. It is commonly accepted in our Western heritage that a whole set of adjectives is necessary when we speak of God, gods, or the divine. These are words that have no correspondence to human experience. Words like infinite, eternal, immutable, omnipotent, omniscient, omnipresent, and ultimate come to mind. Each of these represents something that is really beyond the experience of any of us. How can one speak of that which he has never known? Yet we who live in a world of sense (the five senses), whose very vocabulary is determined by either the affirmation or denial of something in that world of sense, speak of that which transcends our senses. And we somehow feel it must. Everyone does it.

In this, though, the Christian stands in a different position. One may reject the Christian's claims, but one must concede that the Christian's claims are different. The Christian joins in acknowledgment that it is presumptuous for us to speak with any dogmatism about the world beyond sight and sound and touch. None of us has been there to return and report our findings. The Christian believes though that when we could not go there, that world beyond came to us in time and space in a form that could be seen, heard, and touched. That coming was so specific, so real, and so full of meaning that the Christian insists that this coming is the very key to the understanding—the proper understanding—of this world in which we live. The Christian may even call your attention to the fact that those who deny all of this still date their own births; in fact they date everything, by this very event. They note that the birth of Jesus Christ is used as the dividing point for human history.

But who was this Jesus? His impact on our world has been significant. In fact, no other person in human history comes close to him in reverberations caused by his coming. Visit the art museums of the world, especially those in the Western world, or the concert stage with a view to its musical repertoire, or the libraries of the world, or the Internet, or even the holidays of the world, and one will find Jesus inescapable. But who was he?

Those who knew him best and loved him most have left for us a witness. It is found in the pages of the New Testament, written by people whom tradition insists knew him personally and intimately.

They have recorded and left for us the accounts of what they insist came from his own lips or that which they personally observed about him while with him. Most people who give serious time to the study and consideration of these texts seem to feel that they bear marks of authenticity and intellectual integrity supportive of the claims that they make. These texts tell us that Jesus Christ was more than a man. In fact, they tell us that he lived before he was born, that he actually came from that world beyond our reach and of which we feel that we must speak. But when we speak, we speak from our ignorance. He, the Christian insists, speaks with authority because he came to us from that very world. More, the Christian says his reason for coming was, among other things, to clear our confusion and give us certainty where before we could only project our imaginations, fears, and hopes. But we are getting ahead of our story. What do we really know about Jesus?

Jesus was a Jew who lived in what we know today as Israel and Jordan in the first three decades of this era which marks its beginning from his birth. He was born during the reign of the Emperor Augustus (23 BC–AD 14). He carried out his ministry during the reign of Tiberius Caesar (AD 14–37) while Herod was tetrarch in Galilee (4 BC–AD 39). His death occurred under the procuratorship of the Roman Pilate apparently about AD 30. He was one of us, a figure in history, a man among men. That his life and teachings were remarkable seems clear. More unusual, though, were his claims about his relationship with God, the God of Abraham, Isaac, and of Israel, the God of Moses, the God of the Jews. And the God of the Jews was different.

The particularly unique thing about Israel's God was his relationship to the creation, to the cosmos. In contrast to the gods of the peoples around Israel, the Jewish God was not a part of nature. He was not a natural force, nor was he nature itself. In fact, he had no relationship to the creation except that which came through its origination. He was its creator, but this was not in the manner in

HOLY LOVE: A WESLEYAN THEOLOGY

which other people spoke of their gods as creators. His relationship was not that of natural cause to an effect. He was not like Aristotle's First Cause or Prime Mover. His relationship was one of freedom and transcendence. He used no preexisting matter to create. He simply spoke and things originated from his Word. He was not in any way dependent upon his creation. He lived without the creation before he created it. It was not necessary to either his existence or his well-being. He simply chose in freedom and in love to create whatever existed. This meant that all of the other forces that other people worshipped and called divine were simply the result of Israel's God's creative Word. Such thinking about the divine was unknown anywhere in the world except among the descendants of Abraham and Moses.

Israel's God was unlike any of the other gods of the world. The devout Jew believed that, in that transcendent realm that man cannot see, touch, or measure, their God reigned alone. The greatest of all sins would be to assume another beside him. This was what made Jesus such a problem, for he claimed such an intimate relationship with God that he seemed to violate the Jew's most sacred dogma.

Jesus called him Father and spoke of himself as Son, and there was an absoluteness about the way that he used the terms that created problems. His use of the term "Father" was primarily when he was actually speaking to God in prayer or when he was speaking of his personal relationship to God. His use of the simple word "Son" came most often when he was speaking of his private and individual relationship to Israel's Holy One. Clearly, he felt his relationship to God was completely unlike that of anyone else.

The Jews of Jesus' day were familiar with the use of the term "Father" for their God. However, it was used only in relation to their understanding of their election as the chosen people by God. The people of Israel could be called God's son (Ex. 3:21–23; Jer. 3:4, 31:19), God's firstborn. The king of Israel, as the representative of Israel before God, could be called God's son (2 Sam. 7:14, Ps. 89:26–27). But the ordinary Jew did not dare to feel such personal intimacy. Jesus' use of the term "Father" and the references to himself as the "Son" were so offensive to the Jewish leadership that they felt he was blaspheming. He actually seemed to them to be making himself equal to God. This placed on them the clear obligation to see that he was killed (John 54:16–18).

Jesus' response was the beginning of a series of passages in John's Gospel where he developed the concepts of his "sentness" from the Father and of his oneness with the Father. Two Greek words are used for "sent" in the Gospel, and they occur some forty times in John. The syntax in Greek is different from that in English, but the expression in Greek literally reads "the-sending-me-Father" and intimates both the relationship and Jesus' understanding of his mission. The identification in origin and the relationship was so close that a chastened disciple, Thomas, after the resurrection could speak the conclusion of the Gospel and of all of those who knew him best: "My Lord and my God" (John 20:28). Needless to say, this raised problems even in the minds of his most devoted disciples for the firmest affirmation of their Jewish faith was found in the Shema: "Hear, O Israel. The LORD our God is one LORD" (Deut. 6:4 KJV).

But what is the understanding of God that was coming to these friends of Jesus? There were many aspects to it, but perhaps the most crucial one of all was associated with that new name that Jesus had given them for God. It was "Father," and, for his friends, that was a surprise.

For those of us who have twenty centuries of Christian worship and history behind us this may seem strange. But when Jesus said to his disciples, "When you pray, say 'Our Father, who art in heaven,'" he opened a new world of thinking about and relating to God. It is difficult for us to imagine the questions that must have flooded their minds.

It was commonplace for the Jew to think of heaven as the site of God's eternal court where he reigned in power and authority. It was in the royal court that justice would ultimately settle every question. So the Jew naturally thought of God as the king of all the earth. Had not Isaiah pictured him as seated on his throne, high and lifted up, with the seraphim covering their faces and feet in awful reverence as they sang his praises? The prophet was smitten with guilt and dismay because, as he said, "mine eyes have seen the King, the Lord of hosts" (Isa. 6:5 KJV).

The Psalmist also had written about that court:

> *I lift up my eyes to you, to you whose throne is in heaven.*
> *As the eyes of the slaves look to the hand of their master, as the*
> *eyes of a female slave look to the hand of her mistress,*
> *so our eyes look to the Lord our God, till he*
> *shows us mercy. (Ps. 123:1–2 NIV)*

Now, however, a whole new set of associations is being suggested. They are neither royal nor legal. They are those of the hearth, the family table, those of the home. The atmosphere of the one is very different in terms of access, acceptance, belonging, and response. We are not now dealing with slaves before their master or servant girls before a mistress. Social distance and consciousness of class and station are replaced by intimacy, and appropriate fear with respectful affection. Paul picks up this difference as he speaks in Romans 8 of the capstone of the work of the Holy Spirit in the believer's heart. The Christian's first and highest thought about God is not "My Lord" or "O King." Rather, it is "Abba! Father!" and it is that because he has heard a divine voice within that said: "My child!" He knows that he is a citizen of God's kingdom. What thrills his heart and is finally more ultimate is the fact that he himself has become a member of the very family of God itself.

It is important here that we realize that the family language can be used in two different ways. When it is used of Jesus and his relationship to his Father, the meanings are not the same as when

Paul uses the same words about us and our relationship to God. We must be able to distinguish between what is metaphor and what is not. Perhaps this can best be understood with the use of the words *ontological* and *analogical*. When the terms are used of Jesus and the Father, they are speaking of the very being, the ontology, of both Jesus and the Father. They both have the same divine nature. Jesus is the only-begotten Son. His position is unique in that he shares with the Father the same divine nature.

With us, that language is used only analogically. The life of God enters us, and we are called his children, but we are still creatures, and the line between creator and creature is one we can never cross. In fact, it is never crossed but once. That was in Christ's Incarnation, when the eternal Son was joined with Jesus, the son of Mary, and two became one person, Jesus Christ, the God-man. So the language when used of Jesus and the Father is not analogical but ontological and refers to a common essence.

This obvious preference for family language by Jesus and the early church did not mean for a second that the earliest Christians ceased to think of God as sovereign and ruler of earth and heaven. Jesus had told them, "The Father loves the Son and has placed everything in his hands" (John 3:35). This they understood as authority over all people (John 17:2). So when he sent out his disciples after the resurrection to carry the story of him to the entire world, he could say, "All authority in heaven and on earth has been given to me" (Matt. 28:18). Paul picks this theme up in 1 Corinthians 15 and affirms that Christ will destroy "all dominion, authority and power" (v. 24), even death itself, and will reign without rival over all. But Paul is very clear. The final word is not about sovereignty. Christ's authority and power are given to him by the Father and, in the end, Christ will render up that dominion to the Father from whom it came (see 1 Cor. 15:24). The ultimate categories are neither political nor juridical but familial. The legal and the political will pass. The family relationship will endure.

A very significant theological shift is occurring here. One wonders how quickly and how much Christ's disciples understood of what Jesus was really saying. Time is always necessary when we find the basic paradigm with which we conceive something being challenged. It takes time to make the mental shift. In this, Jesus was forcing a remarkable paradigmatic change. The theologians came to think of this as an ontological one because what Jesus was speaking about was not what God *does* but who he *is*. The titles of King and Judge speak of roles that God plays in his relations with his creation. They are applicable to God before time and history. When there was nothing but God alone, before he spoke all things into existence, there was neither ruling nor judging. But before he was Sovereign Judge, he was Father, and we speak here not of an external relation to the creation but of an inner relationship within the very nature of God himself.

Paul was obviously captured by this. One has only to look at the introductions to his epistles. Of the thirteen letters traditionally attributed to Paul, all have an initial greeting in which he prays for grace and peace to be upon his readers. In all but one his prayer is not to God but to "God the Father." The prayer is to no generic deity. It is to the Father of our Lord Jesus Christ. In the one exception, 1 Thessalonians, he has already identified the church to which he is writing as "the church of the Thessalonians in God the Father and the Lord Jesus Christ." When Paul uses the term God alone, it is very clear from his writings that he knows of no God other than the God who is the Father of our Lord Jesus Christ.

The literature of the first few centuries of the church that reveals the baptismal practices of the earliest Christians follows Paul's pattern. No one is ever asked if he believes in God. The question is whether the one desiring baptism believes in God the Father, our Lord Jesus Christ, and the Holy Spirit. The term "Father" obviously has a double use among Christians. God is the father of all who are born of his Spirit, but the term is used analogically. When it is used to speak of God's relationship to Jesus, it is not used analogically but ontologically. It refers to an inner reality, an inner relationship in the nature of God himself. It speaks of his being, his very personhood.

If the foregoing is true, it necessitates a different understanding of more than the nature of God. It means that we have a different context in which to see the family, the human family, itself. Paul caught this. We see the reflection of his understanding so casually written in Ephesians 3:14–15, "For this reason I bow my knees before the Father, from whom every family in heaven and on earth takes its name" (ESV). Apparently, for Paul the origin of the family is not in biology or anthropology. The first father was not Adam. Family relationships did not begin with the creation. In the bosom of eternity before the creation, a father/son relationship existed in the nature of God himself. That means that the use of family terms to describe God and our relationship to him is not a matter of human and temporal metaphors being used to explain eternal spiritual realities. It is the use of human terms to speak of eternal realities, terms that can be used only metaphorically of human relationships to God. That means there is similarity between heavenly realities and some earthly relationships. God, like any good teacher, uses object lessons to make abstract truths clear. So, he has made our world so that we have the categories that enable us, if we will, to understand him and his world. This is especially true in terms of the family, so the most important of all social institutions and the most crucial of all human relationships are drawn conceptually from the very nature of God himself. Sacred overtones can apparently be heard in more places than we thought if we have ears to hear them. The *imago Dei* may have broader implications than we sometimes think.

The most striking thing in all of this was the implication from which any good Jew must recoil. The data with which the first Christian believers were working were remarkably objective. They consisted of the person of Christ, his works, and his words. There was obviously a deeply appealing character to all of this for the disciples. They were attracted strongly enough by it all that they turned away from everything else in their lives to learn more from him, to find more of what he had to give them. As the end approached, they sensed, even if they did not yet fully understand, that following him could be costly. Yet none but Judas was ready to turn away. They accepted this language that Jesus used of "Father" and "Son," but they realized that the language was different when applied to him from what it was when it was used of them. Jesus did say, "When you pray, say: 'Father . . .'" (Luke 11:2). Yet it was clear that he did not include himself in their "our"—that his relationship to the Father was different from theirs. Language that was analogical and metaphorical for them was ontological for him. When he said such things as "I and the Father are one" (John 10:30), "anyone who receives me receives the Father who sent me" (Matt. 10:40 NLT), "Anyone who has seen me has seen the Father" (John 14:9), and "before Abraham was, I am" (John 8:58), they felt like Thomas when he cried out, "My Lord and my God!" (John 20:28). But how could this be?

If God has a Son, an only-begotten Son, of like nature to himself, what does this do with the concept of his oneness? Is God a family rather than one great monad? You and I, with the benefit of the centuries of hindsight that are ours, know that this was the beginning of the development of the doctrine of the Trinity. There is a security for us and a sense of the rightness when we hear the benedictory words: "The grace of the Lord Jesus Christ, and the love of God, and the communion of the Holy Ghost, be with you all" (2 Cor. 13:14 KJV). But when the first disciples began to think through the implications of this, it was undoubtedly an astounding shock.

God has a Son! One can understand why the pagans and the Jews who were not followers of Jesus remonstrated. Now the pagan could say, "You are like us. You have two Gods." And the Jew said:

"You are not one of us. You have two Gods." How was the Christian to reply? He knew that he was no polytheist, and he also knew that he, as Jesus said, was a child of Abraham and that Jesus was the very one whom Moses promised. Christianity has never been an easy intellectual road, and it certainly was not for them.

It must be noted that the New Testament never attempts to explain the Trinity. It assumes it. That means that God does not do our intellectual homework for us. He left that to the young church, living now in that in-between world that was neither Jewish nor pagan, to find its way. And it did.

It is clear that the term "Father" automatically demands that there be an other. One cannot be a father alone. But what now becomes of the oneness of God, a belief so sacred to Israel and all in Moses' succession? The young church seemed burdened with the necessity of believing two things that seemed clearly irreconcilable. They could not existentially conceive of denying either. Apparently, Jesus had believed both. But how could they explain it? They seem to have taken some comfort in the concept of mystery. After all, should the creature be too surprised when he finds that the Creator is beyond his ken? His Maker is infinite and eternal. He himself is finite and bound by time. There is a transcendence in God that God's child cannot know. But that did not satisfy the early church. They felt a compulsion to probe the intellectual possibilities of reconciliation.

Could it possibly be that the contradiction was a demand, a call to a richer conception of God than they had yet achieved? The story of the church of the first four centuries supports this because through their working through the implications of the personhood of Christ and the Scriptures, the church came to an understanding of God, our Source and our Sustainer, that became the source of the richest stream of grace and blessing that the world has yet seen.

Slowly they began to conceive of the possibility of the nature of God as being a unity that did not preclude some internal differentiation that would threaten the oneness of God that is so essential. It was this line of thought, taken by the church in the first three centuries of its existence, that led to the definition of the Trinity found in the Nicean-Constantinopolitan-Athanasian creeds that have been the very heart of the Christian faith ever since.

It is thus the conviction of the authors of the following investigations into Christian doctrine that our Christology should shape all the rest of the study and the Trinitarian implications of that doctrine should mark the entire work. It is in that light that we offer this work to the church.

Abbreviations

ACCS   *Ancient Christian Commentary on Scripture.* 29 vols. Thomas C. Oden, ed. Downers Grove, IL: InterVarsity, 1998–2006.

ANF   *The Ante-Nicene Fathers: The Writings of the Fathers Down to A.D. 325.* 10 vols. American Reprint of the Edinburgh Edition. Edited by Alexander Roberts and James Donaldson. 1885–1896. Reprint, Grand Rapids: Eerdmans, 1979.

BCP   *The Book of Common Prayer.* First published in 1549.

ISBE   *The International Standard Bible Encyclopedia.* 4 vols. Geoffrey W. Bromiley, ed. Grand Rapids: Eerdmans, 1979–1995.

LXX   The Septuagint Greek translation of the Old Testament.

NICNT   *The New International Commentary on the New Testament.* 22 vols. Joel B. Green, ed. Grand Rapids: Eerdmans, 1974–2020.

NICOT   *The New International Commentary on the Old Testament.* 29 vols. Edited by Robert L. Hubbard Jr. and Bill T. Arnold. Grand Rapids: Eerdmans, 1979–2022.

NIDNTT   *New International Dictionary of New Testament Theology.* 4 vols. Edited by Colin Brown. Grand Rapids: Zondervan, 1975.

NPNF   *A Select Library of the Nicene and Post-Nicene Fathers of the Christian Church.* First Series. 14 vols. Edited by Philip Schaff. Second Series. 14 vols. Edited by Philip

Schaff and Henry Wace. 1886–1900. Reprint, Grand Rapids: Eerdmans, 1979.

NT New Testament

TDNT *Theological Dictionary of the New Testament.* 10 vols. Edited by Gerhard Kittel and Gerhard Friedrich. Translated by Geoffrey W. Bromiley. Grand Rapids: Eerdmans, 1964–76.

OT Old Testament

PART ONE

CHRISTOLOGY
AS THEOLOGY

M. William Ury, PhD

---

*I dedicate this work to two consummate and
true theologians who live consistently and boldly
in the reality of our Lord Jesus Christ:*

*To my mother, Elizabeth Callis Ury, whose life has
taught me this one lesson - all that matters is Jesus.*

*And with a heart of grateful love,
To my wife, Diane Nelson Ury,
whose heart and mind are filled with the
beauty of the Incarnate Holy One. You model
for me what it means to fully know that Jesus
has taken our humanity into himself.*

CHAPTER ONE

The Cornerstone

What think ye of Christ, is the test
To try both your state and your scheme.
You cannot be right in the rest
Unless you think rightly of him.

– John Newton

CHRISTIAN THEOLOGY CANNOT EXIST without Christology. It revolves around one axiom: *Jesus Christ is the center of all reality.* He is the Alpha and Omega (Rev 21:6). At the same time, Christology is Trinitarian. Systematic theology draws upon the unified testament of Scripture, tradition, experience, and reason to affirm Jesus Christ as the eternal and incarnate Son of the Father revealed by the Holy Spirit. While attempts to articulate and understand the grandeur of the mystery of his glorious person proves difficult, there is no confusion about his nature in Scripture. The Word of God provides a flawless record of a divinely enabled progressive self-revelation. God desires to reveal himself to humanity. What is presented is neither myth nor mere ideology. Instead, one is confronted with the grandest claim ever pronounced by human lips or conceived by the mind: Jesus Christ is Lord as revealed through his descent, life, death, resurrection, and ascension.

Jesus reveals God. He states, "I am the way, and the truth, and the life. No one comes to the Father except through me" (John 14:6); and "Anyone who has seen me has seen the Father" (John 14:9).

The theological ramifications of statements of such magnitude are profound. Thus, theology can never place him as an addendum to more important theological starting points, such as revelation or the nature of God, for Jesus is the purpose of creation and revelation, and he has shown us who God is. Jesus is the source for comprehending reality because in him alone the Father is revealed. The goal of creation—to be filled with the glory of the personal presence of God—will be fulfilled as the Son offers the Father a recreated physical order and a holy people (Phil 2:11, Col 1:15–20, Rev 21:1–22:5).

The medieval distinction between the philosophical primacy of God's unitary being (oneness) and his Trinitarian essence (threeness) has tended to produce an unhealthy distance between the divine nature and the historical record of the God-Man, Jesus Christ. As subsequent theological formulations continued to appear, this tendency to separate the divine essence from Jesus led to an impersonal focus on a sovereign divine will that is disconnected from the Son of Man. The result had crippling theological consequences. By placing Christology and soteriology beneath notions of absolute determination, the "being" of God was somehow abstracted from the Carpenter of Nazareth. Jesus took second place in theology. Barth puts it this way:

> If dogmatics cannot regard itself and cause itself to be
> regarded as fundamentally Christology, it has assuredly
> succumbed to some alien sway and is already on the verge
> of losing its character as Christian dogmatics.[1]

The central issue in all Christian thought is the person of Jesus. If that is true, then every true Christian is a "Christologian," which, by implication, demands that each also be a Trinitarian. Christian systematic theology offers many distinctives that set it apart from other religious precepts. However, in the final analysis, it all comes down to the radical claim that God was in Christ reconciling himself the world. Jesus Christ, the Lord, is the Savior of the world. Any

---

1. Barth, *Church Dogmatics,* I/2, 123.

aberration of thought that diminishes this core of the gospel results in a loss of truth.

Theology must gather its wits again. That is, no systematic emphasis can be permitted to obscure or sideline Jesus in any way. There is no higher theology than to affirm that Jesus is the Son of God. No complete understanding of God can exist without an engagement with the complete record of the Son's descent from heaven, his earthly life, and his subsequent ascent to the right hand of the Father. In a real sense, there is no fundamental access to reality apart from him. Every other theme in systematic construction must relate to him as the supreme revelation of God. Theology flows from Christology.[2]

The reason for the existence of the Bible is the revelation of the truth that the Trinity is the eternal God. That very truth is inseparable from the person of Jesus Christ. When Jesus claimed that he was "the way and the truth and the life" (John 14:6), he spoke in two important ways. Historically, he declared himself to be the fulfillment of all Israel's expectations. Ontologically, he revealed something about his eternal being. He is the way to Another; his truth is never found in himself alone and the life he offers is that which he co-inhabits with the Father and the Spirit.

The purpose of Scripture in relation to Jesus is not primarily to assist us out of an epistemological problem or an experiential predicament. Its purpose is to offer us a way to relate to the one who is true. The Creator desires to communicate himself to all those made in his image. Through a variety of means, in a Spirit-ordered unity, the revelation of Scripture finds its fundamental promises and fulfillment, its foundation and purpose, in Jesus Christ.

---

2. Nersoyan, *Problems of Consensus in Christology*, 53–54.

HOLY LOVE: A WESLEYAN THEOLOGY

BEGINNING WITH JESUS

The central purpose of the self-revelation and self-communication of a transcendent God is to announce the arrival of the Messiah. The Word of God invites us to view his incarnate life in temporal existence and to reflect upon the only Son of God as he offers us life in the Spirit. Scripture seeks to introduce us to the marvel of Trinitarian reality through the Son. If what we have said thus far is true, then it is logical that theology must find its origin in Jesus. If based upon the historical and verbal revelation of Scripture, the church's message and reality are accurate in that Jesus is the eternal Son of God who became the son of Mary, then Jesus is important in two ways. First, he is God revealed in his personhood as the divine Son. Second, he incarnates the true man as all that the triune God intends for created persons. If this logic is correct, we find our methodological concerns radically altered. Rather than building our prolegomena on a typical model (revelation, followed consecutively by doctrine of God, humanity, and the need for salvation), this work starts with Jesus.[3]

The significance of the person of Jesus undeniably overshadows human history. The power of his words permeates any culture they have ever influenced in the slightest. A theology based upon Christ attempts to discern the reasons for this incomparable grandeur. Dorothy Sayers, speaking of Jesus, has put it succinctly: "This is reality. From the beginning of time until now, this is the only thing that has ever really happened."[4]

Jesus provides the fundamental content for every aspect of systematic theology because it is through him and in the Spirit that the Father is glorified. He is the reason for a doctrine of revelation because he is the one who reveals the Father and the one of whom the Spirit speaks (John 14:7–10). He defines the image of

---

3. Kinlaw, *Let's Start with Jesus*, especially 71–87; see also Appendix A.
4. Sayers, *The Man Born to Be King,* 289.

God because he alone is the embodiment of deity (Col 1:15). He defines what it means to be made in the image of God because he is the true Adam (Col 3:10). He is salvation (Luke 2:30). He is the Lord of the church (Eph 4:5). He opens the seals of every person's future (Rev 5:1–5). No Christian doctrine of revelation can speak of truth without founding it in the person of the Son, the Word of God, who is the truth. Each of the Trinitarian persons is the "way and the truth and the life."

The transcendent Lord is revealed to us and is with us. As Barth argues, "Christology is the touchstone of all knowledge of God in the Christian sense, the touchstone of all theology."[5]

A CHRISTOCENTRIC METHODOLOGY

In the present era, the logic of theology as it was once argued has lost meaningful connection with those in the church and also with those outside the communion of love. Epistemology, ontology, bibliology, anthropology, and hamartiology—important though they are—are not issues which normally compel attention. However, once one encounters the life, sayings and claims of Jesus, an immediate decision must be made. One must recognize the invitation to theology. Either the data is false, or it demands a response of humble love and trust. As one theologian has said, "Without personal identification with Jesus Christ, cognitive specification of who he is remains empty; without cognitive specification of who Jesus Christ is, however, personal identification with him is blind."[6] Though this work draws heavily from consensual theological constructs,[7] the method here presupposes that the God-Man, Jesus, must inform a true and personal theological agenda.

---

5. Barth, *Dogmatics in Outline*, 66.

6. Volf, *After Our Likeness*, 53.

7. "Consensual" refers to the creedal formulations that were ecumenically (universally) agreed upon by the majority of believers. Normally, this term points

Such a pattern is found neither in the magisterial systematic texts nor the typical flow of the creeds. Again, all of the major early baptismal and catechetical formulations start with the Fatherhood of God. In this volume, the emphasis is on the *eternality* of the relationship between the Father, the Son, and the Spirit. Through the incarnation of the Word of God, the declaration that God is love (1 John 4:8, 16) is made accessible to us in a way that is not possible otherwise. The consistent refrain of the best minds in Christian thought has been that the love that God expresses is prior to creation and not bound to it by any necessity. Love, as holiness, is essential to the nature of God. That love is revealed to humanity through the incarnation.

According to Jesus, humanity could never have known the Father as Father apart from the Son (John 14:9). The Spirit is active in the conception of Jesus (Luke 1:35), and he is the one who offers the dynamic of life in the Son (Matt 3:17; 4:1; 12:18; Luke 4:1, 14). The Spirit ever lives to witness to the Son. This mutual dependency is radical. The life of Jesus is not removed from Trinitarian reality. Jesus lives for the glory of the Father. Without the Spirit, the Son would not exist, nor would he be known. This triune relationship has significant theological implications. The creeds presuppose the eternal relationship of the Father and the Son in placing the first article—that of the Father—before that of the Son and the Spirit.

Over the centuries, theological tradition has solidified each of the elements that normally precede Christology in systematic theologies: epistemology, bibliology, theology proper, cosmology, and anthropology. In contrast, the trajectory of this work is both theologically and pastorally driven. The most important fact or idea in history is Jesus Christ. All creation is a context for the revelation of his person and a relationship with him. For only in the Holy Spirit can one call Jesus Lord (1 Cor 12:3) or recognize his being as the

---

one to the basic creeds still used in Christian worship. In Christology, the Nicene (AD 325) and the Chalcedonian (AD 451) creeds are often the consensual referents.

revelation of the Father. Only in Christ do we have access to a full conception of God and the nature of reality. No doctrine or segment of theology can rise higher than its Christological center.

THE CENTRAL ISSUE: COMING TO AN ORTHODOX CHRISTOLOGY

The Sovereign God must convince humanity that he loves and desires us to respond to his grace without coercion or manipulation. He could have deposited a great tome of theology to explain the mysteries of the incarnation, but he did not. He could have offered a never-ending set of miraculous experiences to persuade us. God will not resort to human strategies of persuasion. John Wesley contends that God "draws" persons to himself rather than "driving" them into the kingdom.[8] That reserve on the part of God is an acknowledgment of how important each person is to him.

Nevertheless, with that human freedom, a significant responsibility ensues for the church: that of ensuring the meaningful transmission of the truth of who Jesus is to succeeding generations, not just for creedal affirmation but for spiritual transformation. It took the better part of five centuries for the church to determine the best way to articulate the mystery of the incarnation. In recent times, however, the orthodox doctrine of Christ has suffered strong attacks. A theology of Jesus must be articulated coherently in the face of various ideologies that threaten its centrality. If the church loses this central issue, it has lost everything.

Part of the task of theology is to inquire how the earliest disciples came to discern Jesus of Nazareth as the Creator of the universe who became the son of Mary and Joseph. Surely, they were neither coerced by miracles nor imposing some fantastic messianic vision upon their Rabbi. From the vantage point of retrospect, the

---

8. Wesley, *Notes*, 230.

combined witness of the New Testament is that Jesus is another person who is Yahweh; that he is in some real sense the same God who has manifested himself to us from the beginning. The Gospels could not be more explicit in their main point: the consummation of revelation is found in the affirmation that Jesus of Nazareth is the Lord of the universe.[9] Consonant with that affirmation, the church began the work of worshipful love: clarifying, supporting, defending, and applying the claim that he was indeed the eternal Son of the Father, constituted by the Holy Spirit.

FORMULATING A BIBLICAL VIEW OF CHRIST

Christology is presented first by the straightforward first-century apostolic experience of the historical person of Jesus. God only appeared once in the flesh. The New Testament writers are convinced that incarnation took place in Jesus Christ. There is no other person comparable to him. This ancient commitment has been disputed in various ways but mainly by the rejection of a biblical worldview inherent within some sectors of modernity. The modern conviction that the empirical sciences determine all reality has threatened to limit both the history of Jesus and his divinity.

Clarity on the person of Jesus can never be tied solely to naturalistic presuppositions, which state that what is acceptable as true is verifiable due to repeated experimentation. Believers who claim that those who first called Jesus "Lord" did so out of prescientific mindsets and thus necessarily misperceived reality have imported into Christology the modern correlate that what is real must be determined by science alone. That criticism is an example of the inaccurate bias that has always limited the divinity of Christ. Though never claiming inerrancy of perspective, our forebearers'

---

9. More evidence will be given but one might start with Matt 1:23, 3:17, 12:8, 12:17–21, 14:33, 16:15–17, 27, 28:18–20.

experiences, and reflections upon their experience of Christ, may proffer the most profound key to reality.

A SHORT HISTORY OF THE DIMINISHMENT OF THE PERSON OF CHRIST

Fundamentally, the lordship of Jesus Christ was the central position held in the church until the seventeenth century. The growth of the humanistic tradition in art and philosophy brought a cynicism about orthodox Christian doctrines. Not surprisingly, one of the significant losses involved the abandonment of what some leaders perceived as the anachronistic albatross of Chalcedonian Christology.[10]

A new scientific view of history denied that the biblical text could be considered a document connected to actual history. Scholars argued that what mattered most was the subjective experience of a demythologized Christ. They viewed Christology as offering not a divine person but a human example of high principles. Critics of the New Testament thus denied the deity of Christ. In place of the moral power of the gospel, they substituted their ethical predilections. Biblical studies claimed historical objectivity, but in reality, most of its conclusions severed it from the treasure store of New Testament historicity and the ensuing consensual interpretations of the church.

A principle borne out by the history of doctrine is that over-corrections are almost always wrong in theological formulation. If, as the recent critics state, theology was "Hellenized" (i.e., brought under the rigid and static dominion of philosophical categories), and thus diminished or perverted, then it is also possible to respond

---

10. Though the church has never claimed that any creedal statement is beyond further clarification, the combined influence of the Niceno-Constantinopolitan statement (AD 381) and its successor, the Chalcedonian Symbol (AD 451), have served as the buttress against the nagging recurrences of uncreative heretical perspectives. See the recent criticism of scholars like Sarah Coakley.

in kind by acknowledging that biblical studies were "modernized" (nothing is acceptable that does not affirm the scientific method) and thereby rendered incapable of learning from the riches of past theological affirmations. Maybe a better approach would be to hold both philosophy and the historical-critical method at bay, to be used profitably in assisting doctrinal clarification but not as self-imposed delimiters of theological reality. Earlier theologians saw philosophy and the sciences as handmaidens to the queen, which was theology. Recent Christology has seen an attempted coup in the palace.

Since the Enlightenment, the relationship between dogmatic theology and biblical studies has been a stormy affair. This internecine struggle continues from the Neologs (e.g., Semmler, Reimarus, Lessing, Herder, etc.) to the present debates. Rather than feeding each other productively, there has been an internal ecclesial suspicion with a resultant tragic separation between theology and biblical scholarship. Since the rise of the early critical schools, the recent history of most biblical interpretation has produced a shadow over much of the early church's view of Jesus.[11] The claim to return to the "real" Jesus, or the "kernel" of the gospel, has resulted in the de-divinization of Jesus in nearly every attempt to separate the text from the church's history of interpretation. The first evidence of this in discerning the person and work of Jesus is that we have been cut off from any possibility that the Old Testament might include his self-revelation. It may be that this excision is one reason we struggle to find ways of "proving" that he is who he said he was in the New Testament.

We must take an initial look at how the earliest disciples viewed and interpreted the life and ministry of Jesus in their context, which was based upon the Old Testament and the apocalyptic Judaism of

---

11. See Borg and Wright, *The Meaning of Jesus*. Both authors have written extensively on Jesus and present the basic issues to be confronted in the so-called "Third Quest of the Historical Jesus." As biblical scholars, the scope of their engagement is limited, but it is still quite helpful in laying the framework for discussion.

the era. Any criticism of this procedure must account for the veracity of its own method. Suppose one cannot agree that those nearest Jesus accurately discerned who he was. In that case, that "cultured despiser" must present why his particular critical apparatus is preferable to what the Gospels use. This method of presenting the person of Jesus arose early in the history of the canon. The church rejected the gnostic[12] Gospels, including the Gospel of Thomas, because of the absence of historical verification and for the obvious dualism that permeated such texts.

The early formers of Christian doctrine were not politicizing; they were shepherding believers and protecting them from the vicissitudes of an imposing separation of the flesh and the spirit, which have continued to threaten successive generations of Christians. It was right here that Christology began to be formed. There was an immediate need to protect the reality of the God-Man because without him there was no true connection between heaven and earth, mind and spirit, body and soul. The early church found the key to reality in Christ.[13]

Ironically, despite its many disadvantages and multifarious results, the mood of postmodernism has proven productive in questioning modernity's dogged commitment to rationalistic scientism as the sole basis of discerning reality. The rationalistic theology of the modern era has been rejected for postmodernity's cry for something more real and personally satisfying. Modernism's theological bankruptcy has funded a return to subjective inquiry. Christology

---

12. Gnosticism is the name of a philosophical religion that appeared in the second century AD but whose basic themes are found implied in some of the epistles (Col 2:8–23). Gnosticism was the belief that by a bestowal of a specially endowed knowledge (*gnosis*) a person could rise out of the flesh, either by asceticism or by hedonism, and could move into a realm of knowledge in mind and spirit that would save that person from the evil of a purely physical existence or demise.

13. Irenaeus, Athanasius, The Nicene Creed, etc. are at pains to clarify the relationship between the Father and the Son but also to emphasize the way in which Jesus brings all that is divine to all that is created without being depersonalized or losing any divinity.

HOLY LOVE: A WESLEYAN THEOLOGY

has a new lease on life with the demise of modernity's idols of scientism and rationalism. Where modernity had attempted to restrict the concepts of meaning and truth to historical-critical methodology, empiricism, or phenomenology, postmodernity has raised significant questions that have opened an actual engagement with the text of Scripture and its implications.[14] So, appropriating meaning, truth, and personal reality as categories long absent as acceptable predispositions of reading Scripture are now at the forefront again. The text of Scripture is no longer just for dissection or suspicion, it carries existential import. Nonetheless, without revealed substance founded in biblical content, and without tradition as a subordinate but essential guide to that material, this reaction to modernity will result merely in a self-centered ethical sentimentality that ultimately denies any meaningful, salvific appropriation of the Word become flesh.

---

14. Note the interesting perspective of O'Keefe and Reno in *Sanctified Vision*.

CHAPTER TWO

Building an Orthodox Christology

IT IS EVIDENT IN one of the earliest pleas of the church after the ascent of Jesus that his Lordship was recognized. *Maranatha,* or "Come, Lord" (1 Cor 16:22; Rev 22:20), indicates the place that he held in early Christian worship. The only objective repository for truth regarding Jesus is Scripture. Any rational discussion of the place of Christ must be founded on historical and documentary evidence; otherwise, subjectivism limits what can be known about Jesus. One's experience of the grace of God in Christ is undergirded by the fact that millions of persons prior to any claim to a subjective redemptive event have witnessed the same saving grace from the same person. And Scripture records the reasonable and personal relationships of many with Jesus Christ both in his earthly and heavenly ministry. The goal of revelation is that Jesus would be seen in all of his glory. The entire Bible is included in God's self-revelation; so, the Old Testament and New Testament must be viewed as complementary and irreplaceable sources for Christology.

Because no systematic theology can exhaust all the scriptural evidence given about Jesus, we have chosen a hermeneutic that issues from doxology. The church worshipped Jesus before it produced any creed regarding his personhood. *Christology that does not arise out of worship is worthless.* The cycle of the Christian year revolves around the person of Christ. The creeds that have formed the central themes of worship distill the major components of the biblical record into the key issues of belief. The experience of the risen Christ through the enabling of the Holy Spirit in all ages has been guided by the truths of Scripture as they have been compiled by the church. The church discerned methods of articulating the nature of the incarnate one that were necessary for Christian belief. So, we are using tradition to support the themes that arise out of the early church's worship of Jesus and the texts that came out of their adoration of the Savior.

THE SCRIPTURAL REVELATION OF THE PERSON OF JESUS CHRIST

Lest we enter into post-modern argumentation on the text or its interpretation too quickly, it must be re-emphasized that the writings we call the New Testament arose as a result of worshipping Jesus Christ (*lex orandi*) as the transcendent Son of the Father who became a particular man conceived by the Holy Spirit in the womb of a young virgin of Nazareth, located in a negligible part of a Roman province. The earliest expressions of Christian worship indicate a high Christology (*lex credendi*). Biblical monotheism never excluded belief in a divine Messiah distinct from Yahweh as a possibility. The monotheism of Israel abhorred any form of polytheism but, on the other hand, it was never construed to be strictly monadic. The oneness of God was not a mathematical argument. It was primarily a distinction between the God of Israel and the pantheons of paganism. But that oneness never was construed as a monolithic, static, or pure monadic integer. In fact, the Hebraic notion of monotheism formed the absolute foundation of the Christian doctrine of the Trinity. This is seen in the most fundamental hope of Israel: the arrival of the sent one, the Messiah. The implication of an inherent polytheism in the hope for a divine Messiah never arises in this unique monotheism. If questions regarding the division of the being of Yahweh into separate entities—Lord, Messiah, and Spirit—were ever at play, it is not evident in the Old Testament. The Gospels are full of the same historical desire for a Messiah (Matt 3:3; Luke 1:77, 2:29–32; Mark 8:29; Matt 16:16). It is fascinating to see how the arrival of Jesus initiated a dynamic reconstruction, not a rejection, of a perspective of the inherited monotheism of the earliest disciples. The unity of Yahweh was apparently more inclusive of the possibility of distinction, differentiation, and extension than surrounding philosophical concepts of the One would ever allow.

WORSHIP AND THE THEOLOGY OF JESUS AS LORD

Statements within Scripture like those Thomas spoke on the eighth day after the resurrection in the Upper Room, "My Lord and my God" (John 20:28), confirm that the early community, mainly Jewish monotheists, acknowledged Jesus as divine.[1] But this confession was to mark the church's affirmations each Lord's Day (Rev 1:10). Hymnic doxologies directed to the Lord Jesus Christ, like that of Philippians 2:5–11, formed the basis of all Christian creeds to come.[2] True theology always takes place in proximity to worship. Well known is the dictum: To be a theologian, one must pray, and the one who prays is a theologian. It is beyond doubt that the worship of Jesus preceded any careful theological articulation (Mark 8:29; Matt 28:17). Also, later Christological statements had to be made in order to maintain clarity on the fundamental essence

---

1. Pliny's famous quote is found in a letter to Trajan late in the first century regarding Christians in Bithynia, "They have been accustomed to meet before daybreak, and to recite a hymn antiphonally to Christ, as to a god" (Bettenson, *Documents,* 4). It is woven into the fabric of the Apostolic Fathers explicitly. See also Wainwright, *Doxology,* 46–50.
2. Pelikan, *Credo,* 134–35.

HOLY LOVE: A WESLEYAN THEOLOGY

of Christian worship. The weekly communal recognition of the risen Christ demanded a continual assessment of the claims of Scripture, prophetically and incarnationally.[3] But it is also imperative to note that worship in the church is first an understanding that it is the presence of the triune God who is graciously bestowing love, light, and life.[4] This response of the earliest disciples to Jesus as revealed Lord has continued for twenty centuries, and much was worked out in the period following the New Testament in order to keep Jesus of Nazareth as the central fact in all of time and eternity.

CHRISTOLOGICAL REALITY AND THE SANCTIFICATION OF TIME

The radical nature of biblical faith insists that revelation is historical so that the necessary perception of reality is verifiable within the human parameters of space and time. Much as Israel had used feasts as temporal signposts of both redemption history and theological reflection, the early church punctuated the year with celebrations of the highpoints of the life of their Lord. Even from the earliest extra-biblical references to the followers of Jesus, it is evident that worshipping him was central to their self-understanding. The worship of Jesus included the sanctification of time. The *Didache*, one of the earliest manuals of Christian life we possess, indicated that prayer was to be offered three times a day as an apparent effort to keep prayer central to Christian experience.[5] Jesus was placed where he belonged: with the Father at the center of time and as the basis of all reality. His centrality was repeated in a cycle of annual worship that emphasized equally his humanity

---

3. The debate about the actual day of Christian worship in the early church will never be settled. Both sides of the argument offer their own assessment; the Sabbatarians have Old Testament precedent on their side and the Sunday/Lord's Day camp have church history on theirs. There is enough indication in the New Testament, though, that there was some special worship evident on the first day of the week (Acts 20:7, 1 Cor 16:2).

4. Wainwright, *Doxology*, 242.

5. *Didache*, ANF 7:379. One wonders if this is not a Christian appropriation of the Jewish *tefillah* (benedictions) recited privately three times a day (Dan 6:10).

and his deity. Each of the fundamental points of the kerygma and the later creedal statements about Jesus were rehearsed yearly.[6]

The descent of the Son of God from heaven and assumption of human nature through Mary by the Holy Spirit was recounted in the Advent season.[7] But the actual Advent celebration did not conclude until Epiphany, which marked the offering of himself as light to all peoples. Lent, Good Friday, and Holy Saturday prepared for and revealed the passion and the victory of the Christ in graphic detail. And the vindicating victory of the resurrection on Easter Sunday served both as a climax and an inauguration. It not only spoke of victory accomplished but also opened the way for the Holy Spirit to bring divine life to all. The ascension and session acknowledged the return to glory of the Son and the incorporation of humanity within the Godhead. Pentecost (or Whitsunday), in essence, summarizes or recapitulates the life of Jesus as his own body, the church, turns outside of itself for the sake of others just as her Lord lived with his essence being filled with and continually constituted by the Holy Spirit. Trinity Sunday rounds out the first half of the Christian year in a climactic way by emphasizing that the triune persons have been revealed fully and that ordinary time has the potential of being lived

---

6. Keeping the Lord's Day, Easter, and Pentecost is evident from the apostolic period due to their connection with the Jewish festivals of Sabbath, Passover, and Pentecost, respectively (Dix, *The Shape of the Liturgy*, 336–41). The addition of the other holy days continues into the post-Nicene period. One must also remember that the monastic tradition also celebrated a variety of days and seasons even though there is not as much historical material to access on that account. It is debated just how old the liturgical tradition and calendar of the church really is. The conservative school claims they are apostolic. The less traditional schools of thought look far beyond Nicaea for liturgical origins, emphasizing the inclusion of terms like *homoousion* and *theotokos*. See Cyril of Jerusalem, *Catechetical Lectures*, NPNF2 7:116.

7. Creedal development is easier to trace historically than actual calendrical development. Easter and Pentecost are the most ancient sacred days commemorated by the church. In the Western church, Advent was designated as a period of holy celebration in the fourth century, although the baptism of Jesus and his nativity were connected as early as the late second century. Clement of Alexandria (ca. AD 194) indicates that the Basilideans "hold the day of his baptism as a festival" (*Stromateis*, ANF 2:333). Epiphany was held as a special sector of the year by the West beginning in the fourth century.

HOLY LOVE: A WESLEYAN THEOLOGY

in the glory of that shared life. For centuries in Eastern and Western worship, nearly half of each year focused on the major elements of the life of Christ from incarnation to the sending of the Holy Spirit at Pentecost. Systematic theology at its best is merely a commentary on the issues that arose out of that worship life.

Though these days underscored the crucial elements of early Christology, the gathering of believers was seen to be a distilled recollection of both the person and the passion of Good Friday to his glorious risen presence in the midst of his people every Lord's Day.[8]

It was here, week by week, that the truth of the humanity and divinity of Jesus was proclaimed in a pastoral, doxological, and systematic fashion. Last, it should not be forgotten that the Lord's Supper punctuated the daily life of early Christians as well. The Eucharistic remembrance of real presence of the risen Jesus solidified the constant Christocentric definition of reality in that act and in his presence in space and time.

ADVENT: THE TRIUMPHAL ENTRY AS A CONSENSUAL INDICATION OF THE PERSON OF THE SON

An example of the way the early church reflected Christocentric worship with a clear understanding of the incarnation in time and space is found in the liturgical text for Palm Sunday, the start of Holy Week, which, instructively, is the same text as the first week of Advent.[9]

---

8. The Christian year is divided into two sections. The first is Christocentric. There are no great festivals in the second. Some have said that the church rejoiced only in the completion of the full revelation of the Son and his purposes so that Trinity Sunday, a week after Pentecost, witnesses to that reality. This celebration is followed by twenty-seven Sundays until the Advent cycle begins again. See Dix, *The Shape of the Liturgy*; Wainwright, *Doxology*; Taft, *The Liturgy of the Hours in East and West*; Bouyer, *Liturgical Piety*.

9. "Early church" generally points to the period extending from the apostolic fathers (AD 90) to the time of the Athanasian Creed (ca. sixth century AD). This passage proves to be a pivot to the cross. Apparently, it occurs six days before the crucifixion.

It was the Lord of heaven and earth, and of his church, who came to his own at his birth and would make a final entrance to Jerusalem. As if bracketing the whole remembrance of his life, it was acknowledged that the way he came is the way the Redeemer always comes. Though the Lordship of Christ may not have struck his contemporaries as particularly grandiose, he was no less Lord then than he will be when every eye shall see his second appearing. The eschatological emphasis of the church interpreted the first coming in light of the second advent.

JESUS AS THE ONE WHO REVEALS HOW GOD COMES[10]

The early church fathers found it difficult to understand and define the divine authority of Jesus. He never used his acts of power to wield undue influence on others (Matt 12:23; Luke 9:43). Throughout his life it was easy for contemporaries to miss him or dismiss him because he never coerced anyone to accept his offer of salvation (Mark 5:42–43; Luke 6:46). The early church reiterated the paradox that it was the Lord of glory who chose to borrow the stable for his birth, an animal of burden to enter Jerusalem, and the robe of mockery and crown of disdain to announce his kingdom. He even had to borrow a tomb for his burial. Jesus was employing a different concept of power and authority. At the same time, he is viewed as authoritative over creation (Mark 4:35–41), yet he did not demand subservience. Athanasius wrote:

> Now, if they ask, Why then did He not appear by means
> of other and nobler parts of creation, and use some nobler
> instrument, as the sun, or moon, or stars, or fire, or air,
> instead of man merely? Let them know that the Lord came
> not to make a display, but to heal and teach those who were
> suffering.[11]

---

10. See Matt 21:1–11 and parallels.
11. Athanasius, *On the Incarnation, NPNF2* 4:59.

HOLY LOVE: A WESLEYAN THEOLOGY

From his ministry in the villages of Bethany and Bethphage, Jesus enters a period of messianic political excitement. The King's arrival in Jerusalem is welcomed: "Hosanna to the son of David" (Matt 21:9). For the Jerusalem throng, the statement "He is coming" emphasized that one of the House of David was beginning the long-anticipated rebellion against the oppressors. This revolution would not come in the way they anticipated. He came to his own (John 1:11) and fulfilled the prophecy that Israel's King would once again enter the gates. The purpose for which he came was more far-reaching than anyone could imagine. He fulfilled prophecy; he healed the blind; he led Zacchaeus to salvation; he brought a friend back to life after four days in a tomb, and he demonstrated his knowledge of the future.[12] He revealed sovereignty of a "humble" sort, so there is no entourage parading a resuscitated Lazarus. This is kingship and kingdom of a different order.

The Christology inherent in the early church was a radical reversal of Israel's expectation of a conquering apocalyptic sovereign. Like Israel, thinkers throughout the history of the church have missed him because his revelation did not match their presuppositions. We must accept him as he reveals himself, or we will entertain delusive misperceptions about the Savior. The error has been to define God by categories of absolute power. The almighty "Alpha and Omega" is Mary's babe (Rev 21).

JESUS IN THE CONFESSION (*KERYGMA*) OF THE EARLY CHURCH

The worship cycle of the early church leads us to connect the biblical data on Jesus with the context of worship. Removing Jesus from history is dangerous, and theologizing about him apart from the worshipping community produces little constructive Christology. Another reason for using both calendar and confession to highlight Scripture is the Trinitarian under-girding for all that transpires in them.

---

12. See Zech 9:9–10; Luke 19:1–10; John 11:1–44; Matt 21:2–3, 26:1–5.

The primary witness of the earliest believers pertained to Jesus.[13] We turn to another key place for a full-orbed Christology, which is the preaching of the early church, or the *kerygma*. The apostles confessed in the middle of their evangelism every aspect of Christ's person: the key components of his life and ministry, his humanity, his deity. It is apparent that the post-apostolic fathers did not think it advantageous to impose a foreign structure upon Scripture. Instead, they offered more of an instructive framework by which to allow the theology of the first-century believers to be measured by an increasingly systematic appraisal of the person of the Son which was considered orthodox.[14]

THE METHODOLOGY OF ORTHODOX CHRISTOLOGY

The New Testament canon is the direct witness to Christ, but the entire canon bears a Christocentric shape, even though the person it proclaims is revealed through a diversity of authorship.[15] In the Gospels, the history of the life and teaching of Jesus is offered from four complementary perspectives. Acts records the first Christocentric living and preaching. From Romans to Colossians, Paul offers an increasingly expansive interpretation of the full meaning of the God-Man. The Pastoral and General Epistles, especially Hebrews, underscore major aspects of his Lordship. Without the Book of Revelation, there would be little to draw upon for the eschatological implications of the glory of the Son. John's apocalyptic vision completes the picture of the Eternal Word. He is the Son of God, the

---

13. The usage of terms related to *matur/matureo* in Acts is clear evidence that "witness, testimony, testify" are key elements of the nascent ministry and worship of the church. This family of terms occurs 28 times in the book. See 1:8, 22; 4:33; 22:15.

14. One thinks here of the difference of literary style and theological ruminations between the Apostolic Fathers (i.e., Polycarp or the Shepherd of Hermas) with the Apologists (Hippolytus, Tertullian, or Irenaeus).

15. See part four, *Bibliology*, in volume three of this series.

Lamb of God, and the Lord of all. Critics who wish to limit Christ by comparing him with the rabbinic tradition must circumvent biblical material. While a moral teacher, Jesus is also the source of all being, the apex of all creation, and the judge of all humanity.

Challenges to the church's avowal that Jesus is God would not surprise the earliest theologians. They knew how inadequate human reasoning is to explain the revelation of Christ. What mattered most to those involved in transmission of the earliest theological documents was to recognize and demonstrate that Jesus was the Lord (*ho kurios*). This affirmation becomes the test of faith in the New Testament (Acts 16:31; Rom 10:9; Phil 2:11; 1 Cor 12:3). For the early church, the Christological paradox—fully God and fully man—is both normative and self-evident, though not finely tuned.[16]

THE CHRISTOCENTRIC PREACHING OF THE EARLY CHURCH

The *kerygma* (the content of what was preached concerning the gospel of Christ) formed the foundation for the consensual creeds. The initial preaching of the disciples after Pentecost built on the life and teaching of Jesus.[17] They affirmed that their encounter with the Messiah was not the first witness to his person (Acts 2:25–32, 3:18, 7:52).[18] God had inspired the faith of earlier generations; he longed for them one day to comprehend truth in flesh. Everything that Israel experienced pointed to the eventual arrival of God in Christ.[19]

---

16. Outler, *Christology*, 35.

17. Note that Peter's Pentecost sermon revolves around an interpretation of Joel 2 (Acts 2:15–21) and Psalm 16 (Acts 2:22–34), ending with a reference to Psalm 110 (Acts 2:34–36).

18. In this theological formulation, it is important to remember the relationship between Luke's authorship of the Gospel of Luke and of Acts.

19. To miss this is a form of neo-Marcionism, which erroneously posits that the God of the Old Covenant was not as gracious as the one we meet in the New. Recognizing this theological and historical dualism, which is at the base

Once one grasps the method and the importance of the kerygmatic Christology of the New Testament, it is important to focus on the major aspects of that proclamation of the Word made flesh.

THE LIFE AND MINISTRY OF THE INCARNATE ONE

THE VIRGIN BIRTH

One aspect faces us at this point that is not overtly stated within the sermons of the first apostles but is implied in all they say about the divine nature of Jesus (Acts 3:14–15; 7:52).[20] The uniqueness of the person of Jesus begins with his origin. However, the importance of the virgin birth came to be recognized when heresies questioned the full divinity and humanity of Christ.

The basis for this doctrine is found in two of the Gospels. Following the witness to the historical lineage of Jesus Christ and the birth of John the Baptist, Matthew and Luke focus on the actual history of the infancy of Jesus (Matt 1:18–25; Luke 1:26–38; 2:1–4). Using the language of the day, they indicate that the birth of Jesus was an absolutely unique and unrepeatable miracle. Of the Gospels, Matthew and Luke give an explicit presentation of the miracle.[21] Scripture must set our agenda lest we be swayed by modern epistemology to discount both the veracity of revelation and the eternal deity of the son of Mary. Worship, kerygma, confession, and creed affirm what the modern mind discounts as mythological fiction.[22] The Creator becomes a creature, conceived by the Holy Spirit, born

---

of all heresies, the early church affirmed that revelation in both covenants was progressive and given in an inseparable continuum.

20. Another support would be the usage of *Kristos* (Messiah) and Son of God (Acts 9:20). Mary is mentioned as the mother of Jesus in Acts 1:14.

21. Brown, *The Birth of the Messiah.*

22. Ignatius, *Epistle to the Trallians, ANF* 1:69–70; *Epistles to the Ephesians, ANF* 1:56–57. A comparison of the basic creeds will show the place Mary holds in orthodox statements regarding the incarnation. None of them make any overstatements about her.

HOLY LOVE: A WESLEYAN THEOLOGY

of the Virgin Mary. Aristides defended the faith before a Roman emperor with this statement, "And it is said that God came down from heaven, and from a Hebrew virgin assumed and clothed himself in flesh; and the Son of God lived in the daughter of man."[23] These claims make Adoptionism an untenable position.[24]

He who was eternally God, through the power of the Holy Spirit became man forever through the womb of Mary. Without the assistance of a human father, he took on her flesh, not as a receptacle, but by every normal process of the transfer of life from a mother to her child.

The virgin birth has never been a simple doctrine for the church. Some important distinctives have risen between the Catholic and Protestant understandings of the virgin birth. The Catholic focuses on Mary (her immaculate conception and perpetual virginity), and the Protestant focuses on the miraculous birth of Jesus as the foundation of his atoning work. Both perspectives share an emphasis on the supernatural conception and natural birth of Jesus, but the Protestant assumes Mary mothered other children.

The virgin birth reveals the intimate and personal engagement of God with his creatures and shows the self-giving inherent in the ultimate authority of the Word. God does not intend an act of unrestrained power to overwhelm persons. The Word became flesh to reveal the other-oriented heart of the Holy One. The virgin birth challenges the predilection of modern scientism to dictate the parameters of theological response to Scriptural accounts. Rather than acquiescing to the claim that the virgin birth is impossible and

---

23. The Syriac version of *The Apology of Aristides*, ANF 10:265. Whether it was Hadrian or Antonius Pius to which he addressed these words, which are viewed among the earliest of the "rules of faith," it still places these commitments in the mid-second century with a reiterated resonance to a gospel preached by firsthand witnesses still being referred to as common knowledge.

24. Adoptionism is the heresy that claimed Jesus was merely a human being chosen by God to do a particular task and at that point he became super-spiritual and, in some sense, more god-like than other humans. It was first affirmed by the Ebionites (first century AD) and later by Paul of Samosata (third century AD) and Nestorius (fifth century AD).

thus merely a symbol for unsophisticated people, the consensual voice of the church has been that this is an historical fact, one of a constellation of facts that point to the full divinity of Jesus.

Remarkably, as the church reflected on the uniqueness of Christ's birth in a world of pagan claims to birthed gods, it did not shy away from this stance with all of its potential problems. If we cannot countenance Christ living in Mary's womb as God, we advocate a dualism that separates spirit from flesh. Then there is no true connection between flesh and spirit, and we lose a real redemption. The Word and message are one. God and his Messiah are one. The Savior and the human nature that needed salvation are one. Accordingly, the redemption of humanity deals with the full reality of the state of sin. Mary's voice has become a response to the triune God throughout the ages, "May your word to me be fulfilled" (Luke 1:38). The Word that was spoken was the Word in Mary. The divine life can enter into the human. Humans can trust a God who knows their frame.

This initial point of early Christology revealed the nature of ultimate reality. Even in the annunciation, "Hail Favored One, the Lord is with you" (Luke 1:28), one can find a summation of the biblical worldview. His presence is no longer separated from our humanity. Telescoped here we can find themes of creation, covenant, divine presence, revelation, and the offer of salvation. Granted, the idea of incarnation is not unique to Christianity. There was nothing new about religions advocating unusual births of gods.[25] What is distinctive is the outright rejection of Docetism inherent in this, the virgin birth of Christ.[26]

---

25. Here we can note the incessant flow of comparisons between these pericopes and "apotheoses" (humanity becoming divine) of the era.

26. Docetism is that belief that the divine Christ only appeared (*dokeo*) to be a human. Based upon radical gnosticism, the aversion of spirit from flesh, this doctrine would not allow Jesus to be truly divine because he was of flesh. The virgin birth categorically denies gnostic and Docetic influences, which may explain why it is so often maligned.

If the radical separation of spirit and flesh (dualism) is the only option, as much Western philosophy has made an unquestionable presupposition, then the divine could only *appear* to be human. While the myths are ahistorical, in Christianity the divine enters into human history as flesh. An eternal unity of spirit and flesh—unique in all history, philosophy, and religion—has occurred.

The virgin birth is more ontological and theological than debate allows. We find here an answer to any dualistic framework, which prohibits God ever becoming human. With this response we find a solution to this longstanding dilemma. If the divine is revealed as incarnated without diminishment in a life that is fully human, the contradiction is resolved. Without the incarnation of Jesus, all dualistic strands of thought separate reality from appearance, fact from value, act from meaning, sense from intellect, history from idea, empiricism from theory, and person from work.

These paradoxes have been at the center of some of the deepest concerns about reality through the ages. What early Christology did, rather unsuspectingly, was offer the answer to these ageless concerns in a person, a conceived baby. The meaning of existence and the purpose of all reality are found in Mary's child. In the person of Jesus, we have the permanent and eternal conjoining of divinity and humanity, Spirit and history, being and act, ideal and existence, eternality and temporality, infinitude and space.[27]

For centuries philosophers and theologians have debated the relationship between the one and the many and the universal and the particular. The doctrine of the virgin birth enables a coherent explanation of the relationship between these themes that point to the deepest questions of the human mind. The bringing together of all reality, spirit and flesh, idea and actual experience, is the grandeur of the incarnation. The early theologians thought that

---

27. This list could include unity and diversity, transcendental and real, noumena and phenomena, ontology and economy, uncreated and created, eternity and time, *homoousion* and *perichoresis*, being and energies, essence and accidents, nature and individuation.

Jesus held the universe together and sustained it. Colin Gunton affirms this:

> God comes into relation with that which is not himself through his Son, the mediator between himself and the creation, and the Son is rightly conceived as *Logos*, not only the Word spoken to time from eternity, but the immanent dynamic of meaning which holds space and time together.[28]

Because the people of Israel drew the clearest lines between the divine and the natural, they could not accept this joining of the divine human realities in the virgin birth if it did not have the authority of truth.

The virgin birth affirms that the Son of God is taking on flesh at the point where all human persons begin: conception. The pagan accounts emphasize divine domination and passive humanity. The virgin birth entails a twofold revolution in thought: the transcendent God gladly assumes flesh and at the same time enables an exaltation of the flesh. Revelation in the virgin-born Christ is positive in both directions. He chooses to be with us, the Image of God; and he shows us how important we are to him, made in the image of God.

This birth offers life in a distinctively Trinitarian way. "The Holy Spirit will come on you, and the power of the Most High will overshadow you" (Luke 1:35). This supernatural event is possible because nothing is impossible with God. The virgin birth helps maintain a clear picture of how God desires to relate to his world. If the self-revealing nature of God is based upon the initiative of divine love, then the worth and purpose of created reality is defined by the incarnation. He brings a gracious offer to restore what was lost in the fall. His love is now expressed in human form. He offers himself in gracious self-giving. The incarnation is a direct result of grace, and that grace becomes evident when he takes our nature

---

28. Gunton, *The One, the Three and the Many*, Chapter 6; see especially the conclusion on 178–79.

upon himself to save, heal, and dwell in our midst.[29] He remakes what has been destroyed through the fall. Sinful nature is met with grace. The incarnation must never be separated from the atonement, the nexus where grace and nature communicate perfectly.

Another implication of the virgin birth bears fruit theologically and shows us Christ's nature. The economy of God's act in the incarnation is based upon the ontology (being) of his triune nature. This origin offers a clear picture of personhood. Triune personhood is best understood as three persons in mutual love, not as isolated individuals. Because persons never come alone, it was necessary for Jesus to be incarnated by birth into a human family. The virgin birth is not a deposit of divine spirit into a womb. The ever-dependent Son of the Father is made incarnate by the Holy Spirit's work in and through the full womanhood of Mary. He equally depends upon her. Jesus never ceases to be a divine person, yet he truly becomes a human being. He defines personhood in two directions.

No definition of a person is possible without the web of relationships that comprise existence. The connection between Savior and salvation is made only in Jesus because he participates in both triune relationship with God and complete identification with humanity. Salvation could come only through a divine person who became a human person. No one is saved alone. The church has insisted that the incarnation is a twofold reality. Jesus did not cease being dependent upon the Father through the Spirit. He humbled himself to become dependent upon an earthly mother and father. The incarnation would have been, as Farrer put it, "nothing, but for his relation to his family, his disciples and his nation."[30] His giving and his receiving define his saving nature.

---

29. Augustine (*Sermons*, NPNF1 6:246) argues with force that the inclusion of Mary in the order of salvation history was the only way in which all of humanity could be included. He anticipates many of the arguments put forward by more radical expressions of the feminist theological movement.

30. Farrer, *Saving Belief*, 157. Farrer adds that without these continuing relationships, the ascension of the incarnate Son would be meaningless as well.

The most important conclusion regarding the miracle of the incarnation is the nature of the person who saves: "You shall call his name Jesus." Other Jewish boys had been named Joshua (Heb. *Jehoshua*, or "Yahweh saves"), but this one *is* salvation. We are forced to ask about the nature of the one who was born. The angel announces that *Yahweh* will save (Matt 1:21) and that he is *Immanuel* ("God with us," 1:23). The Gospel begins with these angelic proclamations. The long-awaited Messiah arrives in presence and power. The names of God are applied to one who will be born of Mary. That conception and birth was not of any human initiative. The early church settled on the much-debated term *theotokos*, or "God-bearer," to acknowledge Mary's role in the divine conception of Jesus. The church underscored the full implications of this proclamation by affirming the pre-existent Son of God (in an eternal unbroken relationship with the Father and the Spirit) who became a baby. Any explanation of the union of spirit and flesh must relate to the conception of the God-Man, Jesus Christ: the Word *become* flesh (John 1:14).

We can never divorce theology from history. This particular birth in Bethlehem places Jesus within God's long covenant relationship with Israel. Creation, covenant, deliverance, promised land, kingship, exile, and return from captivity—all reveal the nature of God. There is a correlation between the way God revealed himself to Israel and to Mary.[31] God has always revealed himself to humanity in space and time. However, the self-giving of God never implies a lessening of his divinity. The perfect Son of God takes on a human nature. The divine becomes human by assuming a particular human body and nature.

A certain theological reductionism regarding this important cosmological concept leaves us with the typical formulation: Mary's baby became the Son of God. The proponents of this theme advocate the equation of Jesus with other religious leaders. In Adoption-

---

31. Torrance, *Reality and Evangelical Theology*, 87–88.

HOLY LOVE: A WESLEYAN THEOLOGY

istic modes of thought he becomes another sage, another mythic demigod, another surreal guru, anything but an incarnate Savior. Every confession and creed accepted by the church had some reference to this key aspect of reality, the virgin birth. God's eternal Son became the son of Mary.

Paradoxically, the conception of Jesus in the womb of a virgin stresses the utter humanity of Christ and the radical uniqueness of the historical personhood of Jesus. The central claim of the early Christians is this: Jesus of Nazareth is the only one who, in his own body, can offer full redemption from every sin.[32] This affirmation may have been used by the early church as a defense, but it also ends up being a proof of divine grace. We rightly marvel that he did not "abhor the virgin's womb."[33] In fact, his motive appears to be quite the opposite; he loved and sought and honored that womb.[34]

One can track the importance of the doctrine of the virgin birth by its concomitants. If the means by which Jesus came to his world is an offense, how much more will the discussion of incarnation, or the atonement, or the resurrection, or the second coming be offensive? Without the virgin birth there is no Immanuel. We must recognize that the glory of God took on human flesh and tabernacled with us in every way.

We do not believe in a myth, but we do believe in a mystery. Many have sought to be gods; only one God purposed to be a human. The virgin birth was the Father's means of incarnating his Son in the

---

32. *Didache, ANF* 7:380, "Jesus your servant." *1 Clement*, "Let us fix our eyes on the blood of Christ," *ANF* 10:231; *1 Clement*, "Jesus Christ our Lord, in accordance with God's will, gave his blood for us," *ANF* 10:244. Ignatius, *Ephesians*, "You took on new life through the blood of God," *ANF* 1:49. Justin Martyr, *1 Apology*, "a crucified man that he is the first-begotten of the Unbegotten God," *ANF* 1:180. See also Irenaeus, *Against Heresies, ANF* 1:440–43.

33. Wesley, *BE Works of John Wesley*, 7:505; Hymn #343.

34. "Once the great glove of Nature was taken off his hand. His naked hand touched her. There was of course a unique reason for it. That time he was creating not simply a man but the Man who was to be himself: was creating Man anew: was beginning, at this divine and human point, the New Creation of all things" (Lewis, *Miracles*, 138).

power of the Holy Spirit. The triune God did not send a surrogate, an emanation, an aeon, or a delegate. He came himself. While the cause may not be as clear as we like, the effect is unmistakable. The involvement of the entire Trinity in the incarnation is made clear.

His coming reinforces the self-abnegating love of the Trinity.[35] We miss God if we cannot discern his utter humility. God came only once in human form. If we miss him, we have missed God.

The virgin birth helps us to see that Jesus was not a phantom or a mirage but the divine Son who stepped into his creation. God really became human. Only God can save because he saves precisely as a human for all other humans. And he saves by making himself one with us. He took what is ours and imparted to us what is his. As Mediator, he shares a bodily solidarity with us now and forever. Jesus, then, is not an abstract moral guide. The church fathers are careful to communicate that the atoning reconciliation included the whole of Christ's incarnate life.

JESUS IS REVEALED BY AND FULFILLS PROPHECY

Many prophets in Israel foretold the coming of Jesus. The message of the prophetic texts was assumed in the preaching of his disciples. Some of the earliest debates about the divinity of Jesus revolved around the interpretation of these prophetic texts. The plan of redemption is an eternal, sovereign, and loving expression of the heart of the triune God. Revelation then has no greater purpose than to disclose the nature of the God who came to Israel. The work of the Spirit at Pentecost enabled the disciples to see Jesus throughout the Old Testament. The Son did not wait to be revealed in Bethlehem. The triune God had a history before the manger.[36]

---

35. Self-abnegation is another term for self-denying. "The response to self-existent love is self-abnegating love. . . . When he died on the cross, he did that, in the wild weather of his outlying provinces, in the torture of the body of his revelation, which he had done at home in glory and gladness" (Lewis, *George MacDonald*, 75).

36. Leo the Great, Sermon 24.1 *NPNF2* 12:134–35.

HOLY LOVE: A WESLEYAN THEOLOGY

Prophecy is more than telling the future. In the Hebrew mind, prophecy is the revelatory uncovering of God in time and space and a recognition of his vibrant presence in and through actual occurrences. Even so, we should not ignore the foretelling aspect of prophecy. The number of prophecies that Jesus fulfilled is one of the most remarkable pieces of evidence of the veracity of Scripture.

SCRIPTURE AND JESUS ACCORDING TO THE FATHERS

Justin Martyr, the first post-apostolic theologian, provides a good example of the Christological insight the early Christians found in the Old Testament. He finds Jesus in all of Scripture.[37] In his *Dialogue*, Justin and a Jew named Trypho were antagonists.[38] Their fundamental difference represents a basic contention that continues to this day. Trypho defended a theology characterized by a static monotheism derived from Platonic influences. He insisted the "one" must necessarily mean God as "undifferentiated being." Such a philosophical barrier cannot be overcome even by the promise that the invisible God would send a Messiah.[39] Justin's intriguing exegesis provides the foundation for later thinkers to conclude that a biblical concept of unity in God includes the distinctions of the three persons.

Justin saw the encroachment of philosophy as a challenge to the meaning of the Hebrew text. His first reference to Christ is

---

37. It is important to remember that it was not until the fourth century that a New Testament canon was authoritatively discerned for Christianity. Major portions were used by the earliest fathers, but most did not have access to the entire corpus. The canon of the Old Testament had been determined in the second century BC.

38. Justin, *Dialogue, ANF* 1:194–270.

39. Obviously, if the one sent by God is not divine then it is questionable whether his actions would have any merit, especially of an eternal nature. The entirety of Justin's arguments is based on a Trinitarian schema that challenges the Jewish interpretation of Scripture at every point. The One is the Father, Son, and Holy Spirit. See *Dialogue*, 223–25, 228. He does not move into subtle theology. His main trajectory is to take the text of the Old Testament and show Jesus in it. He does deal with the oneness of divine nature and the begottenness of the Son without division of the One in *Dialogue*, 264. Platonic structuring of reality would not allow the unity of God to be distinguished by the inclusion of another being.

Isaiah's promise that the "Arm" of Yahweh would glorify him. In his summation of nearly all the major points of theological importance in the Old Testament, Justin views the law, the covenants, the Sabbath—even circumcision—as clear prophecies fulfilled only in Christ. He does not hesitate to see Jesus as the Son of the Father in the active ministry of self-revelation *before* Bethlehem, Nazareth, and Capernaum.

The treatment of the Old Testament by early exegetes displays a profound Christological interpretation. Such an interpretation has been rejected by modern attempts to impose the constraints of historical criticism. While the techniques of the fathers may not fully coincide with the clarity of interpretation found in recent scholars, the early believers saw the canon as replete with Christ. For them, the Old Testament was much more than a precursor to Christology. Ignatius of Antioch states the matter plainly: "But to me Jesus Christ is in the place of all that is ancient: his cross, and death, and resurrection, and the faith which is by him, are undefiled monuments of antiquity."[40]

The authority of Scripture is not questioned in the early church. The entirety of Scripture was a Christian book. The fathers strongly believed that we are led to a fuller comprehension by progressive revelation. As Grillmeier avers, "The theophanies of the Old Testament also belong to this historical revelation of the *Logos*: they are a prelude to the incarnation, the beginning of the process of the incarnation in the full sense."[41] The ancient fathers want to substantiate all the claims of deliverance for Israel. For them, the revelation of the Trinity is not confined to the New Testament, but the New Testament must be the exegetical lens through which one views the Old Testament. By its encounter with the Risen Christ, the early church discerned the Christological implications of the Old Testa-

---

40. Ignatius, *Epistle to the Philadephians, ANF* 1:84. I am grateful to J. J. O'Keefe and R. R. Reno who pointed me to this text in their *Sanctified Vision*, 27–28.

41. Grillmeier, *Christ in Christian Tradition*, 1:115.

HOLY LOVE: A WESLEYAN THEOLOGY

ment. Once a biblical scholar acknowledges the dominant place of Jesus in revelation, a deepening Trinitarian framework forms. Then the economy of God can be described as a progressively revelatory expression of God's dynamic personhood.

The fathers consistently point us toward a Trinitarian view of the eternal God. They believed that the essence of the Christian tradition was revealed in Jesus Christ and that the Old Testament pointed to his person in myriad ways. A Trinitarian reading of the Old Testament was the foundation of the earliest creeds. The center of the meaning of the law, the covenants, the priesthood, and Israel was the *person* of the Son.

The interdependence of Old Testament and New Testament in this regard highlights the need for a high view of the entirety of Scripture. The Old Testament is incomplete theologically. The cry for a fulfillment of the covenant is pervasive, but once Jesus was revealed then the dynamic hand of the triune God was read retrospectively by those who acknowledged the three-personed God. Some of the church fathers' insights assist us in remembering that God in *his* triune self-revelation has never changed.

In the huge task of drawing together the strands of Scripture and tradition with philosophy and culture, as systematic theology must do, it is important to remain open to the clearest Trinitarian interpretations. The earlier handling of Scripture with Christocentric lenses kept the nature of a triune God at the center.[42] The focus was different than ours. Early interpreters regarded the Father, Son, and Spirit as active in all of Scripture, but they saw Jesus Christ as the fulfillment of typology, its interpretive center, the

---

42. Radner, *Hope Among the Fragments*. Radner helps with a discussion of the Father's "figural" reading of the text in chapter five. Christ was viewed, he says, as the "original form," as the denotative form which gives all else meaning (11–13). A unified vision of God's being in the world results from the Father's "thematically organizing," "imagistically connecting," "narrationally weaving," the strands of Scripture together (97). This immersion in the text was based upon the "perceived providential power of the Triune God" (100). O'Keefe and Reno give the same type of assessment in *Sanctified Vision*.

key to understanding its meaning. He was the orienting principle behind all exegetical endeavors. This reading of Scripture redefines the merely numerical understanding of monotheism. There is no confusion regarding distinctions within God's own life and revelation. The progress of revelation and dogma inform and prepare us for the revelation of Jesus who is both Lord and Christ.

WHAT BIBLICAL MONOTHEISM INTENDS

Jewish theistic monotheism had the expectation of a divine Messiah. This monotheism was never construed as Unitarianism.[43] In the history of the religions, a unitarian divinity often results in a predisposition to power. Israel was never allowed to project their perception of authority, power, and vengeance upon the one God. They possessed the revelation of the true God in all his fullness. Modes of theology that could only conceive of God as *essence* or *undifferentiated being* were later accretions. By its own nature, biblical monotheism includes the dynamic possibility of the Trinity from the outset. The narrative of Jesus did not begin in the Gospel accounts and is not completed without the book of Revelation. If, as theologians over the centuries have claimed, the center of revelation is the Son, then as Wesley says, he is "the foundation, corner and top-stone of all religion . . . the spring and soul and center of revealed religion."[44]

In this present period of the church's preoccupation with interpretation we must follow the fathers in their Christological sensitivities. Their earliest writings challenge pagan concepts of knowledge. For those outside the Christian faith, *theologia* was a way of thinking that concluded with the mind's apprehension of the divine: an

---

43. Zizioulas, *Being as Communion*, 27–65. Recent scholarship has debated the origins of the relation between power and a non-personal concept of God that arises from a non-Trinitarian theology. Equating personhood with will and not with love is often seen to be at the base of "pathological" theology. See Gunton, *Yesterday and Today,* 188–89, or his *Enlightenment and Alienation,* 65.

44. Wesley, *Notes*, 2:1626, 1516. See also Wesley, *BE Works,* 2:591–92 for a similar hermeneutical statement.

HOLY LOVE: A WESLEYAN THEOLOGY

ever-elusive goal. For those thinkers who had placed their faith in him, Christ engendered a totally new insight and a distinctly Christian *theologia*. God himself had started the process of personal engagement. He had initiated it, and those who wanted to see the face of this self-giving God must turn to Jesus Christ.[45]

The continuity of revelation that issues from the heart of our triune God necessitates that prophecy relating to Jesus be taken in an ever-deepening way. Orthodox Christology insists that the tri-unity of God is found in both Testaments.[46] This God is alive and active—always three persons. At base, then, the interpretive analysis of the early exegetes determined three distinctive modes of revelation. Three basic truths are comprehensible: the God who is never seen, the God seen and met face to face, and the God seen in his people.[47] Indeed, the Son is active in the Old Testament. His person is far more than a logical consequence of the faith of Israel. The Gospels reveal the climax of the revelation of the Three-in-one God, not its beginning.

Jesus at the Temple

The early church's worship of Jesus sanctifies time by observing a liturgical calendar. Another key event prior to the inauguration of his actual ministry is prominent in the church year. The preceding fulfillment motif is underscored by the Christian year during the season that follows Advent. Epiphany highlights the self-manifestation of the Savior, a revelation tied to the covenants made between Yahweh and Israel. One focus is the appearance of Jesus as an infant at the temple eight days after his birth. The structure of Luke 1–2 prepares for the arrival of Jesus. Luke records four "songs" celebrating the marvel of God's redemption in history.[48] Here is an example

---

45. Wilken, *The Spirit of Early Christian Thought*, 15.

46. Note that Irenaeus "demonstrates" what he considers an example of apostolic kerygma concerning Christ by using primarily Old Testament texts in exploring and supporting each of his major points in *On the Apostolic Preaching*.

47. Irenaeus, *Against Heresies*, ANF 1:489–90.

48. Zechariah, Mary, the angels, and Simeon offer songs not only of praise but also of deep theological interpretation and expression of the events surrounding

of the biblical precedent for theology flowing out of worship. As a picture of the full Jewishness of Jesus' family, one finds references to a strict keeping of the laws surrounding the birth of a firstborn son. The Law was always meant to be a relational self-definition of God. Jesus' presentation in the temple thrusts us back to the Abrahamic covenant that originated with a self-revelation in the name *El Shaddai* ("God Almighty").[49] The biblical concept of circumcision was instituted before the birth of Isaac as a seal of the covenant, a vow symbolizing the relationship between Yahweh and Abraham's descendants (Israel). Everything God promised depended upon this child. The destiny of Israel and the "only son" of Abraham became inextricably intertwined.

The rite of circumcision was not meant to represent oppressive patriarchy or a sexualized religiosity as in pagan cults. Nor was it a form of mutilation or self-sacrifice. Rather it was symbolic of covenant responsibilities and blessing, a symbol of renewal and purification because of deep uncleanness. Abraham and his progeny were aware of the inherent responsibility in relationship carried by both parties in this covenant of love. "Walk before me faithfully" (Gen 17:1) carried with it a call to moral responsibility and to enduring faithfulness.

The parallels between Genesis and Luke are unmistakable. In Luke, another "only Son" is present at the place of worship and sacrifice in the temple. Jesus had been born even more miraculously than Isaac. All the promises center in Jesus. He is more than the seal of a covenant. He *is* the covenant. In the temple, the Bestower of covenantal blessings comes as the best blessing.[50] From the beginning of his earthly existence, Jesus chose to join himself to every area of humanity. But here is something even deeper. Note the presence of

---

the birth of Jesus. The *BCP* offers all four hymns as a part of Morning Prayer, which indicates once more the church's awareness that prayer and worship are the proper contexts for engagement with reality.

49. Gen 17:1.

50. The early church expressed this by naming Simeon "theodochus," the God-receiver.

HOLY LOVE: A WESLEYAN THEOLOGY

innocence, of a lack of power and the presence of pain and blood. Even at this early stage of life Jesus undertakes the sin of humanity that he came to bear away. The Clean One comes to our uncleanness to cleanse forever. Circumcision becomes a point of revelation of the nature of the Son. His is not merely an outward identification but a transformative appropriation of all our humanity.

The circumcision ritual is an initial revelation of the life of God, a startlingly clear statement that life is not under the sole ownership or control of the human person, even if that life is the life of the Son of God. Dependence on another for life is one of the hallmarks of personhood and speaks of the origin of life itself. The source of life is never in oneself. This derivation of life from Another was to become a recurrent theme in the self-understanding and ministry of Jesus. The mark of the covenant was an affirmation that the recipient of God's love could not produce anything fruitful in isolation from the gift Giver. This mark was to be the symbol of a personal reality. The faith of Israel was intended as a habitual disposition of soul to walk by faith in the way of holiness. The mark upon Jesus brings him into that ambit of obedient holy love. This is a symbol of the faith of the Son lived out in his humanity. He ever lives with a totality of commitment of heart to his Father. Even in this nascent event prior to actual ministry, one is intercepted with a declaration about the center of all revelation: *holy love*. Jesus, before he speaks a word, reveals the central reality that comprises all of God's life, his redemptive purpose, and the election of Israel as he is carried by his parents to the Court of Women. To love God with all of one's being is the center of Israel's purpose for existence; not a love of him "above all things" but that all loves are loved in relation to the love of the Holy One.[51] The incarnate Son bears in his body the

---

51. "I do not say 'above all things,' for it is both an unscriptural and an ambiguous expression, but 'with all thy heart, and with all thy mind, and with all thy soul, and with all thy strength'" (Wesley, *BE Works*, 2:88).

marks of covenantal love, a love that originated in eternity.[52] This initial mark foreshadows the day when the expected Messiah will be marred beyond recognition to show holy love in a gracious judgment and glorious redemption for all human sin.

ANOINTED AS MESSIAH AND INAUGURATION OF MINISTRY AT BAPTISM

The expectation of the Messiah was fulfilled in Jesus. The inaugural events of the Messiah's coming instruct us further regarding his person. His anointing and baptism made distinct in the early kerygma can be addressed together. First, we will look at the relational implications of the baptism of Jesus and the immediate result of that attestation: his being led into the wilderness by the Holy Spirit. In all the Gospels Jesus is viewed as the climax of the entire Old Testament.[53] They give a clear conception of salvation in the history of Israel, yet that background finds its ultimate meaning in the Messiah's long-anticipated arrival. He is the ultimate fulfillment of the promises of God. Every major image, idea, or word that drew Israel to God finds its ultimate completion in Christ. Resident in the interpretation of the divine affirmation from heaven, "This is My beloved Son," are the meanings of Kingship, Isaiah's Suffering Servant, and the *Akedah,* the sacrifice of Isaac.[54] The deep yearning of the people of God for a deliverer is fulfilled in the person of Jesus.

The church fathers considered space and time as the created means for revelation. A very different type of hermeneutic emerges than that permitted by modern theological constructs. Laying biblical foundations in our day seems to require submission to a narrow

---

52. The only other vignette of the growing years of Jesus is found in the same chapter, where Jesus is once again in Jerusalem at the Temple (Luke 2:41–52). The themes mentioned above can also be discerned here. He is shown as diligently seeking after God with a whole heart. We have the intimacy with the Father as the basis of his life and ministry. And there is an undeniable humility, shown in his deference, towards those he came to save.

53. One recent example of this theme is found in Wright, *The Climax of the Covenant*, especially chapters 1–2.

54. Ps 2:7, Isa 42:1–9, Gen 22.

scientific rationalism. While historical criticism has provided helpful critical tools, it sometimes limits the fullness of meaning that the language of Scripture mediates. In contrast, Ignatius introduces us to a more holistic hermeneutic when he says, "He was born, and was baptized in order to purify the water by the passion."[55] The historical reality of the baptism of Jesus is tied to a deeper theological meaning.[56] Again we see the move from historical witness and verification to illumination on the being and nature of the person. What Ignatius intends is not a denial of the veracity of the actual account. What he intuits is a profound engagement of the divine with our life, in incarnation, inauguration of ministry, and the sanctification of the created order, all of which come together in one moment at the Jordan.

Similar to circumcision, baptism for the Jew was an act of repentance (*metanoia*) and a symbol with a broad range of meanings. Over the centuries Jewish forms of baptism included penitence, submission, conversion, and expectation of a place in the Messiah's kingdom.[57] But there are deeper truths to be uncovered here. No one has ever been able to convincingly disprove the sinlessness of Jesus even though his enemies did falsely accuse him of illegitimacy and of blasphemy. He did not enter the Jordan because of his own sin.[58] John consented to baptize him in order to "fulfill all righteousness" (Matt 3:15). Here we find a revelation of the Trinity that is bracingly forthright. As he is coming up out of the waters, the eternal Son is "anointed" by the descending Spirit; then the Father's voice from heaven proclaims the beloved Sonship of Jesus and God's pleasure in him (Matt 3:17). This is a clear affirmation that Jesus' birth, life, and ministry are suffused with the presence

---

55. Ignatius, *Ephesians, ANF* 1:56–57; *Smyrnaeans, ANF* 1:86.

56. It is illuminating that the early critic of Christianity, Celsus, apparently took as his first two places to discredit Christianity: the virgin birth and the baptism by the Holy Spirit in the Jordan (Origen, *Against Celsus, ANF* 4:413).

57. Beasley-Murray, "Baptism," *NIDNTT* 1:144–46; *Baptism in the New Testament*, 31–44.

58. Matt 3:13–17.

of the first and third persons of the triune Godhead. In the life of Jesus, being precedes function. We are invited into the drama of an eternal and a "new" expression of that relationship in the history of salvation. The power, focus, and direction of the life of Jesus are not found in himself alone. His life and being are from Another.

The baptism, which is his inauguration to ministry, will lead to the cross. At this moment, we find a tri-personal God. God is fully present for the redemption of the world.[59] Jesus is found at the Jordan as a second Joshua who will engage in a complete conquest of love. Notice Jesus is in the Jordan and then the wilderness at the pivotal point in his ministry. If the triune God is to affect our redemption, he must identify with sin (Isa 53:5). An absolute identification with the implications of the fall requires a Trinitarian participation. In this scene, the Spirit who hovers over the waters at creation now descends upon the Son with the same power to produce a new creation.

Israel's God comes to the wilderness, the chaos, the wandering and offers a new order of existence. Where there was once barrenness, a restoration of life can begin. The only way to effect redemption is as one of his own and from within his own creation. No Docetic or gnostic scheme will serve. He comes to the chaos. He starts with the world as it is. He does so by showing us first his triune nature. The triune persons and the work of recapitulation of deliverance are inseparable. This seems very close to the doctrine of recapitulation of the church father, Irenaeus.[60] Reality is revealed

---

59. Augustine, *NPNF*2 6:258–59. Here Augustine raises the issue of the relation between the work of the Father and the Son. He concludes that neither person ever works without the other.

60. The profoundly influential doctrine of recapitulation (Greek, *anakephaliosis;* Latin, *recapitulatio*) was first offered by Irenaeus (ca. AD 130–200) in his magnum opus *Against Heresies*. In the third book he assails every form of Docetism, or the denial of the full humanity of the *Logos*. In the descent and ascent of God in the flesh, Irenaeus saw the full re-ordering, restructuring, recreating of human nature and the universe. Thus, Jesus reformulates all that was broken by sin in his incarnate birth, life, death, and resurrection and because he now reigns at the right hand of God, he assures us of a completion and fulfillment of all the creation.

HOLY LOVE: A WESLEYAN THEOLOGY

when God takes hopelessness into himself. Jesus shows the brokenness in all of us, as exemplified in Israel's wanderings.

MINISTRY MARKED BY THE POWER OF GOD

For a biblical Christology, theological terms must be defined
by reference to Jesus' moral character and ministry. The connota-
tions of terms such as glory, power, mercy, and judgment take on
a remarkably different hue when the person of Jesus is placed at
center stage.

In the Gospel of John, Jesus manifests his glory with his first
miracle at Cana of Galilee (John 2:1–11).[61] The uniqueness of this
sign is connected to this, his first miracle, at the dawning of the
greatest moment in human history, Jesus' life and ministry.[62] Its
grandeur is heightened by the stated purpose of the author in
encouraging belief in Jesus Christ the Son of God (John 20:31). The
ministry of John the Baptist and this first sign inaugurate the history of evidence that leads to belief. We are told he had never done
a miracle till now (John 2:11), but that when he did manifest his
glory, his disciples believed on him.

Notwithstanding the actual transformation of physical elements, the Son shows something of the nature of divine reality.
Here we have revelation of the Son of God in a context of substantial relationships, in the midst of people open to him in a variety of
ways: (1) Mary expressed expectant trust, (2) the steward obeyed
the Lord's command, and (3) the disciples demonstrated belief.
Miracles are the revelation of the triune God at work in the world.
In John, all that Jesus does is intimately connected to the work of
the Father (John 5:19) and the Spirit (John 1:32; 16:7; Luke 4:18).
Clearly this is a disclosure of Jesus as the incarnate God, re-Creator
of all the universe.

---

61. The signs are bracketed by references to glory, see John 2:11 and 11:40.
62. Note for instance the breadth of interest in this miracle in the archaeology
of the catacombs. Of the first fifty-two sarcophagi uncovered in the catacombs,
sixteen had a rosette of this miracle upon them.

With the background of Jewish marriage climaxing in a banquet in the groom's house, this manifestation of Jesus is tied to the real needs of an unnamed couple. Mary's awareness of her son's resourcefulness further elucidates the reality of his power and of his humility. Even though there is a hint of reserve, his response to Mary's request is due to a plan that transcends the particular need at hand. Even so, he is not reserved in assisting the needy couple. To Mary he is saying, "This pertains to more than you realize. What I do always has ultimate significance." His miracle-working power indicates that any situation can be altered for the better by his presence. But more, that such power is always a personal manifestation: a new relationship based upon a new era of revelation.

In the midst of this event, Jesus says, "My hour has not yet come" (John 2:4). John's theological argument points to the hour of glorification, the revelatory, miraculous, and universe-altering glory of the cross. The glory of the Son is always tied to humiliation. So, at the threshold of his sign-filled ministry, the consummation is ever before him. There is a clear sense of the "hour" throughout his life. He will choose when to reveal himself. He is not hurried by anyone. And the need is never the central issue in any miracle. Divine plans and power are always a revelation of the personal nature of God; they affect our actual lives. "You really don't know what you are asking" is not necessarily a rebuke; it is an indication that the most mundane of miraculous deeds has about it the shadow of the cross.[63] In order for the mundane to be transformed, the Creator must recapitulate the creation in himself.

The traces of divine self-revelation are explored by expositors of the early church. His actions are revelatory from categories such as:

1. gracious self-giving (event in the context of intimate care).

---

63. Because all we have are the words and no statement about intention, it is difficult to know if Jesus is truly rebuking his mother for some lack of perception or if this is merely a common way to refer with respect to a mother. The beauty of this nuptial scene in relation to this revelation of holy love would indicate profound respect.

HOLY LOVE: A WESLEYAN THEOLOGY

2. mystery (his will is not exhaustible).
3. self-denying (the groom receives adulation, not Jesus).
4. progressive nature of revelation (God's gifts are better over time).
5. unostentatious generosity (the goodness of God in creation).
6. the sign of abundance (the fullness of the triune Life).

The overflowing grace of the triune God in the Incarnate One always reveals an unexpected quality. At the end of thirty years of silence, the beginning of a whole new vantage point on the humility of glory emerges. Jesus is more than merely human, in that every problem finds its solution in his presence. He always turns the lower into the higher and the common into the valuable.

A question that has occupied the church has been why John included the wedding at Cana as the site of the first sign. Scholars have suggested that John's use of the "first" (Greek, *archon*) here relates to the "beginning" (Greek, *arche*) of John 1:1. There is a distinct contrast between the ascetic of fasting (the theme of the wilderness and John the Baptist's diet) and the joyful aesthetic of this marriage feast. If the revelation of the Son in the Spirit to the glory of the Father is at the base of his miracle-working power, then transformation as the first sign points us beyond the work to Who is manifested. This omnipotence is infinite in power with absolute trustworthiness. This beneficence is about the business of bestowing gifts of grace, the greatest of which is himself. The Catholic tradition has no reservation in seeing the promised feast of bread and wine in this first revelatory act. The titles "Son of God" (John 1:49) and "Son of Man" (John 1:51) find their balance in this initial self-disclosure.

In order to comprehend the reality of God in the flesh, one must recognize how much he has become like us. Even amidst the mundane there is a reiteration of his divine person as the Son of God, the one who bears the "glory of the one and only Son, who came from the Father," (John 1:14) and who makes the Father known (John 1:18). At Cana, another era begins, and a new kind of life is inaugurated. Before the more public and unmistakable re-ordering of the temple, Jesus is placed at the scene of a wedding.[64] The highest level of promised intimacy, which is the only life that God offers, is represented here in origin. As it took Israel centuries to understand God's ultimate purposes, it would take the disciples of Jesus a long time to conceive that nuptial category would be the clearest picture they would ever have of salvation and of the nature of God's own life.

The power of this sign contributes much to our understanding of human marriage. The fall left a deep rift at the center of human relationship in marriage (Gen 3:7, 16–17). The presence of the Son at the sealing of a human covenant of love between a man and a woman points us to the recapitulation of the most sacred of relationships.[65] Without Jesus, human love is a distortion of what he intended. If he can gain access to that relational intimacy, then it might become again what it was intended to be, a sign of an eternal relationship of love-in-distinction between the triune persons.[66]

---

64. Marriage was viewed with an almost sacramental character in second temple period Judaism. There is the constant challenge in the Old Testament of the height of sin being the forgotten spousehood Israel to Yahweh (Hos; Ezek 16; Isa 62:1–4; Jer 6:6–7, 21–24). Unlike the sentimental vacuousness of today's contractual arrangements, marriage was taken very seriously. It carried a dual respect, both sanctity and gladness. It is no wonder then that many exegetes from the early church to Jonathan Edwards saw here more than a mere nuptial agreement but a type of the gospel.

65. One thinks of the intriguing analysis of Frei, *The Identity of Jesus Christ*, regarding the nature of personhood revealed by the inseparable nature of intention and action, that the unique divine nature of Christ and the triune God he manifests is built into the pattern of self-revelation of the Gospels. While Frei believes that the revelation of Christ, as a singular identifiable "unsubstitutable" person, is not truly focused until the Passion narrative begins, he does lay a foundation for the type of analysis shown here in self-revelation at Cana. The persistence, elusiveness, and ultimacy of the person of Christ is experienced in word and action and that is a revelation of his presence.

66. Our preceding discussion of the patristic insight into the text finds an interesting example in the interpretation of this passage. In an otherwise exhaustive Trinitarian analysis of the book of John, Royce Gruenler totally passes over this passage in terms of support for his thesis (see *The Trinity in the Gospel*

If this vignette and the cleansing of the temple (John 2:13–22) are compared, the two major aspects of the nature of God are manifested at the outset of the ministry of Jesus. The first pericope shows the power of God in a relational context, a correct view of the nature of love in creation. The second reveals a wrong understanding of holiness by the religious community. He must correct both because of the importance both institutions bear in revealing the true nature of God.

The first of the signs of the Son of God manifests his glory in the glory of:

1. His person, his purpose, his work.
2. Creation and its purpose—to produce a bride for himself.
3. True reality—he is the only Savior who offers us his life.
4. His tender love.
5. A union through Christ with God vividly imaged in nuptial terms.

Triune reality revealed in the person of the Son is the center of theology. All signs flow from this center; they are the unfolding, the explanation, the result. The glory does not begin on earth; Cana only manifests what was always there from eternity in the Holy One.

MIRACLES AS MANIFESTATION OF
THE PERSON OF CHRIST

In the early church, the worship of Jesus as Lord was closely connected to a continual review of his works.[67] The miracles of heal-

---

of John, 29–30). A survey of most major commentaries reveals the same absence of comment on the blessing of relationship or more, the symbol of marriage in relation to triune reality. See Morris, *The Gospel According to John*, 176–78; Beasley-Murray, *The Gospel of John*, 32–37; Keener, *The Gospel of John*, 1:515. It is intriguing how few of the fathers are mentioned to any extent in these preceding commentaries.

Augustine highlights the presence of the bridegroom who instituted marriage in the middle of the wedding of two persons (*Lectures on the Gospel of John*, *NPNF*1 7:63). Following this, Augustine discerns a Trinitarian theme in the contents of the water jars (66).

67. Chrysostom challenges the readers of his *Homilies on the Gospel of St. Matthew* in light of miracles of Jesus to "give thanks continually. For it is too

ing confirmed the claims made about his divinity. Jesus was much more than a wonder-worker. His signs and wonders always reflected a richness of person more than an attraction to the act in itself. This perfect expression of the eternal life of the triune God is foundational for all the miraculous expressions in the life of Jesus. When it comes to rightly understanding the theological import of the miracles, the logic is crucial. Jesus is not divine because he works miracles. The works of the divine persons draw all things back into the intended purposes of God and serve as perceptible indications of the constant providence of the triune God. He revealed redemptive power in an incarnate life. God never intended the acts of power in creation to be removed from the revelation of the Son. Revelation involves a program of re-creation that is ultimately made possible through the sending of the Son by the Father in the power of the Spirit. When we grasp this, the cross stands out in its true glory, and forgiveness through atonement is understood as a priceless gift.

In John's description of Jesus' ministry, the miracles point to the highest reality we can conceive.[68] Manifesting the glory of Christ is the true essence of Christianity, the church, and the church's mission. Any preoccupation with the immediate results of the miracles or attempts to require their presence is contrary to their divine purpose. They are there to show us the person of Christ. He works them in the power of the Spirit and because they are the work of his Father.

A review of the revelatory encounters identifies at least thirty-six encounters with various people and needs. Major types of Jesus'

---

monstrous, enjoying as we do his bounty in deed every day, not so as in word to acknowledge the favor." And he continues the theme of gratitude to the end of the homily (*NPNF1* 10:174).

68. The cycle of liturgical readings during Epiphany emphasizes the glory revealed through the ministry of miracles. Magi: the inclusion of the Gentiles from the outset; temple: father's business; Cana: relational worldview and transformation of the inanimate; miracles of healing, miracles in his creation, teaching wisdom, transfiguration. For a good example of a Protestant usage of these texts for preaching theologically through the Christian year see Lenski, *The Gospel Selections of the Ancient Church*.

miracles include healings, acts in nature, and raising the dead. Matthew's literary structure demonstrates the close relation of Jesus' work (economy) and person (ontology). The relationship of the inner Trinitarian purposes revealed at the baptism (Matt 3:13–17) and the immediate victory over Satan won in the wilderness (Matt 4:1–11) are followed by the calling of the disciples (Matt 4:18–22) and a preparatory comment: "Jesus went throughout Galilee, teaching in their synagogues, proclaiming the good news of the kingdom, and healing every disease and sickness among the people" (Matt 4:23). In strict chronology, Jesus' preaching ministry is followed by the healing ministry.

The preaching of Jesus in the Sermon on the Mount sets the stage for the healing ministry that follows (Matt 5–7). In Matthew, this narrative serves as a theological bridge to Jesus' broader healing ministry. His astonishing authority is recognized by those present (Matt 7:28). The immediate result of his preaching is the series of miracles that follow.[69] In Matthew 8, Jesus ushers in the kingdom he has already described. Three disparate problems meet with immediate solutions: a leper is cleansed, a paralytic is restored, and Peter's mother-in-law is healed. Just as we see the meekness and mercy of Jesus (Matt 5:5, 7) throughout the book, so we see that Jesus is able to meet every basic human need from this point forward. The climax of this section (Matt 8:16) is a quote from Isaiah: "Surely he took up our pain and bore our suffering, yet we considered him punished by God, stricken by him, and afflicted" (Isa 53:4).[70]

The revelation of the Messiah's kingship (Matt 8–9) is an instructive antitype. The mountain motif points to a second Moses (Matt 8:1); as Moses descended Mount Sinai with the gift of the law,

---

69. Intriguingly, Matthew emphasized each paragraph with a participle of action (8:1, 5, 14).

70. Gregory of Nyssa uses this passage to highlight the *kenosis* of the Son of God, who truly took into himself our infirmities out of obedience to the Father, in his defense of the incarnation against the single-substance theology of Eunomius (*Against Eunomius*, NPNF2 5:121).

just so Jesus descended from the mountainside to offer the Kingdom of God. With Jesus' offer, it becomes possible to understand the victory of the triune God in the redemption of his people both from slavery and from sin. Ten specific miracles follow this initial sermon of Jesus. The similarity between Israel's early mediator, Moses, and the divine Mediator is striking. Each Passover, Israel remembered the ten plagues in Egypt. Jesus, the deliverer, brings people out of a variety of physical bondages. The revelatory nature of these miracles is affirmed by the recurrent emphasis on the presence of Jesus (Matt 8:1, 5, 14). If he is near, there is hope for any human malady.

EXAMPLES OF REPRESENTATIVE TYPES OF MIRACLES

The miracles reveal a self-giving redemptive power. Each Gospel gives examples to verify that Jesus is Lord over every conceivable human predicament. Allowing the principle of holy love to inform our interpretation of the use of power, the following examples aid in thinking theologically about all the miracles.

Cleansing a Leper (Matt 8:1–4)

Following the Sermon on the Mount, Jesus performs a series of marvelous acts. The first of three healings deals with a serious disease with debilitating physical symptoms and radical social stigma.[71] The leper is in a desperate plight. He approaches Jesus trusting in his power.[72] Publicly stepping out in humble confidence, the leper leaves the social isolation brought on by his disease. He acknowledges that the choice to cleanse belongs entirely to Jesus. Represented here is a condition of expectancy with no attempt to manipulate the Master. Trust is placed totally in the Lord's disposi-

---

71. Scholars debate whether this disease is what is called in modern medicine, leprosy (Harrison, "Leprosy," *NIDNTT* 2:463–64).

72. "Prostrated himself," an act of respect but also of urgent distress. "Lord," reveals the utter humility of the beseecher, openness of heart. Leprosy in the first century was living death, kept required distance, but Jesus crosses that line of uncleanness immediately. Note the connection between unclean and what was perceived as incurable emphasized by the recurrence of "clean" in verses 2–3.

tion and ability to restore. But most profound is his apparent belief in Christ as divine. Though never told the source of his faith in the Messiah, we see him lay his life entirely in the hands of Jesus.

The instantaneous healing is indicative of a divine epiphany in time and space. The early fathers of the church discerned that the cleansing of physical leprosy pointed to the need for cleansing of spiritual leprosy.[73] Mark adds that upon seeing him, Jesus was "filled with compassion" (1:41). The unique statement, "I will," indicates that he can conjoin his claims with his actions.[74] Jesus speaks as the Son of God who in the power of the Spirit can heal and forgive. To be cured from leprosy was akin to being raised from the dead. The touch of Jesus expresses an act of power, a willingness to touch the untouchable, and an ability to make pure.[75] In another passage Jesus responds to the questions of the disciples of John the Baptist by listing his wonderful works (including the healing of leprosy) as messianic activities (Matt 11:2–5). The one Israel longed for had come (see Isa 35:4–6). When the Anointed One came, creation began to experience a restorative work. What was undone was re-created in fulfillment of the divine intention.

Restoring the Paralytic (Matt 8:5–13)

The manifestation of the Messiah was intended to reach Gentiles as well as Jews. The universality of grace is evidenced in a miraculous ministry event involving a Roman military officer. A Gentile's home was viewed as unclean in the rabbinic tradition of the day (Luke 7:2). The centurion intuits the absolute nature of

---

73. Origen, *Against Celsus*, ANF 4:416–17; Chrysostom, *ANF* 10:470–72.

74. Each synoptic rendition has this strong unique statement: Matt 8:3, Mark 1:41, Luke 5:13.

75. Rabbinic requirements demanded that any Jew could remain clean if they were 100 cubits downwind from a leper. Jesus is not breaking Mosaic law but fulfilling it by cleansing the man of his disease. Chrysostom writes that Jesus affirmed his lordship over the restrictions of the law and through the touching of the leper he signified himself as "absolute master" (*NPNF1* 10:173).

Jesus' power to heal. Thus, a Gentile first recognizes Jesus' authority to heal someone not immediately present.[76]

Jesus' response indicates the uniqueness of the moment. The term "marveled" (Matt 8:10) is only used of Jesus twice, in this situation and in his response to the unbelief he observed in own hometown (Mark 6:6). The centurion believed that Jesus had the authority to alter personal life whenever it is offered to him by faith. Why is this faith greater than that of Israel? The centurion's faith is based solely on the word of Jesus. It is faith focused more on the person than on the request. As with the leper, the themes of *unclean* and *incurable* appear again, but Jesus justified the man's faith. A statement of Israel's privilege is the climax of this section (Matt 8:11), but it is connected to the larger eschatological reality of the election of Israel. Jesus views this Gentile as the promise of more Gentiles to come, and thus he utters a prophecy concerning the true residents of his kingdom. The healing power of Jesus knows no spatial boundaries, just as his saving grace knows no racial or cultural barriers.

Healing Peter's Mother-in-Law (Matt 8:14–17)

Ministry is not just for public occasions but also for everyday life.[77] The two miracles previous to Simon's mother-in-law involved hopeless cases. Here, in contrast, there is no approach, no request, no fanfare, just Jesus confronting a normal physical problem. Interestingly, there is one similarity to the previous miracles: the rabbis viewed fever as unclean. All that is unclean has the potential of being made new and pure when it comes into contact with Jesus. In this pericope, touch is involved (Matt 8:15, 8:3) and not a word is spoken (Matt 8:3, 13). The Messiah's ability to heal is not dependent upon a proper form of asking. Where Jesus is present, help

---

76. The only two "long-distance" healings are with Gentiles (here and Matt 15:28).

77. Tertullian uses this vignette in his support of the full humanity of Christ and the trustworthiness of his use of his senses (here, touch) against various forms of Platonic idealism (*ANF* 3:197).

HOLY LOVE: A WESLEYAN THEOLOGY

comes due to the re-creative and redemptive power of his life. This act of divine power was twofold: Jesus delivered her from a fever and restored her to service without a period of recuperation.[78]

What do these three miracles manifest? As in all the miracle narratives, the recurrent theme of the authority of Jesus is prominent. They demonstrate Jesus' authority over his creation: stilling the sea (Matt 8:23–27), casting out demons (Matt 8:28–34; 9:32–33), healing and forgiving a paralytic (Matt 9:1–8), stopping an issue of blood (Matt 9:18–26), giving sight to the blind and hearing to the dumb (Matt 9:27–34). More than a mere show of power, this is a messianic fulfillment. The Sent One is verifying the authority of the Father in the power of the Spirit to offer wholeness in every area of life. The disciple is encouraged to trust him, especially his power to heal. And proleptically, the section ends with the authority of Jesus given to his disciples who carry his healing ministry to others (Matt 9:37–10:8).

The supreme works of God have often been distilled to include only the incarnation, the cross, and the resurrection. While entering the debate about suspending natural law or causation (contra Newton, Hume) is beyond the scope of this study, we can say that miracles are signs that God has indeed come. The working of miracles is one aspect of what the triune God does; he creates and recreates. The natural does not produce the supernatural. The fulfillment of the natural is not found in itself. These works are consistent with the revealed nature of God in Christ. In miracles part of prophetic proclamation is fulfilled (Isa 61:1–2; Luke 4:18). He is Lord over his creation (Mark 4:39). Ultimately, all unfortunate results of the fall must be assumed in a self-giving sacrifice in order to be healed (Isa 53:4–5).

Jesus is the gospel incarnate. What is offered in the gospel is *Someone,* not *some thing.* At every point of his ministry, the three classic offices of Christ can be discerned: prophet, priest, and king.

---

78. Chrysostom, *NPNF*1 10:184.

The seal of his prophetic office is disclosed with the logic of all Christology. If he has come from God as God, he will do the works of God. When the Word speaks, what exists conforms to his ultimate intention. Only the human will can resist the speech of God.

Miracles are not new phenomena in the history of Israel. What is distinct here is that all prophetic activity prior to the coming of Jesus is derived power. Jesus' power comes from his very essence as God. The triune God's sovereign and loving reign over all creation finds incarnate expression in Jesus. A proper view of any miracle exalts Christ alone and manifests the implications of his presence. What he speaks is an expression of his being. All of Jesus' prophetic activity in miracle-working power is subordinate to a higher purpose: self-revealing proclamation.

He also discloses his kingly dominion. The intentions of God's kingdom include the restructuring of the fallen created order. Jesus' mighty works resist all the "powers" that repel his coming: guilt, fear, self-deception, demonic powers. The eschatological emphasis of the miracles is strongest in light of his kingly office. The miracles are windows into the reality of what the triune God is doing and will do in creation. The end (*telos*) of creation depends upon its origin and present reality in the supernatural.

The early church saw Jesus' miracles inextricably tied to his priestly ministry. His works reveal the character of Jesus. T. F. Torrance states this plainly: "He embodies what he mediates, in himself, for what he mediates and what he is are one and the same."[79] The entire panoply of human need becomes the appropriated responsibility of the Word. His self-giving authority rebuilds a broken creation from the inside out. Nothing exceeds his ability to rectify and reorder. As Priest, Jesus deals with every infirmity in a cleansing, restoring, and healing manner.[80] He is able to deliver from the con-

---

79. Torrance, *The Mediation of Christ*, 56.

80. See the priestly function in Israel that dealt with the worship life of the people of God but also was engaged with all the elements of humanness in a fallen condition as in Lev 12:1–15:32; 18:1–19:37.

sequences of sin and return to wholeness. Divine omnipotence is conjoined with a self-offering compassion. The Gospel writers elsewhere affirm that all of these acts were fulfillments and verifications of Christ's deity (Matt 1:22; John 20:30–31).

The physical effects of the fall are only symptomatic. A deeper cure was needed: a restorative work to deliver all of humanity from the vicissitudes of sin. Jesus assumed this burden into himself (Isa 53:4). He dealt with the root cause of sin on the Cross. His sympathy and compassion were real, but only his atoning death would ultimately work redemption. All that destroys life or limits its joy is met by the pure, selfless giving of life. There is no healing apart from the cross. What we encounter in the Gospels is part of the "retrospective" application of the freedom offered to us from the cross and empty tomb.[81]

CRUCIFIED ACCORDING TO THE PURPOSES OF GOD

Part eight, *Soteriology*, in volume four of this series, will emphasize the relation between the incarnation and the atonement. Let this point be made here: What Jesus does derives from who he is. Objective notions of salvation are easier to understand than the subjective reality behind them. Paying a debt is easier to comprehend than taking human nature into divine nature and bearing sin for another. The cross reveals the heart of the triune God.

The cross is the foundation of salvation (Eph 1:3–10; 1 John 4:7–19). It reveals the nature of the triune God in a way that nothing else can. Because of his love, God in Christ put himself at

---

81. "Retrospective" pertains to the direction of the nature of the atonement to that which preceded Christ's work. It certainly has to do with time, but it also incorporates the entirety of humanity and the state of sin, which Jesus redeemed us from. Torrance ties this view of the redeeming life of Christ, from manger to the right hand of the Father, to the mediatorial reconciliation of the Son in many of his works. See *The Trinitarian Faith*, 166–68, or *The Mediation of Christ*, 65; Forsyth, *The Work of Christ*, 202. The theological underpinnings for this comprehensive work of Christ are explored creatively in Campbell, *The Nature of the Atonement*, ch. 6, "Retrospective Aspect of the Atonement," esp. 139–42.

risk on behalf of sinners. He loved us more than he loved his own life. His love is the love expressed in the triune Godhead eternally. God's design of salvation was not a secondary plan, one that had to be produced because things got out his control. Salvation is always personal and found in and through the person of the Son. The pre-destined purposes of God are never removed from his nature. Aristides states that "in order that the purpose of his Incarnation might in time be accomplished . . . He himself was pierced by the Jews, and he died."[82] *Purpose* also might be thought of as *economy* or *dispensation.* God's omniscient love discerned the need before it was actualized in the Garden. "The Lamb who was slain from the creation of the world" (Rev 13:8).[83]

The early church thinkers strove to articulate the theological point that Jesus defines the cross, not vice-versa. The Western tradition, following Augustine's lead, has tended to emphasize the power of sin; it has dealt with the eternal purpose of God as primarily providing a redeemer from sin. Though true, theologians holding this perspective have become preoccupied with the work of redemption to the neglect of God's overarching plan for creation. God's purpose was not primarily negative—saving us from something. It was originally positive—making us for another. Thus, Jesus is the revelation of God's full purpose, the uniting of humanity with *himself.* Sin in time and space could not confound an eternal God. Death could not defeat everlasting life. Self-centeredness could not prevail over the absolute self-donation of the Son of the Father in his eternal nature, creation, incarnation, and atonement.[84] The holiness of unchanging triune love is expressed on the cross.

---

82. Apology of Aristides, *ANF* 10:265.

83. "Foundation" or Greek, *katabole,* clearly refers to an eternal, or at least pre-creational, order of reality. See Matt 13:35, 25:34; John 17:24; Eph 1:4; 1 Pet 1:20; Rev 17:8.

84. Nellas, *Deification in Christ,* 38–39, 94–95.

HOLY LOVE: A WESLEYAN THEOLOGY

THE RESURRECTION OF JESUS

In systematic fashion, the early theologians who bore the gospel to the Roman world saw the supernatural reality of revelation most clearly evidenced in the resurrection of Jesus. The preaching of the resurrection was a recurrent emphasis. The unique, comprehensive style of this early preaching incorporated the entire incarnate life of Jesus from conception by the Holy Spirit in the womb of the virgin Mary to the bodily ascension of Jesus in preparation for the *eschaton*.

The early church's viewpoint can be summarized this way: salvation includes both Jesus' supernatural descent into his creation and his victorious ascent by which all humanity is potentially incorporated into the life of the Trinity by grace.[85] They felt a deep reverence for the transcendence of God and a worshipful awareness of the power of revelation. This rich view of salvation proclaims that the one who is holy love descended to our deepest needs as one of us and transforms us in time and eternity.

The confrontation with the dualistic nature of the recurrent heresy of gnosticism is readily apparent here.[86] God has become flesh (John 1:14). The transcendent Creator has taken into his own nature the flesh that he has made. A thorough reconciliation has occurred between God and humanity. All humanity has been made

---

85. Leo the Great, *ANF* 12:132–33.
86. This heresy has plagued the Christian tradition since the first century. Though historically its roots are much older, gnosticism is based upon the belief that there exists an unbridgeable gap (*chorismos*, lit. "chasm or gulf") in reality. The being and non-being, sensible and intelligible, noumenal and phenomenal, the pleroma and the kenoma, are just a few of the many ways this dualism is expressed. What is intriguing is the fantastic mythology (distorted heterodoxy) which ensues, positing a god who is monadic, supreme, and unknowable; who predetermines all that is, issuing in a crushing fatalism only punctuated with a condescending redeemer figure; who either hesitantly, mistakenly, or disobediently engages with the world in the desire to save the elect, the spiritual knowers, the elite. Of course, logically there is an anthropological dualism to mirror the epistemological, so the body and spirit are never at ease with one another. Salvation is always a spiritual reality alone, thus never truly personal, only volitional or mental. See von Balthasar, *The Scandal of the Incarnation*, 1–11, and Torrance, *Divine Meaning*, 25–39, 63–65.

redeemable in the sacrifice of the Son. His enduring, incarnate humanity is one of our strongest guarantees that Jesus continues his priestly work of intercession.

One area of modern debate concerns the actuality of the bodily resurrection of Jesus.[87] The earliest fathers are adamant in their affirmation of his human nature, both body and spirit, coming forth on Easter morning. Clement uses the Pauline theme of "firstfruit" (1 Cor 15:20) when acknowledging Jesus' resurrection and the final resurrection of all who believe in him. In his defense against Docetism, Ignatius offers a doxology at the beginning of his epistle to the Smyrnaeans affirming the spiritual and fleshly components of the Resurrected One.[88] Justin Martyr strongly advocated a physical resurrection because the salvation through Christ includes the body both in time and eternity.[89] Tertullian fought gnosticism by connecting the creation of flesh in the image of God with the assuming of flesh by the Creator in his incarnation (Gen 1:26).

For, whatever was the form and expression which was then given to the clay (by the Creator) Christ was in his thoughts one day to become man, because the Word, too, was to be both clay and flesh.[90] The flesh was neither an afterthought nor an addendum to the Savior's personhood. It was an integral part of the full purpose of God. It is impossible to fully understand the doctrine of humanity apart from the one who became flesh and dwelt among us.

---

87. While there has been a deep division about the actual physical rising from the dead between more liberal scholars and the more traditional perspectives, it is a new phenomenon that even among evangelicals this issue has caused division. See Harris, *Raised Immortal* and *From Grave to Glory*. Harris' argument revolves around the central contention that Jesus could not have been raised a physical body but an immaterial or spiritual body. His post-resurrection body had a dual modality: invisible and nonfleshly and would occasionally take on a visible and fleshly mode in order to assure his disciples of the resurrection. Geisler responded to Harris in *The Battle for the Resurrection*.

88. The heresy that there was not a real union between flesh and spirit in Jesus and thus no true resurrection of the physical.

89. Justin, *On the Resurrection*, ANF 1:297–99.

90. Tertullian, *On the Resurrection of the Flesh*, ANF 3:549.

The resurrection of the Son by the power of the triune God affirmed that what the Word became was not an assumption of a generic humanity that was a mere instrument of salvation to be discarded when the task was complete. He was perfectly human as well as perfectly divine. What he became he always will be. But most importantly, what he became was the expression of the triune life. No one could truly know God except as Jesus Christ. His resurrection and subsequent ascension and session reveal the self-disclosure of God and his ultimate purposes for those made in his image. His defeat of death seals his authority over all that sin threatened to do in destroying creation. He rose victorious, in the flesh, as the re-creator of a broken world and beleaguered humanity. Rahner states it clearly:

> The incarnation is only rightly envisaged if Christ's humanity is not only, ultimately speaking, a merely extrinsic instrument by which a God who remains invisible makes himself known, but is rather precisely what God himself becomes (though remaining God) when he exteriorizes himself into the dimension of what is other than himself, or the non-divine. Even if it is obvious that God could create the world without the incarnation, it is nevertheless compatible with that statement that the possibility of creation has its ground in the radical possibility of God's self-exteriorization.[91]

The resurrection confirms that the human nature of God the Son became an eternal reality and that was God's plan for his created image, to share by a grace-enabled participation in the nature that the second person of the Trinity offered.

Holy Spirit Bestowed

Revelation is never complete in a single divine person. An unnerving reality of systematic theology is the mistaken impression that each section or topic is a discrete statement of reality in and of itself. Worship, prayer, and preaching often articulate real-

---

91. Rahner, *Sacramentum Mundi*, 3:370.

ity more clearly than theology. In the theology of the early church no discussion of either the Father or the Spirit occurs apart from reference to Christ. While systematic theology is necessary, our modern demands for specialization can impose a heavy theological toll, often at the expense of a consistent full Trinitarian awareness. A systematic theology should never attempt to actually divide the being of God. This chapter is an attempt to properly place the revelation of the Son as the highest expression of God's eternal nature.

Jesus' coming was never intended to be an end in itself. The other-orientation of triune love is equally shared. Each person lives for the other two. Jesus consistently points beyond himself. Therefore, it is truly Christological to incorporate the person of the Holy Spirit in credal discussions of the person of the Son. Their eternal relationship is no less real in the incarnation. Jesus depends, experiences, trusts, and is guided by the Spirit in the same manner as all believers are entreated to relate to him. Jesus makes it clear to his disciples that his departure is necessary for the coming of the Third Person of the Trinity (John 16:7–11). The early creeds point beyond Christology to the descent of the Spirit.

Rather than being distracted by philosophical conundrums, the authors of the New Testament developed a dynamic panorama of salvation history. The "descent" of the Son is paralleled by the descent of the Spirit (John 1:9; Luke 24:49–51; Acts 1:8, 2:1–4). The Son came in order to give to us the Holy Spirit. The New Testament does not identify distinct dispensations for the activity of the Son and the Spirit; both are always seen to be active and self-revealing.

The climactic and soteriological "descent" (first of the Son and then of the Spirit) reveals the triune God's intention to dwell with and in human persons. The Son continually points to his Father, and he emphasizes the irreplaceable importance of the Spirit's arrival (John 14:15–17, 16:12–14). A mutuality of glorifying, witnessing, sending, knowing, and loving between the persons undergirds the entire Gospel. One cannot understand Jesus apart from

HOLY LOVE: A WESLEYAN THEOLOGY

the Father, who sent him, and the Spirit, whom he sends. Theology and Christology without Pneumatology are impossible.[92]

The purposes of God are to establish and produce a people who look like his Son. This divine plan could only be realized when the Spirit, who fills the life of the Son, has come to dwell in those created in his image. The gospel narrative and promise are not complete until the Spirit of God and of Christ comes in his fullness at Pentecost.[93]

THE RETURN OF CHRIST[94]

An important feature of early Christology was its future orientation. The *parousia* is ever present in New Testament views of the Messiah. What God begins, he will end in Christ. Accordingly, eschatology was a consistent theme in early Christian thinking about Christ. Any attempt to disconnect Christology and eschatology defaces both of them. God's purposes in redemption were never to be limited to justification alone. The ultimate purpose of the Redeemer (*telos*) can be experienced now, but it is yet fully to be revealed. A biblically promised restoration and re-creation were at the center of God's heart's desire (Isa 66:22; Rev 21:1–5). The *parousia* affirms the original intent of the Creator to dwell forever in the midst of his people. It is a clear sign of Christ's victory over all sin and over all that the devil had attempted to destroy.

Once again, we see the importance of the incarnation and the fulfillment of human nature in Christ's return. The body and the world are affirmed by their Lord. In this sense, then, the full identification of Jesus as God and as human awaits a climactic completion even now. John says, "we shall see him as he is" (1 John 3:2). The full meaning of his re-creative work will be made manifest in and through his incarnate person. Evidence confirms that Jesus is

---

92. See part five, *Pneumatology*, in volume three of this series, for more on the Spirit and revelation.

93. Leo, *NPNF2* 12:134.

94. Pauline kerygma states Jesus "will come again as Judge" (see 1 Cor 15:20–28).

the Lamb of God in the midst of the throne (Rev 5:6; 7:17), but his return will bring about a glorious fulfillment to the revelation of the Trinity (Rev 22:1–5, 17). The Son will glorify the Father and give all that he has won to him. The Spirit will bring about in creation the completion for which it has been groaning (John 17:3–4; Phil 2:11; Rom 8:19–23).

REPENTANCE AND BAPTISM

True Christology must incorporate a full human response to the claims made in the Gospels. Systematic theology without worship or intimacy with the person of Christ is deadening, and mere analysis of Jesus is never appropriate. Jesus lovingly—yet inescapably—demands a volitional response from us (John 1:11; Heb 3:7–12). A personal revelation requires a personal response for a true relationship to occur. Christian theology confronts the human spirit with a declaration of the person of Christ and demands a decision of the whole person.

The self-giving of the Father and the descent of the Son and the Spirit are mirrored in a sinner's repentance. This can be conceived as a volitional "descent" on the part of the sinner. The motifs of dying, burial, and newness of life as soteriological realities symbolize a more profound theological background. Nothing we are required to do is ever removed from the nature of the God who both requires and enables. The Christian kerygma is biblical, logical, and confrontational. Mutually responsive self-giving becomes possible in the light of the incarnation and atonement. One may either turn one's face to God or remain in self-destructive egoism. The preaching of the early church presented Christ in a way that demanded such a response.

Once one repents and believes, fully trusting in the salvific nature of his incarnate self-giving, baptism ought to follow. That sacrament of entering into the gift of the life of God is an initial and life-long symbol of the Lordship of Christ. Baptism indicates life lived as Jesus lived it: glorifying the Father in the power of the

Spirit and in newness of life. Although the act of baptism is completed in a moment, it symbolizes a life of dying to self and resurrection in the Spirit because our life is now lived in the Savior by the Spirit.[95] This life is a constant "descent" out of oneself into the lives of others. Believers die to their own way for the sake of redemptive grace, which can only flow as persons, even divine persons, give themselves away.

The incarnation and the community of the Word made flesh transformed the meaning of everything. Israel's God had released the world from the stranglehold of myth, magic, and meaninglessness. Time and space became a valued arena for revelation. But Israel was always oriented toward a fulfillment that could only become reality in Christ. Once the Messiah had come and sanctified the created order by the assumption of flesh, there was a new orientation to time. The calendar of early Christianity witnesses to the Christocentric nature of the worshipping body of Christ. This kerygmatic outline was a sufficient base for the worship of the early church and provided a practical guide for true Christian witness.

THE DESCENT AND ASCENT OF CHRIST

Kerygma was viewed in the early church as more than preaching. It comprised the non-negotiable framework for true Christian doctrine. Thomas Oden has reminded us of the basic descent-ascent approach to early interpretations of Christ's person and his relation to creation.[96] We have seen how the earliest creedal statements reflect the descent of the Son into full human life. Sent by the Father, Jesus chose, by the power of the Spirit, to come to a fallen creation out of love, which is the essence of divine life.

---

95. Though replete in all the New Testament, see especially Acts 2:23–38 for the kerygmatic foundation of the connection between a self-emptying Savior and baptism "in his name" (2:38). Also note the death and resurrection motif in Rom 6:1–11.

96. Oden, *The Word of Life*, 26–27.

CHAPTER THREE

The Creeds

THE PREACHING OF THE descent and ascent of Jesus Christ was further refined and codified by the creeds. For the average believer, the creeds demonstrated how revelation formed the Christology of the early church. Worship was the normal context for the expression of these insights concerning Jesus Christ.

MARANATHA

The Aramaic prayer, *Maranatha* ("O Lord, Come") was one of earliest responses to revelation.[1] Remarkably this prayer, addressed to Jesus of Nazareth, is a two-word affirmation of the gospel message. Jesus' Lordship in the flesh brings all of reality to its intended purpose. In him we find divine and human, eternity and history, body and soul, present Lord and coming King. This is the Lord sought after in the compact petition, "maranatha." In the context of increasing persecution, the church discerned reality in the descent of the Son. This prayer was neither escapist nor idealist. To claim that Jesus was truly the Lord of the universe was an affirmation that he was the Son of the Father and that he would bring all things to a conclusion in his own time and way. The one who is to come was the Arm of Yahweh, the son of Mary, the Lord of All. The Lordship

---

1. *Didache, ANF* 7:380. Moule looks at the etymological background for the word in *The Origin of Christology*, 36–37.

of Jesus is eternal in its expression; it transcends and incorporates time and space. Without his presence space is meaningless; without his arrival time is purposeless. Jesus, the Man from Nazareth, completes the meaning of history as time unfolds and as it reaches its consummation. The body of Christian theology encompasses the events that prepared for the Anointed One, his actual life, and his everlasting Lordship.

We must not remove this *maranatha* petition from the context of the worship out of which it was born. Such a personal, theologically informed prayer to Jesus has transformative power. Prayer, the earliest Christians teach, is true *theologia*, the only adequate human response to the incarnation. Thus, the earliest creedal formulations were not primarily an attempt to list Christological evidence as objects for analysis or critical assessment. They were responses of prayerful worship, founded on the fact that God first revealed himself fully in Christ.

KURIOS

As often affirmed, the most frequently used title for Jesus was the Greek term for "Lord," *kurios*. It is quite likely that Aramaic-speaking believers first called him "Lord"; if so, the early believers must have been aware of the implications. Of its various possible translations ("master," "sir," "lord"), *kurios* occurs in the New Testament 250 times referring predominantly to Jesus as Lord. The Hebrew *adonai* is the term literally translated as lordship. It is intriguing that the use of the same term in the Septuagint is a translation for Yahweh.[2] Theological reflection has shown that this is more than cultural deference or awareness of some level of spirituality in Jesus. This is a profound identification. To call Jesus "Lord" is a statement that there was no distinction in essence or deity between the one who created the world and called Israel from the one who calmed

---

2. There are over 6, 000 usages of this translation in the LXX.

the sea and called the disciples. This contributes to the theological understanding inherent in the earliest confessions regarding Jesus among the Aramaic and Greek-speaking churches. These monotheists would never have been able to affirm Jesus as Lord if there was not a core of belief supporting such identification. The title *kurios* appears at crucial points to identify Jesus as Yahweh such as when Peter preached his Pentecostal sermon (Acts 2:36). The Christian church's earliest relationship with Jesus incorporated the expectation of his imminent return with his cosmic lordship. One can find the same type of ascription in the *Didache*, the earliest preaching, pastoral preparation, and prayers outside the New Testament.

The staggering Trinitarian implication of this affirmation is that it was spoken by ardent monotheists. The earliest Christians proclaimed one God yet did not hesitate to call Jesus, "Lord." After the ascension seeing that the term "Lord" could be assigned to any conception of deity, they ascribed lordship to his historical human reality as well as his divine reality. The *Logos* had taken on flesh without becoming less divine. Accordingly, Christology was never far removed from the larger Trinitarian discussion. The use of the term *kurios* demonstrates an implicit Trinitarianism running throughout the New Testament.

Ignatius of Antioch provides an example of this doctrinal formulation. The foundational role that he played in early creedal statements cannot be overemphasized. Much has been written about his influence in what was to become known as the Apostles' Creed.[3] The apologetic responses to heresy he constructed served another purpose as catechetical instruction. He brought together a summary of the major ideas surrounding the unique nature of Christ that were circulating before the earliest creedal statements. Clarifying the

---

3. His foundational outline of faith forms much of the later summaries of basic doctrine. The similarity of language is evident in the following: *Epistle to the Ephesians*, ANF 1:56–57; *Epistle to the Magnesians*, ANF 1:61–62; *Epistle to the Trallians*, ANF 1:69–70; note well *Epistle to the Smyrnaeans*, ANF 1:86–87; Leith, *Creeds of the Churches*, 16–17.

HOLY LOVE: A WESLEYAN THEOLOGY

place of Christ's sovereignty for believers was a fundamental step toward confronting and correcting heterodoxy. Both of these forms of incipient systematized theology were to become the foundation for later Christology.

Irenaeus of Lyons wrote of this Lordship as he confronted a diminished Christology: "[His] ascension into heaven in the flesh of the beloved Christ Jesus, our Lord, and his manifestation from heaven in the glory of the Father . . . in order that to Christ Jesus, our Lord, our God, and Saviour and King every knee should bow."[4] Statements like this laid the foundation for what Irenaeus called the *regula veritatis* ("rule of truth") or *regula fidei* ("rule of faith").[5] The rule of faith was the normative doctrinal formulation by which theological statements were to be tested. This Spirit-enabled canon of thought encouraged deeper investigation and served as a measuring line against heretical choices. These doctrines rose out of the biblical revelation that the church received as authoritative. The formula "Jesus is Lord" (*lex credendi*) became the belief of the church because the fathers recognized that he *is* Lord (*lex orandi*).

These early creedal statements possess a clarity often missing in much modern theology. Christian theology would be further developed in later centuries, but these rudimentary statements have not been refuted nor improved upon in a fundamental sense. Defined in personal and relational terms, Jesus' lordship flowed from his essence as the Son of the Father through the Holy Spirit. This was no despotic sovereign ruling by abject power but a relational lord giving life and meaning through relationship and self-giving.

---

4. Irenaeus, *Against Heresies*, ANF 1:330–31; also in Leith, *Creeds*, 21.
5. Tertullian, *Against Praxeas*, ANF 3:598.

THE CREEDS AND THE "PERSON" OF THE SON

The universal lordship attributed to Christ was predicated upon belief in his full divinity. This belief forced church fathers to explain his divine nature as co-equal with that of the Father. Though the term "person" (Greek, *prosopon*; Latin, *persona*) came into theological discourse later in the church's history, the earliest thinkers saw the Son revealed in and through his works. Later philosophical theology has indicated that personhood is an underlying concept for any kind of truly relational being, either divine or human personhood.[6] By the fundamental logic of cause and effect, the person of the Son revealed the Godhead by his work. Historically, it would be one of the greatest struggles of the church's thought life to produce and maintain a proper conception of the person of Christ and his Work. Simply stated, but theologically potent in its implications, personhood always precedes work. It may seem a trivial distinction to say that work is done by a person, but it does distinguish the important fact that the work is not the same as the person. In any period in which Jesus is viewed as an "adopted" human messianic figure, orthodox theology must affirm his work as unique and revelatory of a pre-existent divine nature. The uniqueness of his person is the basis of the effect of the work. Thus, Jesus himself warned repeatedly that to focus on the "sign" could easily mean the obscuring of the one to whom all the signs pointed (John 6:14–15; 26–41).

The Scriptures and the creeds give us insight into Jesus' person and then to his work through his offices. John's Gospel begins with a statement about theological personhood, the Son as the Word, before any messianic activity is mentioned (John 1:1–51, especially

---

6. This is the radical confrontation of the Nicene theologians with all preceding Greek thought. Note the implications of one small example in Athanasius, *Against the Arians*, NPNF2 4:354; Aquinas, *Summa Theologica*, Part 3, Q.43, contra.; Torrance, *The Trinitarian Faith*, 130.

vv. 1–4). Who he is defines what he does. Likewise, the creeds begin by placing Jesus in a co-equal divinity with the Father and the Spirit and give minimal reference to his earthly ministry. This is an onto-logical approach to Christology.[7]

Christian theology is more than a form of philosophy. It is grounded in actual history.[8] God does not demand a belief in ideas without context. His mighty works are culminated in a revelatory way in the acts of Jesus and the work of the Holy Spirit. The person of Christ is prior to his work, but we can only know him through the work he did as Scripture reveals. Once we see the importance of acknowledging that revelation is from above and that God is not tied to the world except by his own self-giving love, the life and min-istry of Jesus can be seen in their proper light. A dynamic reciproc-ity can take place whereby the person of the Son sent by the Father reveals his nature, and the actions of Jesus reveal that same nature. His work, then, helps to interpret his person more clearly.

Theology from below must be grounded in revelation from above. Any orthodox Christological statement must be committed to the radical veracity of the Word. Every modern attempt to his-toricize Jesus or to demythologize the texts has produced a limited and thus heretical Christology.[9]

---

7. Oden points out that the two terms, person and work, are based on the uniqueness of person. They are also conceptually distinguishable, which is important to recognize and know. Modernity says the only way to know Jesus is through his work alone, the implication being that the height of our Christology is determined solely by one's interpretation of his work (Oden, *The Word of Life*, 1–27). One very helpful historical note that he makes is that there is an absence of distinction in creeds between person and function.

8. Origen, *De Principiis, ANF* 4:281; 246–47.

9. Various approaches in recent "modern" Christology include the mythical, existential, emergent, dialectic, functional, historicist, humanitarian, and evolutionary.

THE NAMES AND TITLES OF CHRIST AS PERSONAL SELF-REVELATION

Scripture is the record of a dynamic relationship between the triune God and human persons in producing sacred textual revelation. One aspect of a high view of Scripture pertaining to Christology is that the names found throughout the Bible either speak prophetically of Christ or offer some perspective on how his person is to be understood. No one name for Christ encapsulates all of his grandeur.

Some would say that the names are projections not revelation. They have been placed in the text by hopeful redactors who saw God at work and posited demarcations of divine presence in the form of names. Because of his uniqueness, Jesus became a magnet of the Old Testament names and titles for divine presence. According to this perspective, the early church, after Jesus' death, inserted a further list of names for him that added to the illusion that he was divine. This second perspective holds a restricted view of revelation and demonstrates a preliminary bias against revealed terms that prophesy the coming of Christ; these errors destroy any balanced picture of his character and glory.

OLD TESTAMENT DESIGNATIONS OF THE PERSON OF THE MESSIAH

This systematic theology proposes to start with Jesus, combining his person and his work. Otherwise, we risk being left with a theology that refuses to accept the Old Testament as revelatory of Christ and practices theology as mere functional recitation of the works of God. To assist in this task, it is advantageous to look at how Scripture prepares the earnest believer for the incarnation of the Son.

One of the ways in which the relation of work and person can be examined is the direction Christology takes when the various names for Christ are explored. If our interpretation accepts the reality of the triune God active in Old Testament revelation, a very different trajectory begins. This hermeneutic requires a high view of personal divine revelation. If the works of God are founded on his tripersonal nature, the words that he inspires reveal a personal reality that increases in its expression as Scripture discloses the God who desires to be known.

Of the Old Testament pictures and nuances for Jesus, few are as well-known as Isaiah 9:6 with its prophetic designations of Christ, including "Wonderful Counselor," "Mighty God," "Everlasting Father," and "Prince of Peace." The prophets complete a picture of the promised Messiah in all of his grandeur. The Messiah (Hebrew, *māšîaḥ*, "anointed one") is the supreme title applied to Jesus based upon the promises of the Old Testament.[10] These concepts leave a serious theological conundrum for the monotheist. Yahweh sends his arm, his angel, his Messiah, his king. And the work that this personal being performs is that which God alone can do. The New Testament authors assume that the reader understands these revealed attributions regarding Jesus.[11]

From every sector of the Old Testament early theologians selected what they identified as revealed concepts of the Son. They understood these to be prophetic in nature. Incipient forms of the messianic reality were explored with great vigor. These messianic descriptors became apparent in the worship of the first centuries. He was seen as the promised "rock," "deliverer," and "kinsman redeemer" in the same manner as the God of Israel was believed to be to his people. Thus, from its earliest days, the Christian mind has connected the work of God in the salvation of God's people to Jesus. They were keenly aware of the telic nature of the prophecies regarding the personal being sent from God. He had not yet come in all of his glory, but they anticipated his arrival consistently.

---

10. *Heidelberg Catechism with Commentary*, 70–71.
11. See 1 Cor 10:4; Heb 3:2; 7:22.

New Testament Designations
for the Person of the Son

Many Old Testament terms are fulfilled by the arrival of Christ. A sample of references to Christ in the New Testament highlights their inclusive nature: Cornerstone (Eph 2:20), last Adam (1 Cor 15:45), Alpha and Omega (Rev 1:8), Great High Priest (Heb 4:14), Stumbling Block (1 Pet 2:8), and Bridegroom (John 3:29). When the question is raised as to the actual meaning of these designations, we are confronted with two possibilities. Either they are, as some say, mere additions to the "simple gospel," or they are revealed terms that give a fuller understanding of Christ.

Early confessions of the church affirmed God as the Father of Jesus Christ. All other religions focus on impersonal divine power or fate. Whereas the Christian creeds all begin with a clear affirmation of belief in "God the Father Almighty." Yet, it is a reasonable statement to say that early theology was mainly Christological. The amount of space in the creeds given to the second person of the Trinity testifies to the truth that the triune God and the nature of reality are most fully disclosed in Jesus Christ. Even before Trinitarian thought had been clarified, the elements of differentiation between the Son and the Father were written into liturgies, catechisms, and baptismal formulations. Through an intense inquiry into the person of Jesus, the church began to understand more deeply the relationship between the Father and the Son.

Oscar Cullmann has given a formative, though incomplete, outline of the major titles of Christ that mirror the descent-ascent trajectory of the early church:

1. Titles that focus on the earthly work of Christ (Prophet, Suffering Servant, Priest).
2. Titles that center on the future work of Christ (Messiah, Son of Man).
3. Titles that emphasize his present state or present work (Lord, Savior).

4. Titles that deal with the pre-existent state of Christ (Word, Son of God).[12]

According to Cullmann, terms that pertain to pre-existence produce the most consternation for modern scholarship. The tendency is to historicize the titles and other Christological terms, reducing the theological freight that these designations can carry. Those who attempt to remain orthodox typically choose a different order than Cullmann for these categories. Christ is first pre-existent, the Son of God, the Word of God, eternal Lord. Second, he is the incarnate God whose work as Messiah flows out of his person as the Son of Man. Third, his prophetic and priestly works culminate in his role as Suffering Servant, Savior, and King now at the right hand of the Father.

The bias of much modern theology is that Jesus is not the pre-existent God that consensual thought has always claimed he is. It is important to note that the titles of Jesus give us a complete view of the person and work of Jesus.[13] As Cullmann's study indicates, a full-orbed view of the titles provides a comprehensive picture of the Second Person of the Trinity as eternal Son, the reigning eschatological Lord.

Exploration of Two Titles[14]

Although many titles for Jesus appear in Scripture, two form an outline for the way the titles can be effectively approached: "Son of God" and "Son of Man." From a Trinitarian perspective, sonship is a key factor in understanding the person of Jesus Christ. Our

---

12. Cullmann, *The Christology of the New Testament*. It would appear that several of the ideas he propounded were in an earlier work: *Christ and Time*, 108–9.

13. No recent work has come close to the inclusive breadth of scriptural language in all of its categories for systematizing the biblical materials in relation to holiness, including a strong Christological strand of names, titles, roles, and sub-roles, than is found in Coppedge, *Portraits of God*, 64–65, 106–10, 145–49, 180–85, 216–17, 260–66, 308–9, 338–40.

14. Other works have delved into many of these titles extensively. Our foci are twofold: first, to emphasize the divinity and humanity, and second, to offer an example of the kind of work necessary to come to a theological understanding of these delineations to encourage the student of theology to continue to investigate the implications of these revealed concepts throughout a lifetime of inquiry.

Christological starting point leads us to a Trinitarian conclusion. The first title, "Son of God," refers to the divine essence of the one who came from Heaven; the second, "Son of Man," expresses his own self-understanding.[15] These titles are given as examples of the way revelation occurs in an historical context. They illuminate the Christian understanding of reality by which God reveals his nature in space and time. This background is crucial to understanding how distinctive Jesus really is. Jesus shows himself in categories that are humanly understandable but never exhaustive of his divine person.

Son of God

The task of theology in the worship life of the church is to identify the major themes in revelation and Christian experience and to present those concepts for increased spiritual understanding. Of the many titles that denote the person of Christ, one ties most of the concepts together: "Jesus Christ, the Son of God."

Historical Context: Sonship in the Ancient Near East and Israel

Distinction: Transcendence, Discontinuity, and a Rejection of Polytheism

The cultures around Israel had no trouble advocating filial relationship within the pantheon or viewing human rulers as the offspring of gods. Due to its theology, Israel employs *sonship* in a unique way. The actual title "Son of God" seldom occurs in the Old Testament.[16] Nearly all of the Old Testament references indicate the

---

15. Cullmann discusses the general implications of the titles in *The Christology of the New Testament*, 162–63. Although he disagrees with too strong a divine-human correspondence, he does see that Son of Man carries a distinct theme of humiliation and, thus, humanity with it.

16. Three titles that occur in the Old Testament need to be considered. First is *Bar Elohim* (Dan 3:23). *Bar* is an Aramaic term for "son"; therefore, *Bar Elohim* is rendered "Son of God." The second is *Ben Elohim*. This is found in Ps 29:1 and in Ps 89:7. This term is also found in Gen 6:2, 4 and Job 1:6, 2:1, and 38:7. In all of its usages, with the exception of Gen 6, one finds a type of supernatural being in relationship with God. It is also found in reference to Israel (Exod 4:22)

transcendent God is relating to the "sons of God," angelic beings who interact with Yahweh in a supernatural environment.[17] These beings are not divine in the same way as God himself. This brings to mind the picture of a heavenly court. These supramundane entities (angels, heavenly host) are never identified with God. This discontinuity sets Israel apart from any other cosmology in history. The "sons of God" are viewed as being separate from God himself, preventing any identification with polytheism. In the Old Testament, one encounters "sons of God" pictured as intimate with God, but inferior to and subject to the Creator.[18]

Royalty

In the ancient Eastern cultures, the "sons" of the gods were royalty. In the Egyptian and Canaanite cultures that surrounded Israel, the kings were acknowledged as gods or sons of gods. This was the center of the issue in Samuel's divinely inspired rebuke when Saul made an unholy sacrifice (1 Sam 13). He crossed a cultic and moral line laid down by God. Saul gave the impression that he was a divine being, a priest-king.

The royalty of a particular "son" of God in the Old Testament is focused upon David and his lineage. Second Samuel 7:12–16 provides the divine promises made to David regarding the establishment of a house and kingdom that will last eternally. The "son" of that kingdom would enjoy a double sonship: one with David and one with Yahweh.

Aside from the unique references to royalty, "son" of God carries three underlying themes in the Old Testament context: Sonship as unique relationship, Sonship as trusting obedience, and Sonship as representation.

---

and in conjunction with the son-father intimacy of the Davidic royal line (2 Sam 7:12–14).

17. Gen 6:2, 4; Job 1:6; 2:1.

18. Jacob describes it as a distinction between adoption and begetting (*Theology of the Old Testament*, 236).

Sonship as unique relationship pertains to an intimacy shared between God and his "son." In some places the nation of Israel is described as "firstborn son" (Exod 4:22, Hos 11:1). This distinction did not mean that the people of God were viewed as divine beings or persons endowed with superhuman qualities. Israel was to conceive of itself as divinely chosen. This was a relationship by grace not by nature.[19] In particular, the "son" usage described a people called to participate in a special relationship with Yahweh. Israel is not ever called to be an elite group but "chosen" as a singular messenger for the sake of the whole world (Exod 19:6).

Sonship as trusting obedience pertains to the concept of obedience out of the trust engendered by placing faith in an unwavering object. Therefore, the Old Testament focuses on obedience so that "sonship" is not assured by bloodline. Neither is it guaranteed by attempts to impress God. Only obedience to God establishes this familial relationship. The other ancient religions emphasize obedience to the gods, but as a fate-based, forced, or contrived obedience. In contradistinction, Israel was offered a familial intimacy founded upon grace and faithful love. The condition for Israel's "sonship" was life in agreement with the revealed character of God.

The phrase "my son" also carried a tie to the Servant of Yahweh (Isa 42:1, 49:3; see 2 Esd 7:28–29, 13:32, 37, 14:9). The LXX *pais* ("child" "son") often translates the Hebrew *ebed* "servant."[20] This draws two strands of relationship together in the Messiah as Servant-King. He is a son, but he is also a servant as a direct expression of his sonship. The election of this one presupposes a divinely appointed task (Isa 52:10–13). This task is uniquely suited to the character of the Servant of Yahweh with a sustained endowment of the Holy Spirit (Isa 42:1; 50:10). He alone brings about the restoration of Israel, and he alone is the "light to the nations" (Isa 49:3, 5–6).

---

19. Jacob, *Theology of the Old Testament*, 202.

20. Braumann, "Child," *NIDNTT* 1:283. In this section of Isaiah, Jacob or Israel is referred to as the servant of God (44:1, 21; 49:20). See Cullmann's discussion in *Christology of the New Testament*, 52–69.

This work includes exaltation by extreme humiliation, so graphic that those who look upon the Servant are horrified by the marring of his countenance (Isa 52:13–15). This Servant bears the burden of sin so that the sinful and broken ones can be set free (Isa 53:1–12). In him all of the grief-filled results of sin are borne.[21]

The Hebraic concept of "representation" means that the *whole people of God* can be referred to as a single individual, such as *the king* (Ps 2:7) or Isaiah's Suffering Servant (Isa 3:11).[22] In the third theme, *sonship as representation*, then, "son of God" can represent the whole people of God. Yahweh intended the nation of Israel to be a kingdom of priests for the sake of the whole world (Exod 19:6). But the history of Israel shows that the people of Israel never understood and never lived up to this divine call to sonship. So, God chose a succession of individual priests, judges, kings, and prophets in the hope that one might fulfill his will. Any one of these can represent God's intention as an example of the expectation lived out in an individual.

One finds in Jesus Christ the pristine expression of these basic Old Testament themes: He is not absolutely identified with the Father but retains his own identity as the Son. Jesus is unique in his relationship with God and thus bears a certain royalty as divine King. Jesus as the Son exemplifies perfect and complete dependence upon the Father for every facet of his life and ministry. Out

---

21. The four main passages that deal with the suffering Servant motif in Isaiah are: 42:1–7; 49:1–7; 50:4–9; and 52:13–53:12.

22. See Jacob and Israel, David, and the people as a whole, the notion of the Passover Lamb and Israel's atonement. Cullmann states in the conclusion to *Christology of the New Testament* regarding the principle of representation that:

> The path leads first of all from the many in progressive reduction to the one, and from this one, who represents the centre, back to the many. It leads from creation to humanity, from humanity to Israel, from Israel to the "remnant" to the incarnate Christ; then it leads from the incarnate Christ to the apostles, from the apostles to the Church, from the Church to the world and the new creation. (324–25)

Earlier he discussed the issue of representation as the nexus whereby Jesus fulfills all of the Old Testament and sets the trajectory for the New Testament people of God (Cullmann, *Christ and Time*, 115–18).

of that intimacy and through trusting obedience, Jesus Christ is the representative who brings all of the life of God to all humanity. He is, in himself, the middle point of all human history, the one who offers reconciliation to all who trust in him. The church spent centuries dealing with the relationship between the Father and the Son in order to clarify misunderstandings that arose in that regard.

Scripture distinguishes all other forms of sonship from that Jesus enjoys with his Father. The language of sonship, particularly the use of "Abba" as the distinctive means of identifying his relationship with the Father, clarifies a vital theme in Christology. The New Testament idea of the Son in relation to the Fatherhood of God is a fulfillment of the relational themes expressed in the Old Testament. However, a number of the titles relating to the divine Sonship of Jesus appear frequently. In fact, the primary thrust of Scripture as to the essential nature of Jesus is that he alone is the Son of the Father. All that he is flows from that ontological relationship. Many sons and daughters come by adoption, but only one Son is begotten. What we experience by grace, he possesses by nature.

Sonship in the New Testament

The Father sends his Son in the power of the Holy Spirit, expressing the inner life of the divine persons. Jesus' personhood reveals the nature of all true personhood. The filial relationship in the Gospels presumes a basic understanding of the Old Testament idea of sonship. But the New Testament inaugurates a whole new order of intimacy in essence and in relation.[23] References to sonship appear in crucial theological passages, giving importance to this element of Christology. Immediately following the heavenly benediction, when the Father affirms the sonship of Jesus, the devil's first temptation is aimed directly at the unique personhood of the Son of God (Matt 4:3). Ironically, Satan acknowledges Jesus' son-

---

23. "But the New Testament Christology is not simply reducible to such Jewish ideas. It is completely original and represents an unparalleled innovation" (Kasper, *The God of Jesus Christ*, 174).

ship to the Father. Note the same emphasis in Luke by a contrast of origins. In Luke 3:38, the name "Adam" ends the genealogy as a "son of God" by physical birth, whereas Jesus' uncreated sonship is challenged by the devil: "If you are the Son of God." What is emphasized is a unique origin, one of incarnation rather than creation.

At the pivot of the ministry of Jesus in Caesarea Philippi, Peter acknowledges Jesus as "the Son of the living God" (Matt 16:16). The Old Testament relational themes of trust and obedience in the "son of God" are perfectly met and exceeded in the burgeoning understanding of what a full relationship between this "Son" and God entails. The New Testament points to an intimacy that, when seen in Jesus, places him as the Servant above all others and as the one and only begotten Son of God.

The clearest development of this theme is found in Mark. This Gospel prepares the reader for the verification that will come from every sector; even abject enemies declare that Jesus is none other than the Son of God.[24] All he does and says ultimately finds its origin and purpose in that triune relationship he shares with the Father and the Spirit.

Jesus is next identified as the Son at the Jordan River with his baptism. The Gospels record three incidences—two in Mark—where God speaks from heaven at pivotal points in the revelation of the Son and his ministry. In each of these remarkable events, the filial relationship of Jesus of Nazareth and his Father is clearly emphasized. The first is related by Mark when a key preparatory statement is given from the Father: "And a voice came from heaven: 'You are my Son, whom I love; with you I am well pleased'" (1:11). Some might wonder how Mark could record that Jesus was actually the Son of God unless Jesus was perceived to be much more than a sage or a miracle worker.[25] The second incident in the New

---

24. The actual references to this title in Mark in order are as follows; 1:1; 1:11; 3:11; 5:7; 9:7; 12:6 (implied); 13:32; 14:32; and 15:39.

25. There is evidence that in the spiritual realm Jesus is recognized in a filial relationship unique to him, as found in Mark 3:11 where unclean spirits state of

Testament is when the Father speaks of his Son at the transfiguration in Mark 9:7. Jesus stands with Moses, the chief exponent of the law, and with Elijah, the representative of all the prophets. It is illuminating that the context is sonship. Again, the ontological foundation of the gospel is decidedly Trinitarian in scope. From the essence of God as Sender, Sent One, and the Spirit, the redemption of the world is made possible. The third vocal affirmation of sonship is not as overt, but the relational implication is unmistakable. It occurs in a pivotal text in the theological argument of John, just prior to the Passion narrative. The Apostle records the voice from heaven responding to the request of Jesus for the Father to glorify his name. The Father responds, "I have glorified [my name] and will glorify it again" (John 12:28). The glory of the Father is united with the Son in the work of self-giving love expressed in the atonement.

In Mark, the demons and unclean spirits know who Jesus is, often in contrast to those who supposedly have been trained to recognize the Messiah. Mark 3:11 records one of those encounters with a demoniac. His cry immediately orients the event towards the sonship of Jesus. If one ties this incident to the first encounter with the demonic in Mark 1:24, "What do you want with us, Jesus of Nazareth? Have you come to destroy us? I know who you are—the Holy One of God!" then the responses of the unclean beings can be seen to bind the concepts of sonship and Holy One together in an instructive way.[26] The highest epithet for the God of the Old Testament ("Holy One") is conjoined with the highest statement about the essence of the person of Jesus ("Son of God"). When Jesus confronts Legion, the immediate response is the reaction of evil to the

---

Jesus, "You are the Son of God." The same is true of Mark 5:7 when a possessed man, whose name is given as "Legion," states that Jesus is the Son of God.

26. An interesting comparison of attributions of the holiness of Jesus can be found in John 6:69 in the resignation of Peter and the other disciples after Jesus shocks the crowds with his statements regarding his body and blood, which must be consumed. Also, in John 10:36, Jesus himself states that the Father set apart (Greek, *hagiosen*)—as in, made holy—and sent into the world the one who bears no blasphemy in stating he is "the Son of God."

presence of holiness: "What do you want with me, Jesus, Son of the Most High God?" (Mark 5:7).

The recognition of relationship between Jesus and God is meant to be more than mere title, as if Jesus were one of many "sons." This language is intended to evoke the eventual theological identification of persons who are equal in essence. The logic of New Testament theology discounts any polytheistic or adoptionistic ideas. What is presented is a linguistic revelation of a historical event that reveals an ontological correspondence. Of all the analogies used to reveal the nature of Jesus as God, none more clearly evidences the Father-Son relationship in its eternal and its historical moment than "Son of God" or "Son of the Father."

Jewish monotheism, as interpreted in the Second Temple period, is the backdrop for an increasing theological debate in each of the Gospels centering on the title "son of God."[27] Jesus foreshadows reality at a redemptive level when in the parable of the wicked tenants the father sends the son whom the tenants ought to respect. Here, Jesus uses an allegory that is a strong prophetic allusion to his sonship and the cost of being sent by the Father. When the son of the vineyard keeper comes back to the vineyard, he is violently killed (Mark 12:6). The revelation of the sonship of Jesus is a costly one. Based upon divine personhood, personhood is going to be truly explored as self-giving for the sake of another.

Laying aside of the use of divine attributes, Jesus states, "But about that day or hour no one knows, not even the angels in heaven, nor the Son, but only the Father" (Mark 13:32). This kenotic ("self-emptying") passage is balanced with the previous verse that indicates the eternal nature of the words of the one who is the Son of God (Mark 13:31).

The last and climactic use of this title in Mark is the centurion's uninformed yet adequate assessment that this broken person is

27. The recurrence (Mark 2:7; Luke 5:21; Matt 9:3; John 10:36) of attributing blasphemy to Jesus is one strong indication that the essence of monotheism, as understood in the time period, was being challenged.

surely "the Son of God" (Mark 15:39). In radical contrast to the tenants of Israel's vineyard (12:1–12), Mark's argument is sealed by a pagan centurion when confronted by pure self-giving love. The centurion may have spoken better than he knew, but out of his mouth comes a theological climax to the book of Mark.

These references in Mark indicate that Jesus was fully human but radically different from any other human person. What we find is a progressive revelation based upon the Spirit-enabled reflection of the Gospel writer. Like Mark, other writers cover the themes of election, obedience, and sonship. The being of God is defined in a new familial way; God the Father and God the Son are sharers in the nature of divinity. Work (function) and being (ontology) are indivisible in the person of the Son if one is to understand what he came to do and who he claimed to be. In fact, his work bears a certain ontic reality. The clarification that comes from the revelation of the Son of God in history points us beyond all the Old Testament categories for this title. All of the previous references could be distilled into function, but in the Gospels that is not the case. The work of Jesus reveals his being, always a personal and relational being. His work is to come from the Father for the sake of others. A relational reality is revealed in all he does.[28] His divine reality permeates every situation, so the title "Son of God" is a revelation of the one whose words and works alter the lives of those who accept him.

The Personhood of the Son in Johannine Literature

When it comes to Father-Son language, John's theology is distinctive enough to merit its own discussion. The Johannine material assists our systematic endeavor to understand the nature of God as interpersonal triune love. John's titles are distinctly unique from the Synoptics. The use of *logos* ("word") is found mainly in John.[29] The seven "I am" statements of Jesus provide unparalleled self-dis-

---

28. Kasper, *Jesus the Christ*, 166.
29. John 1:1–18, 1 John 1:1–4, 5:7; Rev 19:13. There is a strand of thought here that would include Heb 1:1–4 and Col 1:15–20.

closure.[30] Jesus reveals the glory of his divine eternality as Yahweh when he states, "Before Abraham was born, I am" (John 8:58). He is called "Rabbi" ("teacher" or "master," John 1:38, 49), and John 4 refers to him as Messiah (vv. 25–26). The unmistakable implication of John 14:16 is that Jesus will send the *paraclete* ("comforter") to complete the work of redemption in human hearts. John uses these titles in a profound way.

Four major titles in the Book of John deal with sonship. Contemporary theologians are often asked whether Jesus understood himself to be the Son of God in an ontological sense. An assessment of these titles confirms that both Jesus and his contemporaries were clearly declaring his unique nature in relation to his Father.

Son of God

John uses the title "Son of God" in much the same way as Mark, but there are differences as well.[31] The Baptist's recognition of the divine messianic sonship of Jesus offers the foundation for understanding the Lamb who takes away the sin of the world (John 1:34, 29). Nathaniel uses the term in recognizing the Rabbi Jesus, who is also the King of Israel (1:49). Three times Jesus uses this designation for himself; each can be seen as distinctively self-revelatory (5:25, 10:36, and 11:4).[32] Religious minds of the day recognized the relevance of the Son's eschatological glory. They were fully aware of the ontic claims in Jesus' use of this title. Jesus affirmed intra-Trinitarian self-giving love, mutuality in the economy of salvation, and identity of essence between the Father and the Son on the temple mount when challenged regarding the healing of the lame man (5:19–24).

The dependence of the Jesus upon his Father is impossible to miss. In the theological crisis that precipitates the crucifixion, the

---

30. Bread of life (6:35); light of the world (8:12, 9:5); the door (10:7); the good shepherd (10:11); resurrection and the life (11:25); the way, the truth, and the life (14:6); and the true vine (15:1).

31. John uses the title 23 times (O'Collins, *Christology*, 132).

32. It is also implied that Jesus is the Son of God in John 9:28–29 and 9:35.

title "Son of God" draws the accusation of blasphemy (10:22–42, esp. 36). At the center of his ministry in the next chapter, Jesus indicates the true meaning behind the death of Lazarus (11:4). The glory of the Father and the Son is closely connected to the resuscitation of this friend. The response by Martha illuminates the divine nature of her Friend: "I believe that you are the Messiah, the Son of God, who is to come into the world" (11:27).

Monogenes

"Only begotten" (*monogenes*) is found twice in the prologue to John's Gospel concerning the incarnation of the Word (1:14, 18), but it is also found in John 3:16 and 18 in the teaching of Jesus himself. Though the meaning of the term is multi-faceted, John uses it for an important theological reason.[33] The traditional interpretation has been to see it primarily as an indicator of distinctness. Begottenness can be construed spiritually, as in God begetting children by faith, but a much deeper connotation applies to Jesus.[34] His relationship to the Father in the Spirit is unique, so distinctive that in order to describe it a new terminology has to be produced or existing words redefined. In the earnest attempt to keep the ori-

---

33. The early church saw much more in the term *monogenes* than is allowed by most modern scholarship. It was assumed that the term clearly indicated a Father who begot and a Son begotten from eternity. See Origen, *De Principiis*, ANF 4:376. Augustine, *On the Gospel of St John*, NPNF1 7:267–68; 296–97. Leon Morris clarifies the etymological origin of *monogenes* from *ginomai* and not *gennao*. From that he discerns that a purely metaphysical origination is not John's intention. The term is used for "only" or "unique" in other places (Luke 7:12, 8:42, 9:38; Heb 11:7). John uses it also in 1 John 4:9. Morris does say that it is an important term in distinguishing the absolutely unique sonship of Jesus. He writes, "No other is or can be the Son of God as he is" (*The Gospel According to St. John*, 105). Interestingly he takes a more "metaphysical" interpretation of John 1:18 and the reference to the "bosom" (*kolpos*) of the Father (114). Köstenberger sees an *inclusion* from John 1:1 to the usage of *monogenes* in John 1:18. He translates it, "one-of-a-kind Son" (Köstenberger, *John*, 48–50).

34. 1 John 5:1 offers insight into a transition of thought regarding "begottenness" within the New Testament with the uses of the participle *gennao*. The Father is spoken of as the one who begets, and Christ as the one who is begotten. The context is not that uniqueness but of a type of generation. Debate will continue on this matter, but one is left to find adequate language to envision the mystery of the triune life and its most helpful descriptors.

gins of the Son of God outside of creation, the Alexandrian Fathers made much of the essential derivation of the Son from the Father *in eternity.*[35] The Only-Begotten One shares the nature of the Father. He is not made like the rest of us. His sonship by nature makes our adoption by grace possible.

Some modern scholars argue that *monogenes* ought not be read in an ontological manner; instead, the term simply refers to the uniqueness of Jesus. They believe any allusion to divine begottenness should not be interpreted as John's Gospel does; eternal generation must be a later theological gloss. The modern interpretation supported the adoptionism that marked the Christology of the nineteenth and twentieth centuries.[36] Although subtle ontological references were nuanced in the theological debates of the second through fifth centuries, this crucial term for Jesus was one of the supporting arguments that he, and he alone, was from the Father. He was in an absolutely unique relationship with the Father from eternity.[37]

Son

"Son" is the most-used title in John's Gospel for Jesus.[38] As a term employed without qualification, there is the option of generalizing its meaning ("sons" as a term for anyone's relationship with God) or particularizing it ("son" as unique to Jesus). Repeatedly Jesus introduces the term "Son" almost as an afterthought. This usage appears utterly unpremeditated, as if it were the most natu-

---

35. Athanasius, *Statement of Faith*, NPNF2 4:84–85.

36. I know of no Christology that aligns itself with the trajectory of rejecting concepts like "generation" or "begottenness" as indicating ontological relationship that does not end up with the usual result of a diminished Christology (Kasper, *Jesus the Christ*, 174).

37. Recent scholarship in the manuscripts of John show that John 1:18 reads more accurately, "his one and only, who is himself God." If that is the case, then John is underscoring the relationality between the Father and the Son with this unique term (1:1–4, 14) and he is affirming the deity of Jesus as well. See Köstenberger, *John*, 50; note page 98 for other scholarly agreement.

38. The title, "Son" by itself is only found two times outside of John: Matt 11:27 and Mark 13:32.

ral thing in the world, even though this was utter blasphemy to the Jews of that day.[39] It is a means by which Jesus claims identity with the Father in nature.

Liberal interpreters often say that orthodox believers claim to know Jesus only through salvific experiences. At this point, care must be taken not to deny Jesus' divine reality before his actual work of salvation begins. There must be an absolute ontological origin for all that we claim in our experience; otherwise, salvation takes place outside the nature of God. Colossians 1:14–17 shows that Jesus has the position and power to establish a saving relationship with those who believe in him. Paul states that he is the linchpin of all reality so that we in turn can be a part of all of his reality.

From the beginning of the Gospel of John to its climactic priestly prayer, Jesus repeatedly refers to God as Father (over 120 times). Jesus is not just *a* Son, but he is *the* Son of God (John 17:1).[40] Jesus' distinctive use of *Abba* has been a fruitful anchor point for Christology for decades.[41] As theologians drew the materials together, it became clear that the term "Father" in the mind of Jesus was much more than an epithet of deity. *Abba*, an expression of his eternal personal relationship with the Father, is the distinguishing name by which Jesus began his prayers. We are given a glimpse of the perichoretic life of the Trinity in the unsurpassed communion of the Son and the Father.

Son of Man

"Son of Man" is the fourth Johannine title (John 3:13, 14). The theological rationale of John first includes a discussion of Jesus as the only begotten Son of God followed by "Son of Man" language. Jesus gave Nicodemus, an informed Jewish religious leader, an option to interpret the world differently. The context reveals that

---

39. John 5:19–23; "Son of God," 25; "son of man," 27.

40. See Thompson's interesting yet exclusively biblical analysis of the place of the Father in the Gospel of John, *God in the Gospel of John*.

41. Pannenberg, *Jesus—God and Man*, 158–60, Bornkamm, *Jesus of Nazareth*, 126–29, Kasper, *The God of Jesus Christ*, 170–71.

Jesus offered to Nicodemus a clear, uncoerced choice. Jesus does not force himself upon anyone, but he always gives enough information for a meaningful response. He wants us to make the decision to believe he is who he claims to be. This "Son of Man" language was not new to Nicodemus or his theological heritage. What may be shocking to the reader is Jesus' claim to be the "Son of Man" about whom Ezekiel and Daniel prophesied and that a first-century Jewish leader was given the choice to believe that or not.

The next pericope in which "Son of Man" takes on deep theological significance is when the Greeks request to see Jesus:

> Now there were some Greeks among those who went up to worship at the festival. They came to Philip, who was from Bethsaida in Galilee, with a request. "Sir," they said, "we would like to see Jesus." Philip went to tell Andrew; Andrew and Philip in turn told Jesus.
>
> Jesus replied, "The hour has come for the Son of Man to be glorified. Very truly I tell you, unless a kernel of wheat falls to the ground and dies, it remains only a single seed. But if it dies, it produces many seeds. Anyone who loves their life will lose it, while anyone who hates their life in this world will keep it for eternal life. Whoever serves me must follow me; and where I am, my servant also will be. My Father will honor the one who serves me.
>
> "Now my soul is troubled, and what shall I say? 'Father, save me from this hour'? No, it was for this very reason I came to this hour. Father, glorify your name!"
>
> Then a voice came from heaven, "I have glorified it, and will glorify it again." The crowd that was there and heard it said it had thundered; others said an angel had spoken to him.
>
> Jesus said, "This voice was for your benefit, not mine. Now is the time for judgment on this world; now the prince of this world will be driven out. And I, when I am lifted up

from the earth, will draw all people to myself." He said this to show the kind of death he was going to die.

The crowd spoke up, "We have heard from the Law that the Messiah will remain forever, so how can you say, 'The Son of Man must be lifted up'? Who is this 'Son of Man'?" (John 12:20–34)

That the Son of Man would be lifted up is necessary to his hour of glorification. A remarkable unselfconsciousness is revealed in Jesus' use of the "Son of Man" in this context. The reader is included in a personal triune discussion. The Son speaks of himself not in divine terms alone but in very human terms as that self-chosen sacrifice for those he came to save. This section describes the crowd's queries seeking the meaning of the title in question (John 12:34).

Although it is misleading to overemphasize one nature of Christ over the other, it is clear that this list of titles revolves around a single theme and bears enormous theological weight. The filial nature of revelation in Christ is unmistakable. The self-perception of Jesus, the focus of his ministry, and the culmination of all salvation comes together under the aegis of his sonship in the Father. Jesus' descent into human history revealed his relationship to the Father by the Spirit. Jesus, the one true person, came to an impersonal and fallen humanity and, by a life and death of self-giving love, extended the hope of salvation. That salvation, however, was not something ancillary to God's own life. It was neither a decree by divine fiat nor a physical ransom paid out, nor even a payment of a commercial debt. Salvation was, and is, Life; the life of the only true God and Jesus Christ whom he has sent through the agency of the blessed Holy Spirit. Reconciliation with God is true life; this life is offered by the Son of God whose origins are eternal. Only in the Son of God can anyone ever hope to find life eternal, and once that life is inaugurated, every vestige of self-will is confronted by reconciling grace.

SON OF MAN

We have already begun this discussion above, but it deserves a deeper treatment here. Systematic Christian thinking must always attempt the balance of divine and human categories in Jesus. This title, uniquely connected to Jesus, connects the transcendent with the immanent in a powerful way.

Jewish and Non-Jewish Sources

The "Son of Man" is a Semitic phrase with a variety of nuances. No solid Christological argument based on the "Son of Man" motif has been developed because scholars tend to think of Christ primarily as Messiah. Even though "Son of Man" was his preferred title, we find it rarely used in contemporary worship.[42] We seldom pray to the Son of Man, and we hesitate to preach about the Son of Man.[43]

A Mere Human Being

In the ancient Near East "Son of Man" could mean a mere human being or humanity in general (Ps 8:4, see Heb 2:6). Ezekiel is referred to as a "son of man" (Ezek 2:1, 3, 6, 8), apparently designating a non-divine person chosen by God.[44] He is a representative of Israel who receives the word of God on behalf of the nation. "Son of Man" was also used to identify a person with a certain group. For example, a liar could be referred to as a "son of lies." A "son of

---

42. See the discussion in O'Collins, *Christology*, 62–63.

43. David Wells says of this title that, "There are few places in the New Testament which exhibit more plainly the mental and spiritual distance which sometimes exists between ourselves as interpreters and the biblical writings we are interpreting than the Son of Man sayings" (Wells, *The Person of Christ*, 77).

44. In Ezekiel the title occurs some 93 times. The distinction between God and the son of man is clear in these references (Michel, "Son," *NIDNTT* 3:613). Zimmerli interprets its usage as a means of expressing "an individual within the created order, the servant, who is summoned by his master in an act of unprecedented condescension by his divine Lord" (Zimmerli, *Ezekiel 1*, 131). In the fourteen usages of the title outside of Ezekiel, only one, Daniel 8:17, addresses the prophet as Ezekiel was. The remaining uses are all in poetic literature where parallels to "man" or human being are clear (see Job 16:21; Isa 51:12; Jer 51:43). (Aune, *"Son of Man," ISBE* 4:574). Daniel 10:16 has a reference connected to an angelic figure.

wealth" might be considered a person of means. Another example is found in lists of kings with *ben,* meaning "son of," followed by the king's name meaning "son of the king."[45] This is comparable to *ben Adam,* which means "son of Adam." What Jesus seems to mean by applying this title to himself is, "I am truly human. I fully identify with the human condition." In his repetitive references to total identification with humanity, Jesus willingly humbles himself in the incarnation. Paradoxically, the God who is not like man (Num 23:19) has become mortal. The use of the title in both Ezekiel and Daniel gives the impression that the "Son of Man" is *unmistakably* human but not *merely* human. What we find is an early statement that the one Israel awaits is both human and divine.

The Christian tradition has consistently maintained that Jesus' application of *ben Adam,* "Son of Adam," to himself is more than an affirmation of human existence. Jesus' usage of this title presumes his hearers understand the Old Testament background.[46] But at the same time, as we shall see, he is adding his own definition to this term.

The Gospels record eighty-one times when Jesus and the title "Son of Man" are clearly connected. Of those, Jesus uses the title with self-reference seventy-nine times. In two instances Jesus is called "Son of Man"—by the crowd in John 12:34 and by Stephen in Acts 7:56. In the apocalyptic vision of John, it is almost certain that "Son of Man" (used without an article) refers to the regnant Christ (Rev 1:13, 14:14). The term "Son of Man" is never used in the Epistles and seldom in worship or theological reflection—in spite of the many uses of the term by our Lord.

---

45. Schweizer, "υἱός," *TDNT* 8:336–37; Cullmann, *Christology of the New Testament,* 138.

46. Moule mentions the intriguing analysis of J. W. Bowker that the mere humanity emphasis of this title is borne by Jesus even into heaven. So, Jesus takes "frail, mortal man into the heavenly court" (Moule, *The Origins of Christology,* 12).

HOLY LOVE: A WESLEYAN THEOLOGY

Apocalyptic Redeemer

The Son of Man is viewed as an apocalyptic redeemer in the Jewish tradition. In Daniel 7, the prophet portrays the Son of Man establishing dominion as he comes in glory on the clouds of heaven.[47] This redeemer figure has been interpreted as a representative of the saints (Dan 7:18, 21, 22); some even attest that it is an angelic figure coming to save his creation.[48] The Jewish tradition, even in extra-biblical literature, related the Son of Man to messianic patterns.

Hebrew philosophical culture had deliberated on the concept of an original man, that is, an archetypal man who appears in a messianic context.[49] This heavenly being will come at the end of time to redeem Israel from its beleaguered situation. In the New Testament this archetypal man is viewed as the incarnate Lord, not merely a heavenly being or a kind of pre-existent human. The orthodox Jewish mind could accept the idea of an archetypal or a supernatural being, but the conception of an incarnate divine-human being was extremely difficult to grasp. This idea challenged the transcendent monotheism with its attendant cosmology. Divine and human could not mix or merge, but the one who claimed to be the Son of Man was crossing these barriers.

---

47. One also finds similar themes in apocryphal literature, as in 2 Esd 7:28 and 13:32, 37 where the Son, the Messiah, is seen coming out of the sea.

48. The saints in mind are apparently persecuted faithful Jews. See Cullmann, *Christology of the New Testament*, 146; O'Collins, *Christology*, 62. The angelic interpretation is tied to Daniel 10:16.

49. Cullmann, *Christology of the New Testament*, 140–52. Pannenberg offers some critique of Cullmann in *Jesus-God and Man*, 196–97. Wright's consistent criticism of a pious over-reading of the texts (516) or the earnestness to find Trinitarian glosses (523, 526) shows here when he assesses what first-century Jews would have heard in the title. He deems that it was unmistakably messianic (518), vindication and exaltation (524), and representation (Wright, *Jesus and the Victory of God*, 525; see also 360–68). Wright is convinced that the Son of Man title would be perceived primarily as an historically-based metaphor of the "vindication of Israel after her suffering at the hands of the pagans" (*New Testament and the People of God*, 292).

Usage in the Gospels

In the Synoptic Gospels, the title "Son of Man" occurs fifty times from the mouth of Jesus.[50] Although the titles "Son of God" or "Son of Man" challenge human abilities to grasp the full meaning of either description, the Gospel writers insist on their use. The difficulty is not one of textual ambiguity but of an exceeding richness of content.

The four major areas of usage of the title in the Gospels are evident:

- The Son of Man as preexistent (John 3:13; 6:62).
- The Son of Man working on the earth (Matt 12:8; Luke 5:24).
- The Son of Man and his passion (Matt 16:22; Luke 9:44; John 3:14).
- The Son of Man and his coming again (Matt 26:64; Luke 18:8; most of the references to this title fall in this category).

The usage of this title reveals Jesus' self-perception. The phrase "Son of Man" carries an authority that dismays the religious elite (Mark 2:10) and promises judgment of sin at the end of time (Matt 16:27, 19:28). Mark lays the groundwork for this title.

Mark begins his Gospel by announcing that Christ is the Son of God (1:1). The quotation from Isaiah 40:3 in Mark 1:2 proclaims the majesty of the one who is announced. He is named as Son by the Father (Mark 1:11). In Mark's description of the paralytic's healing, the significance of the entire event is the claim that Jesus makes regarding himself: "'But I want you to know that the Son of Man has authority on earth to forgive sins.' So, he said to the man, 'I tell you, get up, take your mat and go home'" (Mark 2:10–11). The Jewish teachers rightly held that only God can forgive sins. By forgiving this man's sin, Jesus identifies himself, the "Son of Man," as God.

---

50. Sixty-nine times if one includes parallel passages. John uses this term twelve times (thus eighty-one occurrences).

HOLY LOVE: A WESLEYAN THEOLOGY

The authority of the Son of Man as Lord extends even to the holy Sabbath (Mark 2:28).

Jesus' contemporaries respond to his actions and titles in a variety of ways. The Pharisees accuse him of being Beelzebub (Mark 3:22). His family has questions about his sanity (3:31). His own townspeople deride him as merely the son of Joseph (6:1–3). Herod fears that he is the resurrected John the Baptist (6:14). The devils say he is the "Holy One of God" (Mark 1:24). At the pivotal paragraph of the book (Mark 8:27–33), Mark records the major question precipitated by the events in the first half of the Gospel when Jesus turns to his disciples and asks, "Who do you say I am?" Peter's answer testifies to the fulfillment of messianic promises (Mark 8:29). When Jesus begins to talk about his passion, he uses the title. "The Son of Man must suffer many things and be rejected by the elders and the chief priests and the scribes and be killed and on the third day be raised to life" (Luke 9:22). Mark 8:31 points back to Daniel 7:13, but it also provides new insight on the Son. Peter disavows the possibility that a heavenly redeemer could ever suffer. The Son of Man came to judge not die. Peter envisioned a triumphant Messiah who would end oppression and injustice. To him, Jesus is redefining this title in an unexpected way.[51]

Peter, an example of the Hebrew mind of his day, anticipated a messianic deliverer. The Jews did not fully comprehend how the Son of Man could descend to earth. Jesus' disciples could not conceive how the divine Son could further descend to die. Thus, two different levels of descent are revealed here. On the first level, the disciples could accept a glorious Son of Man (example, Daniel 7). On the second level, they could not understand the idea of a Son of Man who would die to inaugurate a kingdom. Jesus is using the culturally familiar first meaning as a basis for adding the second meaning. He starts with the familiar and transforms its content.

---

51. O'Collins states that the "innovative reinterpretation" of "kingdom," "Father" (implying Son of God) and "Son of Man" almost thoroughly sums up the ministry or Jesus (*Christology*, 66).

Three passages in Mark deal with the cross (8:31–34; 9:30–32; 10:32–34, 45). Here, Christ as "Son of Man" is central. These are the familiar verses where after the transfiguration Mark deals with the crucifixion. The strongest statement on the atonement in Mark is distinctly tied to the Son of Man and reveals a direct link with Daniel (Mark 13:26). The Son of Man becomes a servant who will ransom Israel through vicarious suffering.[52] This passage reminds us of Daniel's eschatological "Son of Man" coming in the clouds. Mark 14:21 again shakes the disciples' messianic theology of triumph with the reality of suffering and rejection. In an ironic twist, the chief priest asks, "Are you the Messiah, the Son of the Blessed One?" (Mark 14:61). Jesus' telling response shifts the conversation: "I am . . . And you will see the Son of Man sitting at the right hand of the Mighty One and coming on the clouds of heaven" (Mark 14:62).[53] Jesus is using the title "Son of Man" to emphasize his unique divine/human nature. His identity cannot be construed from the divine side alone.

Mark emphasizes the authority of the Son of Man, affirms the messianic identity of the Son, and connects these with Jesus as the Son of God. Matthew uses the title as one of the means by which Jesus refers to himself (Matt 5:11, 10:32, 16:21) and to point out the righteous judgment of Jesus at the end of human history (Matt 16:27, 25:31). Luke also has an eschatological focus much like Matthew's (Luke 17:22, 30; 18:8). John includes the only clear pre-existence motifs in his unique use of title (3:13, 6:62). Several times John connects the exaltation, the glory of the Son of Man, to the recurrent theme of Jesus' impending suffering and death (8:28, 12:23, 13:31).[54]

---

52. Bruce, *New Testament History*, 192–94.

53. In Matthew and Luke he says "you say," but here, his reply is recorded as "I say, 'I am'."

54. Paul does not use the term but shows vestiges of the title in his contrast of Adam with Christ, or the earthly man and the heavenly man (Rom 5:12–21, 1 Cor 15:42–50). Hebrews 2:6 is a quote from Psalm 8:4. Rev 1:13 and 14:14 clearly depict the picture of the Son of Man found in Dan 7:13.

In the Gospels, every Old Testament prophecy of the Son of Man is fulfilled. Jesus is viewed as fully human—made like us in every respect.[55] Like the prophets he too is called upon to speak in the midst of a perverse generation. Yet the authority he bears causes all who come in contact with him to expect something extraordinary. His words and actions are recognized as radically different, perhaps even "heavenly." The predominant focus of the Gospel usage is to emphasize his incarnation. His judgments are strong but always fair. He stands against all injustice. He is an advocate of the faithful.[56] In his power to forgive and heal, an undercurrent of self-giving transcends mere human sympathy. Most shocking, however, is the connection to suffering.[57] The cross is fundamental to the Gospel depiction of this Son of Man. The only way to receive his revelatory descent in its fullness is to encounter the Son of Man who bears all the implications of sin. His redemptive, descending likeness, deriving from divine life and love, enters fallen human existence.

In these passages also, the Son of Man, individual yet representative, descends to make saints of those who are his own. Christ represents humanity to God, but he also represents God to humanity. The Son of Man descends to make others holy. Saints are identified with him. They share his character and suffer with him (Dan 7:25).

---

55. Ethelbert Stauffer contradicts the scholars who say use of this title was to emphasize that Jesus was a mere man. He writes, "'Son of Man' is just about the most pretentious piece of self-description that any man in the ancient East could possibly have used!" (*New Testament Theology*, 108. See also 244–45 for the centrality of this title for pre-Christian apocalyptic).

56. Bruce, *New Testament History*, 174–75.

57. Cullmann is quite helpful here. He states that the use of the title "Son of Man" is chosen by Jesus over the "Servant of Yahweh" motif because the former is more inclusive of present and future work. The relation of the two ought not to be missed. "Son of Man" incorporates the highest concepts of exaltation while the Servant motif involves the deepest humiliation. This, Cullmann says, is an "unheard of new act" (*Christology of the New Testament*, 161). F. F. Bruce says that Jesus' application of this title in contradistinction to both Daniel and the "Son of Man" theme in Ethiopian Enoch and 2 Esd "marks a creative advance in its use and significance" (*New Testament History*, 133).

"The Son of Man" and the Shema

The consistent use of this title challenges the theology of the *Shema* (Deut 6:4). The eschaton is the context for the descent of the Son of Man. The interpretation of the title "the Son of Man" is that the Father and Son are so close they are inseparable by time and space. The Son of God is no less God when he becomes the Son of Man.[58] This is the language of revelation. "Son of Man" indicates a mutual relationship between divine persons, only one of whom became human. Jesus speaks passionately in John 17 about his oneness with the Father. The clearest example of this oneness is found in verse 21: "I am in the Father and he is in Me." He also desires that we be *in him* (John 14:20; 17:21–23). This reinforces the language that we are to become like Christ, holy as he is holy.[59] In the Old Testament "holy ones" is to be interpreted in the context of God's coming to redeem and to make saints out of human persons.[60] Jesus comes to make men and women like himself; he is the image of full humanity and personhood.

SUMMATION ON TITLES: TWO MAJOR VIEWS

THE TITLES RELATE MAINLY TO THE WORK OF CHRIST

The theological worldview of the early church has suffered by the interpretations of modernity and postmodernity. The radical reduction of the person of Christ as a result is a tragedy for the church.[61] An historical account would need to explain the origins of this Christological minimalism. Our point is that none of the detractors of the supernatural worldview has offered any substantial reason why one should worship Christ.

---

58. Tertullian, *Against Marcion, ANF* 3:359.

59. Hippolytus, *Treatise on Christ and Antichrist, ANF* 5:209.

60. *Kadeshim* can also refer to angelic figures.

61. Bultmann, *Theology of the New Testament*, 33–37, and *Jesus Christ and Mythology*, 13, 16. In agreement with the assessment of Philipp Vielhauer, Käsemann, *Essays on New Testament Themes*, 43–44; Lindars, *Jesus Son of Man*; Perrin, *Rediscovering the Teaching of Jesus*, also have attacked the apocalyptic, transcendental redeemer figure.

A consideration of these two major titles, "Son of God" and "Son of Man," shows that they are meant to emphasize the two natures of Christ. The "Son of God" title, tied with the filial themes of the Old Testament and New Testament, strongly supports the foundational belief that Jesus is the Son by nature, not by adoption. His relationship with the Father and the Holy Spirit is far above all other types of sonship. On the other hand, the title, "Son of Man," provides the immanence motif that includes judgment, vindication of the oppressed, and identification with humanity.[62]

The formulators of the creeds discerned more in the titles than modern scholarly minds are willing to allow. As a theme in this entire work, it is advanced that revelation does unequivocally presuppose a Creator who is able to redeem because he is divine, not bound by our limitations. Biblical claims do not necessitate unwarranted leaps of thought. Those who would apply an Ockhamistic razor to every title of Jesus end up equally as nominalistic as the medieval philosopher himself.[63] Ernst Käsemann is reflective of the genre of "minimalists." On the title, "Son of Man," Käsemann states matter-of-factly that "we ought to take note here that it is very questionable whether Jesus in his lifetime claimed for himself the title 'Son of Man.'"[64] Though we have no desire to leave any important

---

62. Moule's conclusion is that Jesus' use of the title implies a "vindicated human figure of Dan. 7 and as a symbol for the ultimate vindication of obedience to God's design" (*The Origin of Christology*, 17).

63. William of Ockham (1285–1347) produced a radical reductionistic approach to philosophy and theology. All superfluous (to him) notions were to be shaved away and only the essentials left. Thus, the "razor" motif. More effective though was his denial of universals (they were to him simply names, or *nomos*, and thus, nominalism). He advocated a belief in only those things that he called "individual things." This nominalism, or conceptualism, deeply affected the epistemology of the Reformation and modern periods. The focus on the tangible and the proveable as the sole source of truth was contrasted to the intangible and the revelatory.

64. Käsemann, *Essays on New Testament Themes*, 37. One is stultified by the influence of this work. The lack of evidence for some incredibly large assessments is surprising. One gets the distinct impression that detracting from the tradition of the Son of Man sayings is all that is needed. For him what is "obvious" (38), "very questionable" (38), "a bewildering confusion" (35), or the statement that we can "no longer assume the general reliability of the Synoptic tradition about

debate on Christology untouched, we must begin with a solid commitment to the veracity of the biblical texts and a belief that the Holy Spirit has guided the church.[65]

The atoning work required a divine person, and Jesus Christ came to do that work. His person originated from another world. If that origin is truly divine, then he must be God. And if he is God, then what he offers to us as delineations of himself in the titles bears life to the soul. Uniqueness of mission is only as strong as uniqueness of person.

THE TITLES RELATE MAINLY TO THE PERSON OF CHRIST

The other school of thought, taking seriously the meaning of these designations, views the work of Jesus as the revelation of his person. Here we are thrust into the middle of the economic (divine activity) and immanent (divine essence) debates.[66] This volume emphasizes the significance of Jesus' historical life and mission and grounds its theological structure and formulation on the belief that the triune God precedes all that is. God's self-giving nature is the ontological foundation for understanding creation, revelation, anthropology, and soteriology. Thus, the words and actions of

---

Jesus" (34). All these astounding assessments are based, it seems, on Käsemann's unquestioning acceptance of higher criticism and thus no necessity implores him to verify or substantiate his grandiose claims. Although Pannenberg's magisterial opus, *Jesus—God and Man*, offers many helpful insights, his trajectory is clearly limited. He takes the line of the historical schools who all have their own presuppositions to replace the antiquated ones. Recurringly, he argues against the consensual understanding of titles as theological statements that, "Dogmatics seems in this case to have preceded historical research" (57).

65. We will deal with this more under our discussion of Christology from "above" and "below" (see page 238).

66. Karl Rahner is attributed with this distinction in its twentieth-century rendition. Most references to discerning reality from below focus on the economic Jesus. Those who choose to emphasize his deity start their discussion from biblical delineations of the immanent Trinity. Whatever Rahner's original intention, the concept that there is no immanent trinity that is not the economic trinity has been used to severely limit discussion about pre-existence. The result is an over-historicizing of Jesus and the resulting diminishment of his divine personhood.

Jesus are not viewed from a merely historicist position or from an overly-simplistic fideist perspective.[67] A dynamic self-revelation is involved in every event of Jesus' life and ministry.

When the Son of God became the Son of Man in the flesh, he took on our humanity so that we might be one with him. The meaning of Christ's titles is not esoteric or mystical but salvific. Christ reveals a God who is abundantly generous in offering salvation to human persons. The roots of this self-giving love occur throughout the Old Testament. The New Testament is the fulfillment of the promise that Immanuel would come. The prophets could only point in a redemptive direction. The Gospels reveal the Son of Man as the *Incarnate Christ*.

YAHWEH AS KURIOS

The personal self-revelation of God to Israel is focused in a name: Yahweh. The life and ministry of Jesus equally reveal that Yahweh *in the flesh* forms a new Israel by redemption and transference into his kingdom. The Greek word for lord (*kurios*) is used to translate the personal name of Yahweh in the LXX.[68] The rendering of Yahweh as *kurios* in New Testament quotations from the Old Testament provide a fascinating look into the view of Jesus' contemporaries. They connected their theology of Israel's Yahweh with Jesus of Nazareth. He is the Lord of heaven and earth (Ps 102:5; Heb 1:10). "Prepare the way for the Lord" is the introduction to this theme in each Gospel.[69] The early church was built upon the

---

67. Fideism is the commitment to the rejection of proving doctrine by reason and the belief that only by faith (*fides*) can one establish the truth of a doctrine. Ockhamism led to some forms of radical fideism.

68. Though affirmative of the divinity in Jesus and the references that could be drawn on to support that thesis, the other names of *elohim* or *adonai* and the Aramaic *mar* take a secondary place in relation to the personal name of the God of Israel, Yahweh. See Cullmann's discussion of the surrounding cultural use of *kurios* (*The Christology of the New Testament*, 196–99).

69. Drawing from Isaiah 40:3, each of the Gospels confirms the ministry of the last prophet of Israel before Jesus as pointing to Yahweh's arrival (Matt 3:3; Mark 1:2–3; Luke 3:4; John 1:23.) Matthew, Luke, and John each include a mention of Isaiah in the context. See Luke 1:17, "And he shall go before him [John the Baptist]," in relation to Malachi 3:1 and 4:5–6. Though not exhaustive, see

premise that the name of Jesus was the saving name because it was identical to the name of the Lord (Acts 2:21; Rom 10:13; Joel 2:32). The church fathers saw the mission of the church as one given by Yahweh himself in the person of Jesus (Acts 13:47; Isa 49:6). The worship of Yahweh is indistinguishable from the homage offered to the Son (Isa 45:23; Rom 14:11; Phil 2:10). Jesus is honored as the judge of the whole earth (2 Thess 1:9; Isa 2:19).[70] These are references to the personhood of the Son. Though differentiated from the Spirit and the Father, he is fully and irrevocably divine. When one hears the voice of Jesus, one is hearing the voice of Yahweh.[71] The titles and names of Jesus Christ coalesce into a climax of the salvific history found in Israel. All of the metaphors, symbols, and stories of Israel become predicates of the reality Jesus. "God was in Christ" literally. He was not an adoptive agent or a receptacle of divinity but a co-equal and a co-sharer in the divine nature.

THE NATURE OF TITLES AND
A HERMENEUTIC SPIRAL

In the discussion of the relation between titles and the person of Jesus, one can discern a hermeneutical spiral within an orthodox Christological interpretation of the data before us. He is the life, and death can only be understood properly in light of that eternal life. His death interprets his life but only as his life enables us to understand his death. If his resurrection interprets his lordship,

---

Eckman, "The Identification of Christ with *Yahweh* by New Testament Writers," 145–53. The connection between actual quotes from the Old Testament and their usage as references to the divinity of Christ as Yahweh is clear in Luke 4:18–19; Acts 15:17; Rom 14:11; 1 Pet 2:3. Of sixty-three Old Testament quotations that include references to Yahweh, twelve at least belong to the class Eckman refers to as "undeniable" in the sense that they definitely place Jesus as the recipient of the same adulation, prophecy, or power that was attributed to Yahweh in the Old Testament.

70. Some examples are Matt 3:3, Luke 3:4, Rom 10:13, 2 Thess 1:9.

71. Cullmann shows a scholarly reserve in his assessment of the name *kurios*, although he does end his discussion with the conclusion of the early church that "the pre-existence of Jesus (like the existence of the *Logos* with God in the beginning) should be understood in the light of the present lordship of the *Kyrios* Christ" (*Christology*, 235).

HOLY LOVE: A WESLEYAN THEOLOGY

his eternal life informs the meaning of that reality beyond physical death. The person and work of the Son are inseparable for a well-rounded doctrine of Christ.

Here the discernment of a systematic principle is instructive. A dynamic view of revelation and careful reflection upon the historical events must guide our perspective. As we shall see, Christology is the only inclusive way to understand reality. Without the personal unity of the creature and the Creator in Christ, no true redemption is possible. That is why the church has taken these titles, words, and actions of Jesus so seriously. Orthodox thinkers have resisted, up until this era, all attempts to minimize the dynamic of Trinitarian self-revealing and self-giving. The only way truly to know Yahweh is to know Jesus Christ (John 17:3). The entire ministry of the Holy Spirit could be summed up as making the Son known (John 15:26). Apart from Jesus, the Christian believer can easily fall into an over-philosophized view of God. The separation of the transcendent from the immanent reduces Jesus to a mere sage or rabbi and forces theology into an impenetrable sphere epistemologically.

The hermeneutical spiral of life and death, of person and work, is important because at no point do we merely have to do with a man. God is dealing with us. Everything about him reveals the Trinity. The history of apophatic theology, with its assumption that God's inner nature is unknowable and hidden, is a denial of the full meaning of revelation and of incarnation. Without claiming universal comprehension, Trinitarian Christology that forms the rudiments of this inquiry provides the logic of all reality. We believe in God because we have seen him in Christ (1 John 1:1–2). Being is revealed in Yahweh, who is not defined by the unspoken tetragrammaton (*YHWH*) of the Jews or the Unknown of Plotinus, but by Mary's son born in Bethlehem. The words, works, and life of God are shown in Jesus, so we are encouraged to excavate the themes that illuminate the full depiction of God. Irenaeus helps to summarize this discussion of titles and other references to Jesus by speaking from a variety of vantage points concerning the deity and the humanity of Christ. After listing many biblical allusions to Jesus as the Son of God, he turns to those who are unsure Jesus could have ever really taken on a true human nature:

> Again, there are those who say, "He is a man, and who shall know him?" and, "I came unto the prophetess, and she bare a son, and His name is called Wonderful, Counsellor, the Mighty God;" and those [of them] who proclaimed him as Immanuel, [born] of the Virgin, exhibited the union of the Word of God with His own workmanship, [declaring] that the Word should become flesh, and the Son of God the Son of man (the pure One opening purely that pure womb which regenerates men unto God, and which he himself made pure); and having become this which we also are, he [nevertheless] is the Mighty God, and possesses a generation which cannot be declared.[72]

BEYOND FUNCTION TO FILIAL CENTER

In the titles that describe Jesus as the Son, the church's best insights revolve around the interpretation of them as indications of the revelation of God's inner nature. Jesus lives life in the presence of his Father with the same dependence and mutual love that he did as the Son in eternity. The central reality of that unique filial relationship—a reciprocal and dynamic love expressed in time and space—the incarnation in which the only-begotten Son of God is constituted by the Spirit—is the message that permeates all the titles, all the miracles, all the teaching of Jesus of Nazareth. He does not live only to fulfill a role. He lives out of an eternal relationship. When Jesus claims sonship and affirms his Father's eternal relationship with him, it is from a concept of reality, which makes no sense if it is merely an adoptionistic understanding of his person. The personhood of Christ is an eternal reality. The filial relationship that he shares in the Spirit with the Father is the foundation for comprehending all of his earthly life and ministry.

---

72. Irenaeus, *Against Heresies*, ANF 1:509.

A PREEXISTENCE OF LOVE

We must not start with Jesus' function as Savior. We have begun our discussion with the relational, eternal existence of Jesus. His being as the Son is the only verification that his work is efficacious for salvation. Though inseparable, the essence and the function of the triune persons must be logically distinguished because of the crucial nature of revealed personhood.[73] The history of salvation reveals that the dynamic of the triune life makes the best sense of biblical data concerning the nature of Israel's God.

SCRIPTURAL INDICATIONS OF THE PREEXISTENT PERSONHOOD OF JESUS

Angel of the Lord: ma'alak Yhwh

The Son reveals to us a life, a person, who has been "sendable" from eternity. The sending of the Son by the Father does not create a new relationship. One theme of interest in this regard is the Old Testament record of representatives Yahweh sent on his behalf. Whether theophanies or Christophanies, the Angel of the Lord was a source of encouragement, guidance, and enabling. He always dealt with Israel in a redemptive manner.[74] When biblical persons acclaim the deity of this Angel of Yahweh, their belief in the one true God is not altered.[75] The consensual agreement that God does not offer his life through emissaries negates the possibility of this Angel being less than divine. Though rejected as a pre-incarnate manifestation by most modern scholarship, the early church saw much in

---

73. Ridderbos, *Paul: An Outline of His Theology*, 77.

74. Both singular and plural usages occur. *Ma'alak Yahweh*: Gen 16:7–11, 22:11–15; Exod 3:2; *ma'alak ha'elohim* or *elohim*: Gen 21:17; Exod 14:19; Judg 6:20; 1 Sam 29:9; 2 Sam 14:17–20. See part two, *Theology*, in volume two of this series.

75. Hagar says, "I have really seen God and remained alive" (Gen 16:13). Jacob is convinced he has wrestled with God, which is confirmed by his opponent (Gen 31:11, 13).

this figure that reminded them of the Son.[76] If this is a direct intervention of the one, true God, though incomplete, what concerns us is the identity of the Angel of Yahweh.[77] Earlier theologians saw Jesus in these passages.[78]

Though not equivalent to the fullness of revelation that comes only with the incarnation, there is preparation for understanding the sent-ness of and the person of the Son in this important element of progressive revelation of the triune God.

Word of God (dābār Yhwh)

"In the beginning was the Word" (John 1:1). The Hebrew *dābār* ("word") carries an interpersonal meaning. Communication, then, is an event, a thing: "the Word" has an existence. The Word of God was the declaration of the will of God. When God spoke the universe as he intended, it came into being (Gen 1:3, 6, 9, 14). The Word, for Israel, was the foundation of the moral code that permeated their historical relationship with the Holy One (Exod 20:1, 34:1, Deut 4:10). In a way similar to the sovereign ordering of the universe, yet allowing for freedom of response, this powerful word guided Israel by various forms of legislation, by true prophetic utterance, and by offering wisdom. There is a clear theological connection between the *Word of God* in the Old Testament and the *Logos* in the New Testament.

---

76. Edmond Jacob calls the Angel of Yahweh "elusive and perplexing" (*Theology of the Old Testament*, 75). And again, "[he] is so little a person in his own right" (77). von Rad surmises that the Angel, as with other indications of heavenly beings, "never rises above a certain colourlessness and indistinctness" (*Old Testament Theology*, 1:285). It is interesting that von Rad notes that regardless of our interpretation, this "representative" figure always seems to take center stage (286).

77. Eichrodt says, "In the quasi-human form of the messenger he can temporarily incarnate himself in order to assure his own that he is immediately at hand" (*Theology of the Old Testament*, 2:27). But on the following page he is quick to discount an ontological relation to the Son, stating, "[t]his [*Logos*] interpretation has rightly been abandoned on all sides, since the God who reveals himself in the *ma'alak* is in no sense present in a human body or as a permanent personal being." He settles for a tenable "primal form of revelation" (28).

78. Novatian, *Treatise Concerning the Trinity*, ANF 5:627–31; Augustine, *On the Trinity*, NPNF1 3:47–49.

John's commitment to the creative Word (Gen 1–2) underlies his usage of the term *logos* (word). In the Greek world *logos* was more ratiocentric (emphasis on reason); *logos* was the principle that ordered the universe. There is a strong probability that John was aware of the Hellenistic concept of *logos*. But in an essential move away from the philosophical idealism and pantheism of the Hellenistic *logos*, John, under the inspiration of the Spirit, personifies the *Logos* as Jesus. John applies both dynamic and personal meanings to *Logos*, which now truly is the Word become flesh.[79] That theological move is anticipated in the Wisdom tradition of the Old Testament (Prov 8:1, 22). In John, *Logos* is used as the beginning of the sustained theme of Jesus' pre-existence as the Son sent by the Father. This Word that brought all of creation into existence is connected distinctly with John 1:3: "Through him all things were made." John 1:14 makes the connection between the Word of God (*Logos*) and the incarnation: "The Word became flesh." The Word was the expression of God's face-to-face love to Israel. This personal God now came, in all of his divinity, with the face of a living human being.

John supports the relationship between the Word of God and the incarnation with a series of "I am" statements. These statements ought to alert any student to the "I am," which is the foundation of divine self-bestowal in the Old Testament. Direct statements that Yahweh makes about his nature and character in the Old Testament presuppose his being (Exod 3:14).

The Word that was with God was God. The Word who is Yahweh and the Father who is Yahweh existed in indissoluble unity even

---

79. Eichrodt's treatment of *dābār* is not only eloquent but also the only place where he specifically uses the term "trinity." He states that it is the concept of the Word enfleshed that incorporates otherness and immanence, the personal and the spiritual, creation and redemption, the permanent and the new, the present and the future. He states, "All this was only possible by applying the absolute fullness of the Old Testament concept of the Word of God to the person of the Redeemer; and that is why the New Testament development can only be understood on the basis of the Old" (*Theology of the Old Testament,* 80).

"before the world began" (John 17:5). There was never a time when the Son was not. All of the sovereign majesty, creative will, and providence of the Yahweh of Israel's faith is resident in Jesus of Nazareth when he declares his own being. "Before Abraham was born, I Am" (John 8:58). Although he laid aside the expression of his power during his earthly ministry, he shares it with the Father and the Spirit for eternity. The biblical concept of existence is distinct from the philosophical. Being, in Scripture, is always relational, never independent. The "I Am" is not a *static being* but an *eternal relationship* of three persons who are the "I am."[80]

OTHER TERMS THAT DEAL WITH PREEXISTENCE

"Only Begotten"

This term (*monogenes*) occurs nine times in the New Testament.[81] Two major interpretations of this term are identified by scholars: uniqueness and aloneness. Jesus shares in a unique and incomparable sonship with his Father.[82] While the term does not

---

80. Jacob, *Theology of the Old Testament*, 52.

81. See the previous discussion on page 120.

82. How the only-begotten Son of God is called firstborn: He who is first begotten is called firstborn, whether he is only-begotten or the first of a number of brothers. If then the Son of God was called firstborn, but was not called only-begotten, we could imagine that he was the firstborn of creatures, as being a creature. But because he is called both firstborn and only-begotten, both senses must be preserved in his case. We say that he is firstborn of all creation because both he himself is of God and creation is of God, but as he himself is born alone and timelessly of the essence of God the Father, he may with reason be called only-begotten Son, firstborn and not first-created. For the creation was not brought into being out of the essence of the Father, but by his will out of nothing. And he is called firstborn among many brethren, for although being only-begotten, he was also born of a mother. Because, indeed, he participated just as we ourselves do in blood and flesh and became man, while we too through him became sons of God, being adopted through the baptism, he who is by nature Son of God became firstborn amongst us who were made by adoption and grace sons of God, and stand to him in the relation of brothers. Wherefore he said, *I ascend unto My Father and your Father.* He did not say "our Father," but "My Father," clearly in the sense of Father by nature, and "your Father," in the sense of Father by grace. And "My God and your God." He did not say "our God," but "My God:" and if you distinguish with subtle thought that which is seen from that which is thought, also "your God," as Maker and Lord (John of Damascus, *Exposition of the Orthodox Faith*, NPNF2 9:77).

refer to a physical or temporal relationship in the Godhead, it can be easily misunderstood as pertaining to a time when the Son was uniquely "begotten." That heresy made infamous by Arius was soundly defeated in the Nicene era because of its radical implications for both Christology and soteriology.

"Begotten"

Related to the term *monogenes* ("only begotten"), *gennao* ("begotten") pertains more to the doctrine of the Son's eternal generation.[83] In the context of a discussion on love between brethren as a symbol of the life of God in the human heart, 1 John 5:1 makes an interesting comparison statement. Belief in Christ produces incorporation into the family of God as children. But then John adds, "and everyone who loves the parent loves the child." Literally, it reads, "everyone who loves the one who begets also loves the one begotten of him." Augustine claims forthrightly, "Who 'begat'? The Father. Who is 'begotten'? The Son. Everyone who loves the Father loves the Son."[84] Most modern biblical scholars are uneasy with interpreting the word "begotten" as an essence statement about Jesus in relation to the Father. However, the verse makes little sense unless Jesus is identified as the "begotten one." Even Bultmann says, "It therefore seems that Jesus Christ is to be understood" by this phrase.[85] Intriguingly, few scholars relate 1 John 5:1 and 5:18. Love for the triune God as mentioned in this discussion of *begetter* and *begotten* defines the intimacy of Jesus with the Father.[86]

---

83. See: 1 John 5:1; 1 John 5:18; Acts 13:33.

84. Augustine, *Ten Homilies on the Epistle of St. John*, NPNF1 7:521.

85. Bultmann, *The Johannine Epistles*, 88.

86. Examples of modern approaches: Dodd, speaking of 1 John 5:18, submits that it is the "Son of God *par excellence*, the eldest Brother of the family" (*The Johannine Epistles*, 138). I. H. Marshall steers clear of any theological use of *gennao* in this chapter (*The Epistles of John*, 226–27). Strecker does not see Jesus involved at all. He interprets it all within the community of keeping one another (*The Johannine Letters*, 175). Kruse compares the use of birth language in John's Gospel and epistles and finds that it is never used of the divine persons in relation for the obvious reasons of misuse, but when he comes to 1 John 5:1, he

This, or any discussion of generation, does not entail that Jesus was created or that he had a beginning. He began to be a human being, but he never began to be God. God is under no necessity to produce a Son. Such interpretations are perversions and heresies. Rather, *gennao* is a term used analogically to emphasize the unique, eternal relationship between the Father and the Son.[87] Hilary explores this vividly when he says, "The Son draws His life from that Father Who truly has life; the Only-begotten from the Unbegotten, Offspring from Parent, Living from Living. . . for the Son is born of the Unborn."[88] While not immediately ontological, this term offers a window or metaphor into the mystery of the eternal nature of self-giving.

"Firstborn"

The ancient title "firstborn" was used literally of the first child in biblical times.[89] But its application to Jesus in "firstborn over all creation" (Col 1:15) is an example of another common usage of the term. When Yahweh called Israel and David his firstborn, the connotation was not physical but rather a term of exaltation, uniqueness, or paramount importance.[90] Only one was prior to and supreme over all of the creation. We must put this term in context theologically. Jesus, then, is viewed as preeminent in all of the cosmos not because he is originally part of it but because, as Paul further points out, by him "all things have been created" (Col 1:16) and "he is before all things" (Col 1:17). Christ is, then, the exalted Creator and Lord of the universe, who precedes all that is.

Paul refers to Jesus as the "firstborn among many brothers and sisters" (Rom 8:29). This designation suggests that while his like-

---

states, "it is best interpreted as Jesus himself" who is begotten (*The Letters of John*, 195).

87. Augustine, *On the Creed*, NPNF1 3:371–72; John of Damascus, *Exposition of the Orthodox Faith*, NPNF2 9:6–7.

88. Hilary, *On the Trinity*, NPNF2 9:55.

89. Exod 4:23; Matt 1:25.

90. Exod 4:22; Jer 31:9; Ps 89:27.

ness includes a full humanity, it must always be viewed in light of the resurrection. He is the "divinely human" person.[91] The firstborn of humanity, Adam, brought sin into the human heart. This second and greater Adam, as Firstborn in a soteriological sense, paves the way for the reconciliation of the Godhead with humanity. Chrysostom employs the term not as descriptive of dignity and honor but as a clear reference to the "firstborn of the dead" (Col 1:18), that is, the firstfruits of the resurrection. Chrysostom emphasizes the identification implicit in the term. He uses "firstborn" as a foundational concept, one that binds Jesus to all creation, all humanity, all sin and death. At the same time Jesus as the Firstborn liberates creation from sin and its consequences by his reconciling self-sacrifice.[92] In the broader context, "Firstborn" entails a voluntary submission of the Son. As Athanasius says, "For the term 'Only-begotten' is used where there are no brethren, but 'First-born' because of brethren."[93] The one who is prior to all is born of Mary on our behalf. His humility, so closely connected to his own creation, reveals the love inherent in his willing identification with us. He bears our lineage of brokenness.

"Equality with God the Father"

The Son is viewed as co-equal and co-eternal with the Father. His enemies recognized that he was claiming identity with the Most Holy One.[94] Paul overtly claims that Jesus was before all things. Philippians 2:5–11 may well be a confessional hymn of the early church. Here Paul exalts Christ because he is equal with God (Phil 2:6). He is preexistent in the form (*morphe*) of God. For Paul and the other authors of the New Testament, the Son shares the

---

91. This phrase is used eight times in the New Testament. See: Col 1:15, "First born of all creation;" 1 Cor 15:20, "First born from the dead;" Rom 8:29, "First born among many brethren."

92. Chrysostom, *Homilies on Colossians*, NPNF1 13:270–72.

93. Athanasius, *Four Discourses Against the Arians*, NPNF2 4:382.

94. Mark 2:5–7, 14:61–64; Matt 26:63–65; Luke 22:70–71; John 1:1–4, 18, 5:19–24, 8:42–59, 10:29–33.

very nature of God.[95] The Son fully shares the divine life with the Father, not as a subordinate being but as truly one in divinity.

"Creator"

An important aspect of pre-existence concerns the relation of the triune God to Creation. Each person of the Trinity is involved in the origin, formation, and sustenance of the created order.[96] The consistent reference to the work of the Son in creation supports the view that he is both preexistent to creation and equal to God in all respects. No mythic demigod is involved in trying to restore a material world to spirituality. "He is before all things, and in him all things hold together" (Col 1:17). *In him* all things were created (Col 1:16). God deeply desires to share his divine life with humanity. What he made, no matter what has happened to it subsequently, can be remade, reformed, recreated. *Through the Son* all things visible and invisible were created (John 1:3; Col 1:16). The agency of the Son in creating the universe gives it a personal basis. The Son creates and sustains by the Holy Spirit. His person offers meaning to all existence. All of life has a personal origin and theological implications inseparable from the Son.

For him all things were created (Col 1:16). The wonder of the creation is that it has a telic (from *telos,* "goal") or purposeful end. Everything has its purpose in God, a purpose defined by the Son. The picture given in Scripture is truly Trinitarian. At the end of human history when the Son has completed all of his redemptive work and judgment, he will have done so only for the glory of the Father (Phil 2:11). This world and all the created order will find its ultimate purpose in the triune life of the creator.

---

95. Note the way Paul uses the title Son of God: 1 Cor 1:9, 2 Cor 1:19; see also Heb 1:3.

96. Gen 1:1–4, John 1:1, Heb 3:3–4.

"Sustainer"

In order to sustain the creation, Christ is the agent of providence as well as Creator.[97] By his preexistent Word, God creates and sustains. The *Logos* is with God in the beginning and powerfully creates as God intends.[98] All things were created *through* him (John 1:3, Col 1:16). Creation's purpose is to demonstrate God's holy nature and saving activity. It is fitting that Christ sustains all things (Heb 1:3; Col 1:17). All things are held together coherently by the one person of the Trinity who took on human flesh. The person of the Son is the unifying factor in all reality. Though never separated from Father or Spirit, he is the principal cohesive factor in the universe. His sustaining power is resident in his eternal nature and manifest in the order and majesty of the universe (Ps 19:1–4; Rom 1:20).

These strong statements emphasize the importance of the incarnation. Jesus is the Word by whose word the universe is held together. Without his personal presence all existence would fall apart. He is both the source and the sustaining providential end of all created reality. Creation is in him as the source of all being, but he is not in creation as a part of the whole. The sustaining of the universe by the personal reality of the Son of God enables true personal freedom in humans. He does not coerce but guides; he does not drive but leads. His sovereignty flows from the loving holiness of the Godhead. His eternal sustenance has a purpose, and for those made in the image of God, it includes the distance, separation, and otherness necessary for true personhood. "Perhaps," as C. S. Lewis muses, "there is an anguish, an alienation, a crucifixion involved in the creative act. Yet he who alone can judge judges the far-off consummation to be worth it."[99]

---

97. See John 1:3; Heb 1:2.
98. Gen 1:1–2, John 1:1.
99. Lewis, *Letters to Malcolm*, 41.

"Sent One"

Christ made "all that is" prior to the incarnation. Thus, he is equal to God. However, the truly unnerving element of the gospel for many is that the Creator was also the one sent to redeem his sinful people. The radical humiliation involved can produce either worship or consternation. The Gospel of John, as we have said, explores the "sentness" of the Son more than any other New Testament book, but the theme is present elsewhere. Only one who existed before creation could be sent to offer true redemption. No other form of mediation was sufficient to regenerate human persons. Had he not been divine, Christ would have been a part of the created order and incapable of providing any true deliverance. The Father sent the Son "in the likeness of sinful flesh."[100] Christ was sent into creation to redeem it.[101]

The "sentness" of the Son reflects the inner mutuality, the other-orientation that demarcates the life of God. Self-giving is to "go," as it were, to another. So it ought not to surprise us if, in order to redeem, the triune God sends Jesus in the form (*morphe*) of a slave and in the likeness (*homoioma)* of humanity (Phil 2:7). The sending of the Son cannot be reduced to mere obedience. The coming of the Son reveals the heart and life of the Father and the Spirit conjoined with the Son in offering what sinful humanity needs most. The "sentness" of the Son reveals the Sender.[102] This descent into his creation is a loving and willing embrace of what he had made.

"Revealer"

In both testaments God reveals himself to us. In an ever-clearer way through progressive revelation, God expresses his nature and his will (Ps 19, Heb 1:1). Through the eternal Word of God, he discloses himself; all previous revelation pales in the light of the cli-

---

100. Rom 8:3.
101. See Gal 4:4–5. See also Phil 2:6–11; 2 Cor 8:9; Rom 8:32.
102. Hilary, *On the Trinity*, NPNF2 9:66.

mactic revelation of God in the person of Jesus Christ.[103] While the church refused the notion that Jesus was the revelation of a divine "man" from eternity because of the incipient gnosticism in such a perspective, it clearly affirmed that Jesus reveals the nature of God.[104] Hilary comments, "The human aspect He wore could be no aid towards the mental vision of the incorporeal God. But God was recognized in Christ."[105] Jesus stated often that the reason he came was to reveal the Father (John 12:44, 13:31–32, 14:8–11, 17:26). The self-revelation of the Son enabled the human mind and heart to grasp the nature of the Holy One. Ridderbos says it well: "God sent His Son, and this sending does not create Sonship, but presupposes it."[106] Revelation is thus initially and primarily from above; it is not tied to our conception of God. All revelation has a filial center, the Son in the Spirit making the Father known. Consequently, we are reminded of two important points. First, the Revealer and what is revealed are the same. God, the Revealer and the Revealed, meets every need of the human spirit. Second, revelation is always fundamentally personal.

"Redeemer/Reconciler"

Salvation must come from outside of our human situation. Most religions have some idea of deliverance from beyond our human sphere. Someone other than the offender must pay the price or restore the relationship that has been broken. The problem comes in offering a rational assessment of a truly transcendent redeemer who at the same time knows the inner workings of the human heart. Early Christian thought, distinct from all other views of salvation, produced the hermeneutical spiral (the reconciler is both human

---

103. See Gen 21:17; Exod 3:2; Judg 2:1–4; Zech 1:12–13; John 1; and 1 John (*Logos* statements).

104. Käsemann's and Cullmann's esoteric discourse based on gnostic hellenism on the Heavenly Man in the latter's *Christology in the New Testament*, 166–77. See the response to that perspective in Ridderbos, *Paul, An Outline of His Theology*, 76.

105. Hilary, *On the Trinity*, NPNF2 9:134.

106. Ridderbos, *Paul, An Outline of His Theology*, 69.

and divine).[107] If humanity is lost and dead in sin, then only a divine person can offer redemption. The one who comes to reconcile us to God has to be one with God in nature and also the full revelation of God's nature to us. The creature, no matter how good, can never unite its sinful nature with God. Deity alone can unite humanity with deity. Thus, the one who redeems from sin and the one who becomes one with humanity and reconciles us to God must be God himself. Another step remained in order for divinity to be in proper relation to humanity. For there to be total identification with the human predicament, that reconciler had to be not only fully divine but also fully human.[108] The two natures informed one another and had to be perfectly conjoined in one person for all the facets of redemption to cohere. From soteriological reasoning the doctrines of the Trinity, Christology, and Pneumatology were worked out. Only Jesus Christ of Nazareth fit all the requisite categories for true reconciliation. A divine person assumed a human nature in order to offer a free and full salvation to created persons.

"Image of God"

We have already explored the importance of understanding Christ's being as basic to his activity. His preexistent being must be fully in view to have a complete concept of his person and work. Another concept, one that provides a solid ontic base, is the Pauline description of Jesus as the "Image of God."[109] The image of God is a title of the pre-existent Christ; he reflects the perfect living likeness of God because he shares in the nature of the Original eternally. Jesus is the image of God revealed. This perfect divine image par-

---

107. See *apolutrosis* (redemption) in Mark 10:45, Rom 3:24, Rom 8:23, 1 Cor 1:30, Eph 1:7, and Col 1:14, *katallage* (reconciliation) in Rom 5:8–10, and *apokatallage* (reconciliation) in Eph 2:16 and Col 1:20–21.

108. Athanasius, *On the Incarnation*, NPNF2 4:36–66; Anselm, *Cur Deus Homo?*, 119–20.

109. Heb 1:3 is a *hapax legomena* using *character*, which is translated "image." *Eikon* is used twenty-three times in the New Testament: five of those refer to the stamp of a coin, eleven refer to an actual idolatrous image, five refer to humanity in the image, and two, 2 Cor 4:4 and Col 1:15, refer to Jesus as the *Imago Dei*.

ticipates in the eternal Godhead as the Son who perfectly images the Father. Though mysterious, it is evident that the Son as image draws his life from the Father. His incarnation offers a full revelation of the nature of God. He is the perfect image of the Father in both divine and human terms.

There is a certain duality in the use of the term "image" here. Jesus is the *only Image of God*. Humans are made *in the image* of God. They image the relationality of the triune God in their personhood, but it is the Son who specifies, articulates, and defines that image in them. As Irenaeus says:

> We should therefore not seek after another Father besides him, nor [look for] another substance from which we have been formed, besides what was mentioned beforehand, and shown forth by the Lord; nor another hand of God besides that which, from the beginning even to the end, forms us and prepares us for life, and is present with His handiwork, and perfects it after the image and likeness of God. And then, again, this Word was manifested when the Word of God was made man, assimilating himself to man, and man to himself, so that by means of his resemblance to the Son, man might become precious to the Father. For in times long past, it was said that man was created after the image of God, but it was not [actually] shown; for the Word was as yet invisible, after whose image man was created, Wherefore also he did easily lose the similitude. When, however, the Word of God became flesh, He confirmed both these: for He both showed forth the image truly, since he became himself what was his image; and he re-established the similitude after a sure manner, by assimilating man to the invisible Father through means of the visible Word.[110]

To have a full Christology, one must understand the Son's power and glory in his pre-existent state. A real, as opposed to ideal, pre-existence affirms an eternal loving relationship between the three persons of the Godhead. Dunn explains ideal pre-existence as the

---

110. *ANF* 1:544, 550.

belief that God had Christ in mind from eternity, but there was no actual person or being who pre-existed.[111] The orthodox doctrine of real pre-existence is not merely the result of a few statements from John's Gospel but is also found in Paul, whose writings began just two decades after the resurrection. The church in the creedal era was earnest about affirming the full humanity of Jesus so that the doctrine of Christ's pre-existence did not overemphasize his divinity in an unhealthy way. If these elements are held in dynamic tension, coherently and intelligibly, the saving power of the Son of God comes to the fore. The ecumenical councils of the church made Christ's pre-existence clear. The Nicene Creed states that the Son is "begotten of the Father as only begotten, that is, from the essence [ek tes ousias tou patros] of the Father, God from God, Light from Light, true God from true God, begotten not created, of the same nature [homoousion to patri] with the Father." The ontological perception gained a universal agreement, in the early consensual statements, that the Word was eternally generated from the Father, without beginning. Christ is "God before all ages."[112] As the Second Council of Nicaea stated in AD 787, "Not an ambassador, not an angel, but the Lord himself hath saved us."[113] Each of these statements implies that the Creator entered into his own creation and actively participated in the history of salvation. Pre-existence, then, is crucial for soteriology. Any other proposed form of redemption that included a non-pre-existing person would have been forced

---

111. Dunn, *Christology in the Making*, 55–56.

112. Niceno-Constantinopolitan (AD 381): "The only-begotten Son of God, begotten from the Father before all time." Chalcedonian (AD 451): "He is of the same essence as God [homoousion to patri] as far as his deity is concerned . . . Before time began he was begotten of the Father, in respect to his deity." The Anathemas of the Second Council of Constantinople (AD 553): "If anyone does not confess that God the Word was twice begotten, the first before all time from the Father, non-temporal and bodiless, the other in the last days when he came down from the heavens. . . ." It is interesting to note that most of the subsequent creeds after AD 787 do not spend much time on intra-Trinitarian discourse. Much of that is incorporated in their use of the earlier creedal statements, but it also can mean that serious reflection for the most part on this issue ceased to take center stage.

113. *NPNF2* 14:541.

into adoptionism. Adoptionism is the heresy that Jesus, a mere man, was endowed with divine spirituality to accomplish certain tasks but was never truly or eternally divine.

All of the preceding biblical ideas have formed the classical belief in the full, real, and personal pre-existence of the only-begotten Son who eternally lives in the love of the Trinity. That loving pre-existence is the foundation of all creation, covenant, incarnation, redemption, and consummation ("bringing many sons and daughters to glory," Heb 2:10). In contradistinction to any notion of the divine life as static, impersonal, or volitional, these concepts offer insight into the marvel of the divine life.

When the words used about Jesus or by him pertain to his divine existence prior to Bethlehem, they are not impositions on the text by misguided disciples. They are gifts for the probing heart to discern that everything created can and eventually will be restored, and that every fallen human who believes in Jesus Christ will be made new.

Pre-existence, as a doctrine, has fallen on hard times.[114] Once pre-existence has been secured and, as Hilary says, "with the Holy Ghost speeding our way, we are approaching the safe, calm harbour of a firm faith," the next emphasis must concern how the eternal Son becomes the son of Mary and the implications of that descent into the world, which he created and sustains.[115]

VOLUNTARY RESTRAINT OF INDEPENDENT EXERCISE OF DIVINE POWER

The position in this volume is founded on the conviction that the divinity of the Son of Man is unquestionable.[116] Christology must not lose the element of divinity or humanity. The *Logos* voli-

---

114. Note the cleverly disguised adoptionism of Schleiermacher, *The Christian Faith*, 2:398–402. This point is denied by the authors of *The Myth of God Incarnate*, John Hick, ed. A necessary but questionable response to that work is found in Dunn, *Christology in the Making*. He is more than reserved on pre-existence outside of Johannine materials, including John 1:1–18, in *Christology in the Making*, 39–43, 82–95, 244–45.

115. Hilary, *On the Trinity*, NPNF2 9:218.

116. Augustine, *On the Trinity*, NPNF1 3:37–38; 98–99.

tionally emptied (*kenosis*) himself of the independent use of certain divine attributes when he took on human flesh. He did all that he did in the power of the Spirit and under the authority of the Father. He never stepped outside the bounds of that eternal love and that divine purpose. He submitted himself, limited himself, humbled himself so that no one could claim that God has ever coerced or manipulated anyone in the particular terms of salvation. Jesus did show throughout his ministry his divine power, but total revelation is always held in reserve.

DIVINE GLORY/MAJESTY

In the early church many felt that Christ gave up eternal glory in order to humble himself to become both an incarnate person and a servant.[117] His heavenly glory and majesty were hidden. Speaking of the relationship of the incarnation and human needs, in the context of the barren fig tree in Mark 11 and the mentioned hunger of Jesus, Hilary of Poitiers said:

> This was the mystery of his hunger, grief, and thirst, that the Word was assuming flesh. His humanity was entirely exposed to our weaknesses, yet even his glory was not wholly put away as he suffered. . . . When he ate and drank, it was not a concession to some necessity external to himself, but to show his full participation in the human condition.[118]

Other examples of reserved glory include some intriguing passages. First, when he went up to Jerusalem, his disciples "were astonished, while those who followed were afraid" (Mark 10:32); the context cryptically implies they comprehended something of his glory, and a glimpse of it overwhelmed them. Second, at his arrest, the cohort sent on that mission "drew back" (John 18:6) when he responded to their query, "I am he." They were awe-struck and

---

117. Origen, *De Principiis*, ANF 4:249, Peter of Alexandria, *On the Godhead*, ANF 6:280, Athanasius, *Four Discourses Against the Arians*, NPNF2 4:329, Hilary of Poitiers, *On the Trinity*, 311, 328, 404, 472–75.
118. Hilary, cited in Oden and Hall, *Mark: ACCS* 2:157–58.

afraid of this unarmed individual due to nothing other than his glory and majesty. Thus, it would seem that the glory that Jesus shared eternally with the Father (John 17:5) and expressed most clearly at the Transfiguration (Matt 17:1–8 and parallel accounts) was at certain points of his ministry disclosed as he chose. When the person of Jesus is present, true glory is defined by the absolute interdependence of the mutually honoring persons of the Trinity. In a real sense, glory must be redefined by the incarnation. The glory of the cross is the exact representation of the glory of the triune Godhead. No more authoritative divine revelation has ever occurred. No other glory saves.

OMNIPOTENCE

A line of thought in theology is drawn from the philosophical concept of immutability. A perfect, transcendent being cannot share in the same feelings as created beings. Hence, the concept of *apatheia* or a non-feeling deity. As the divine Son of God, Christ could not have really suffered.[119] Though it is impossible to discern exactly what the divine nature senses or feels, one can distinguish between created and uncreated natures. An omnipotent divine being would not suffer physically. Accordingly, Jesus voluntarily laid down the use of that power, a power that was most evidently his to use (John 1:10; Matt 8:26). In a similar manner, Jesus had authority to lay his power down and thus the authority to take it up again (John 10:18). Jesus gave us a glimpse of triune power and its relational base when he said, as he was taken captive, "Do you think that I cannot appeal to my Father, and he will at once send me more than twelve legions of angels?" (Matt 26:53). At the cross, our understanding of omnipotent power is redefined. Jesus' cry from the cross indicates the depth of his submission to suffering and death on our behalf: "My God, my God, why have you forsaken me?"(Matt 27:46). Here we see the paradox of *omnipotent weak-*

---

119. Athanasius, *Letter 59 to Epictetus*, NPNF2 4:572, *On the Opinion of Dionysius*, NPNF2 4:179.

ness. He voluntarily restrained the exercise of power that was available to him. He could have directed legions of angels, come down from the cross (Mark 15:31–32), and annihilated his enemies. That power was available to him at any moment, but in order to forgive and redeem sinful humanity he offered the only power that saves— the power of self-giving love.

OMNISCIENCE

The question of what Jesus knew and did not know is of great interest and greater importance. In some passages he has complete knowledge, and in others he does not. Often, he knows the minds of people (Mark 2:8, Luke 6:8) and future events (Mark 10:33), but at other times he expresses surprise at learning something or professes ignorance of facts (Mark 6:6). No one can state definitively what Jesus chose to know. Most times Scripture indicates that he knows the hearts of people as he confronts them with the truth. Many scholars take Mark 13:32 as the primary text indicating that he had laid down his omniscience: "No one knows except the Father." One possible assessment is that the divine *Logos*, who in self-emptying unto death and laying aside his omnipotence also laid down his omniscience. What is captivatingly absent from the interpretations of this passage is any reference to the previous verse indicating Christ's understanding of the eternality of every word he spoke (Mark 13:31). He is always the *Logos*. He knows as much of reality as he chooses to know. He is the Word of God for eternity. He knows all eventualities and all causes and effects, yet as incarnate *Logos*, uniting himself with humanity, he voluntarily subjects himself to human limitations—ignorance, temptation, suffering, and death. As eternal *Logos*, he is equal to God the Father, but in his humiliation, he becomes subject to time and finitude. He had access to the full range of eternal foreknowledge, but it was not a continual reality that he drew upon. Jesus knew some things, and he chose to not know others, but there was no necessity laid upon him other than that which he chose to experience.

Thomas Oden quotes Gregory the Great, that the incarnate Son knew the date and hour of judgment *in* his human nature, but he did not know it *from* his human nature.[120] The distinction is that when Jesus says the Son does not know, he's talking primarily out of his human nature. He is not saying the eternal Son does not know. He's saying that in the incarnate state of his self-abdication, his self-effacement, he chooses not to know this. One must be cautious of an over-emphasis on a dichotomy of natures. Though each nature is intact and unchangeable, their unity is also inseparable. To say that the human Jesus knew something and the divine Christ did not is problematical. All knowledge was his to access at any point, but the self-donating nature of the incarnation involved taking on a fully human mind.

OMNIPRESENCE

Jesus was not everywhere at all times as the incarnate *Logos*. He encountered humanity in history at a specific, verifiable time and place. However, the *Logos* did not cease to be during the incarnation. This is one of the paradoxes we have mentioned before. The *Logos* is not some impersonal principle who chooses to descend and fill a particular human body on earth while maintaining another existence in an ultra-transcendent state. The *Logos* "indwelt" the body of Jesus; he fully joined himself with this human body. So, we have the *Logos* incarnate in a particular man, Jesus.

An obvious question, then, is this: When Jesus became incarnate, what happened to the second person of the Trinity? The Scriptures never say that the *Logos* ceases to be; the *Logos* is eternal. It is the incarnate Christ who suffered, God the Son. The *Logos* is not in some essential way diminished in the incarnation. We must be cautious about saying that one-third of the Trinity left that eternal

---

120. Oden, *The Word of Life*, 90.

unity or in some way became imperceptibly disconnected from the Trinity. Nor can we diminish the *Logos* and claim to know what the *Logos* perceives in either eternity or incarnate state. What we cannot do is divide the divine and human natures in Jesus at a fundamental level.

Nonetheless two major points must be made. First, the eternal *Logos* became incarnate, and second, the eternal *Logos* suffered and died as incarnate man. No dualism occurs on the cross. Creation continues to be because of the triune relationship in which the *Logos* eternally participates. As the Son, he freely laid aside some eternal perception in order to be fully human. What we do not have is an impersonal divine essence called the "*Logos* principle" keeping things together while the Son is gone (incarnation). However, we need to be very careful when we talk about God becoming man not to infer that God left heaven, that he left his Father and the Spirit and lived independently by himself. The Son is an eternal person, which means he is never an individual. He is always in eternal and mutual relationship. He has never used his power in a non-Trinitarian, non-relational manner. The simplest answer to the question of the universe and the *Logos* is that one needs to think Trinitarianly and not individualistically. All three persons are involved in creation and its sustenance. In the same way, all three are committed to providing a real redeemer and not a gnostic or Adoptionistic one. Jesus is not the only divine person to be involved in kenosis. Only he took on flesh, but triune self-bestowal is an eternal reality, the foundation of the incarnation and the atonement.

Since the nineteenth century, this issue has become a problem that the orthodox church has had to respond to. If care is not taken with these most recent perspectives, one soon begins to lose the capacity to affirm the divinity of Christ. The liberal tradition has no problem looking at Jesus' humanness, but they have difficulty talking about his divinity. As evidence of what it means to have "emptied" himself, Jesus voluntarily chose not to grasp for himself divine powers. He laid them aside. "Grasping" is a metaphor for the essence of sin. He came to redeem grasping mankind by refusing to grasp for himself.

In the incarnation the Son of God took upon himself the weakness of humanity, but he did not relinquish the power of God in an essential sense. He chose not to use those powers in any form of coercion or manipulation. He laid aside his glory so that the true glory of his person could be recognized.

The Shorter Catechism of the Westminster Confession summarizes the orthodox position as follows: "Who being the eternal Son of God became man and so was and continues to be God and man and two distinct natures as one person forever."[121] The church has consistently refused to say that in his resurrection, Jesus left his physical body behind and ascended in a solely spiritual state. Some have misinterpreted the church's doctrine to say that the spirit/human unity was split at the resurrection.[122] The orthodox church has always kept the unity through the centuries without denying that Jesus is in a glorified state after the resurrection. The unity of Jesus, spirit and body, had to be permanent if he was to redeem and continue to redeem sinful humanity.

---

121. *The Shorter Catechism*, 7.021, Q.24.
122. Pinnock and Brown, *Theological Crossfire*, 162–72.

CHAPTER FOUR

Discerning the Incarnation: One Person, Two Natures

The worship of the church affirmed that Jesus is the God-Man long before it was worked through by theological minds and councils. Besides the Trinity the incarnation is the distinctive doctrine that most radically distinguishes the Christian faith from other religions. The two natures, divine and human, have been the crux of debate for many centuries. A mystery cannot be solved by reason alone, but it can be explored worshipfully and intelligently. Amid the myriad theories regarding how the natures relate in the revealed Christ, the issue is which theories are closer to the revealed word of God. The church has always had to confront and respond to oversimplifications of the person of Christ. Arguments for a "return to the kernel of the real Jesus" undistorted by so-called "Hellenizing" effects of the church councils fall short. The essence of the true gospel pivots on the nature of the Savior, so it was worth half a millennium of critical biblical analysis for the church to arrive at a statement that kept mythology and philosophizing out of Christology.

THE MYSTERY OF THE PERSON OF CHRIST

At the heart of all high religion is mystery.[1] Rudolph Otto's term, *numinous,* referring to that which is beyond the confines of human understanding, is quite adequate here; the *numinous* does have a place in Christian thought. To claim that one comprehends the incarnation is virtually ludicrous. Yet systematic thought encourages a reasonable assessment of data in light of revelation and experience within the limits of an orthodoxy sensitive to deepening conception over time. A profitable Christology must skirt the Scylla of apophaticism and the Charybdis of dead creedalism. Jesus Christ is a revealed mystery. His life is based upon historical fact. The best doctrine of Christ is based upon doxology and confession. To those given charge of protecting Christian thought from corruption, the only worship of God possible was through Jesus the Son of God.[2] Outler says, "The Mystery cannot be analyzed but its correlates can be analyzed in part, and this is the business of Christology."[3]

From the witness of those who had been transformed by meeting the risen Christ, creeds arose that later came to stand alone as holistic statements about what it meant to believe that Jesus was God.[4] Christology became the chief concern of the church. No geographically constrained issue, the same sorts of issues were stated in both the Latin and Greek segments of the church.[5] There is evidence of a universal commitment from various groups that continually challenged all suspect thinking about Jesus.[6] Something beyond a basic

---

1. Otto, *The Idea of the Holy.*
2. Lactantius, *Divine Institutes, ANF* 7:133.
3. Outler, *Christology,* 60.
4. See for example the liturgies of St James or St Mark for recurrences of the highest Christology without the nuances of later creeds (*ANF* 7:553–54, 562).
5. One of many examples that could be given would be the first Latin systematic treatise by the apologist Lactantius (AD 240–320), *Divine Institutes.* On his Christology, see *ANF* 7:106–26.
6. The best expression of this interpretive canon is found in Vincent of Lérins, *Commonitory, NPNF*2 11:132. He died before Chalcedon (AD 451), but note the clarity of his Christology (140).

commitment to revelation was required to clarify the centrality of Christ. This universal and mutual quest to understand the mystery of Christ fostered further exploration.[7] The continued concern of the church was to maintain the worship of Christ in an intellectually credible manner without losing any of the reality of his presence. Written documents, though absolutely necessary, can quickly become forms of intellectualized dogma that threaten to separate the person of Christ from the correct Christology.

We have looked at the kerygmatic elements that formed the basis of the worship life of the early church. The names and titles for Christ, both revealed and reflected upon, give us a view of the place he held in the church as her lord but also the diachronic theological elements that put Jesus in the center of Israel's hopes and thus the world's deepest needs. The next area of theological assessment must be addressed: the Christological creedal statements. Systematic Christology depends heavily on the consensual interaction of previous theological minds. No one dare start out alone when it comes to discerning the person of Jesus. To do so is to welcome heresy.

Dom Gregory Dix informs us that creeds entered soon after the rite of baptism became a necessity. They were also used apologetically to combat the cavalcade of gnostic challenges to creation, history, incarnation, crucifixion, and resurrection. Dom Gregory writes that more was needed than to simply affirm that Jesus was the Messiah. In Gentile groups one had to "furnish security that the convert was not simply accepting 'the *Kyrios* Jesus' as one more 'Saviour' among his 'gods many and lords many.'"[8] Biblical truth invites the deepest ruminations of the human heart. When one considers that the largest number of authors of the creeds were pastors and shepherds of common people, it is difficult to dismiss tradition

---

7. For a criticism of the Vincentian Canon, see O'Collins, "Criteria for Interpreting the Traditions," 327–39. He alleges even Newman found the Canon yielding hardly any "satisfactory result" (332).

8. Dix, *The Shape of the Liturgy*, 485.

HOLY LOVE: A WESLEYAN THEOLOGY

as "over-intellectualization" or as "hellenization."[9] Much has been written about politics and power-plays behind the scenes of creedal formation, but humble, worshipful, and prayerful servants suffused with Scripture used their giftedness to develop the creeds.

THE THEANDRIC UNION

A systematic theology that begins with Jesus first must acquaint the church with the major scriptural evidence of the divinity and humanity of Jesus Christ. Second, it must provide the historical interpretations of this scriptural evidence. In this spirit, we intend to introduce the major issues of a systematic Christology and place it within its historical framework. Like gnosticism, theology can be removed from history, from the church's engagement with the actual presence of the risen Christ in successive cultures. Most Christians will realize that anyone who does not know history is at the mercy of the most recent theological or philosophical fad. We need a generation of Christian disciples who fully believe Scripture, are aware of the development of doctrine, and are committed to right thinking about divine realities.

No single volume of systematics can adequately compile the abundance of material from every sector of Scripture regarding the person of Christ. Nor can it reproduce the amazing yet arduous historical struggle that accompanied the church's grand attempt to describe the majesty of the incarnation. This chapter summarizes many significant issues that arose in the formation of the creeds. These creedal statements are distillations of multiplied centuries of worship, prayer, liturgy, ministry, and exegesis.

As this fascinating history of transformative ideas unfolds, the tendency will be to move too quickly to practical application. The history of the church's thought about Christ has shown repeatedly

---

9. Theology then is to "explore the problems we are reminded of by our awareness of his presence" (Outler, *Christology*, 56).

that overly simplistic formulations of the Savior's being (the two natures) have always depleted the gospel of its power. Heretics have been for the most part kind, good, well-meaning individuals, but as their thoughts were explored, serious weaknesses were revealed that undermined the true faith. Error beneath the surface of theology is always hard to detect and more difficult to remove. Orthodoxy is viewed as an arbitrary authority by the autonomous spirit. But if one wants to live a truly full and free life, every vestige of perverted thinking must be revealed for what it is and eliminated.

THREE MAJOR TRADITIONS

Three major traditions highlight the significant, theological differences regarding the incarnation. These three perspectives assist in organizing the lists of names and councils that accompany the saga of orthodox Christology. First, the Alexandrian Christians (Alexandria was the premier Hellenized city in Egypt) were conversant with Neo-Platonic thought. Because of their emphasis on philosophy, the *Logos* concept became predominant in their theology. This philosophical bent was evangelistic in connecting Christianity with the highest pagan thought available, but it needed constantly to be corrected. Recent biblical scholarship has all too quickly assumed that what resulted from a collaboration of Hellenic categories and biblical monotheism was an aberration of the gospel. In fact, the argument can be made that as the gospel was preached in the Alexandrian context, the Greek mind understood the gospel as incarnational. Accordingly, terms from the Jewish and Greek intellectual heritage became the language of the Creeds.

A second approach to Christ was found in Antioch of Syria (the largest Mediterranean city after Alexandria and Rome). This *Antiochene* tradition emphasized Hebraic sources and, therefore, focused on the "Word." Whereas Alexandria moved immediately to philosophical constructs, this school turned to the use of *dābār* in the Old Testament and its counterpart *logos* in the New Testament. Here one finds a mix of philosophy and theology but with a heavy historical component. But more important is the deeply entrenched Hebraism. There is a love in Antiochene thought for the actual life of Jesus and for gospel history. No school of thought was unbiased, so the openness to philosophy in some Antiochenes diminished the value of this train of thought (Paul of Samosata).

The third approach, the Western, is normally connected to the Latin theologians of Rome and Carthage. Tertullian's famous and helpful delineation between nature and person (*natura* and *persona*) became one of the key insights of all Christian thinking.

TERTULLIAN'S DISTINCTION

The Western tradition focused on Johannine literature. Less prone to the esoteric philosophical theology of Alexandria, it emphasized practice. The Western view did not stress gospel history as did the Antiochene approach. At times the Western emphases produced a helpful balance to Alexandrian philosophical proclivities. Here the Father/Son relationship became a primary category due to the focus on Johannine intra-Trinitarian language. Ambrose, Augustine, and Hilary were major figures in discussion of Jesus from this perspective. However, their advance did not produce the relational accent of the East due to the more functional background of Latin theology and even the Latin language itself. Not until just before Chalcedon, through Pope Leo, did the West really offer anything formative to the Christological debate. After that Council, Western thinkers began to gain prominence but not specifically in Christology.

In all of the discussion to follow one major issue must be kept in mind: the relation of the divine and human in the person of Jesus Christ. Trinitarian implications appeared throughout, but the majority of the debates hung on the relation of natures in Christ.

Early Christology faced many philosophical difficulties. What was an absurdity to the Greek mind (a god taking on flesh) was an anathema to the radical, transcendent monotheism of Jewish thought. The Jewish mind had always exhibited a vibrant concept of God's nature, but the Jews had not yet engaged with the full meaning of an immanent, historical incarnation in one person.

The streams of thought that surrounded, and sometimes influenced, late-first-century and early-second-century Christianity included Jewish monotheism, Platonic idealism, Aristotelian particularism, Stoic skepticism, Epicurean subjectivism, superstitious mystery religions, and other folk religions. Though it is a common misperception that early Christology was a simple set of truths universally agreed upon, that notion is far from the truth. From the earliest stages there was an urgent need to distinguish Jesus Christ from prevailing philosophical moods. The Late Roman Empire offered no accepted philosophical or religious consensus but a virtual disavowal of authority. Christian thought was hammered out in a complicated pluralistic religious and philosophical world where spiritual experimentation was rampant.[10] The irony of heresy is that heresy forced the church to evaluate what was preached and taught. Because heresy demanded a response, it was actually an important incentive to orthodoxy. Vigilance for the truth about Christ is as old as the New Testament itself (Col 2:1–15).

One basic continuing threat was the cosmology of radical dualism, the fundamental belief that true, transcendent being and temporal existence are separated by a huge chasm. The heretic Marcion, for example, solved this problem by positing a "demiurge" as the only option for an interrelationship of any sort between heaven and earth. The demiurge was a concept advanced by Plato in the fourth century BC. He posited an intermediary between the ideal and sen-

---

10. Acts 14:8–18, 17:16–32. Note Charles Cochrane's graphic description of the end of *Romanitas* in *Christianity and Classical Culture*, 354–55. Robert Wilken's inviting style incorporates a readable assessment of this interaction in *The Spirit of Early Christian Thought*, 62–63, 294–95.

sible worlds. But Marcion made the God of the Old Testament the demiurge.[11] This creator God, focused upon legality, was fickle and despotic, not the supreme God of love. Jesus Christ's appearance had to be disconnected absolutely from the capricious and cruel demiurge. Jesus simply appeared out of nowhere in Capernaum. The immediate counterpart to dualisms of this nature is Docetism. Docetism held to its most basic commitment of escape from the physical by constantly rejecting divine enfleshment.

The student of Christology must always be aware of the persistent, fundamental difficulties of crossing the boundary (whether in reality or in the mind) between the divine and the natural, the one and the many. When a small group of thinkers who worshiped Jesus as God began to talk of conjoining both natures in one person, the debate began to rage. No one had so shaken the conceptual substructure of the universe as these Christians. If being and act could be conjoined in one person, if the universal could be contracted to a particular, then all prior thinking about reality would be proven inadequate. This epistemological move was met with contempt; it was a scandal for some, an absurdity for others.[12] The task of orthodoxy is to chart a course between theoretical extremes, between paradoxical notions, between false disjunctions.

---

11. Read Irenaeus' diatribe against Marcionism in *Against Heresies*, esp. ch 30 on the demiurge (*ANF* 1:403–6). Robert Jenson underscores the importance of ejecting Marcionism from theologizing by stating that we must "begin with confession of the God of Israel, in view of the predominantly gentile church's perennial temptation to evade it. The temptation was early overcome dogmatically, with the rejection of Marcion, but it remains the church's most regular occasion of apostasy" (Jenson, *Systematic Theology*, 1:42).

12. Albert Outler uses "*skandalon*" for the offense of Christ to the Jews and "*morian*" for the impact Christology had on the Greeks from 1 Cor 1:23 (*Christology*, 50–54).

THE EBIONITE APPROACH[13]

What was the earliest Jewish Christian approach to the paradox of God become man?[14] The Ebionites, strongly steeped in Jewish thought, were especially committed to strict numeric oneness in their definition of monotheism. While trying to maintain an allegiance to Jesus, this group denied the deity of Christ altogether. The virgin birth was discounted; Jesus was taken to be the natural son of Joseph and Mary. Though they believed he was predestined to be the Messiah, they could not accept the genuineness of his deity. He was merely human, but quite noble. Historical accounts of his teaching and acts were assumed to be true. For the Ebionites, Jesus took on a heroic status, much like the ancient prophets. The paradox of two natures was untenable for this early group. The church quickly dispensed with this option because it involved the adulation of a mere human person. Most of the heresies that followed were modifications of the same basic flaw of the Ebionites. Any diminishment of Jesus' divinity starts here.[15] Much of the search for the historical Jesus ends up with similar ideas, as did Protestant liberalism and most recently the Jesus Seminar.[16]

---

13. Another term for this trend of thought is *psilanthropism*, that is, man alone. Jesus is seen as any other prophet who is Spirit-endued but nothing more.

14. Some have connected the *evionim* (Hebrew for "poor men") or the Ebionites with the Nazarenes, another early sect who denied Christ's divinity. Justin Martyr may refer to them in *Dialogue with Trypho*, ANF 1:218; Irenaeus in *Against Heresies*, ANF 1:351–52; Tertullian in *Against All Heresies*, ANF 3:651.

15. A quick overview of the minimalist schools regarding Jesus' human nature would include gnosticism, Marcionism, Modalism, Monarchianism, Arianism, Apollinarianism, and Eutychianism.

16. Schweitzer, *The Quest for the Historical Jesus*, 396–401; Jenkins, *Hidden Gospels*; Wright, *Jesus and the Victory of God*, 3–124.

DOCETISM

Certainly, Jesus was more than a spiritual man, the conclusion taken to an extreme by the Docetists. Thus, the ancient problem of spirit/flesh dualism inherent in gnosticism once again threatened the orthodox view of Jesus. Where the Ebionites eliminated divinity, the Docetists excised his humanity. He was either merely a man who pretended to be God, or as the Docetists preferred, a phantom figure (God *appearing* in the form of man).

Some have concluded that Docetism is the most seductive of all heresies because it can come across as "normal" in Christian circles, an acceptable heresy.[17] Docetism is deceptively prevalent and hard to discern because it is an aggregate of confusing reservations about Jesus rather than a full-fledged assault on his person. If the nature of God is first viewed as ineffable, immutable, or impassible, then divine nature cannot have a real union with humanity. As a result, Jesus and Christ are separated in a variety of ingenious, deeply flawed, non-salvific theories.

One can see immediately that Docetism is similar to gnosticism. Gnosticism asserts that spirit needs liberation from the corruption of matter. By divine emanations in a process of mediation, persons can be released by a touch of spirit. Some persons can rise to the truly spiritual level that Jesus came to represent.[18]

The most fundamental conundrum, then, is faithfully defining the divinity of Jesus of Nazareth. Thus, the earliest responses to these one-sided solutions came from the bishops and shepherds of worshiping communities. They needed to know in truth the nature of the object of their worship. Ignatius, Polycarp, and Clement did not see anything fundamentally offensive to Old Testament theology in advocating that the Creator in his transcendent glory

---

17. Outler, *Christology*, 76. With his usual wit, Outler avers that "[t]here is a residue of Docetic dye in many orthodox garments" (77).

18. Outler, *Christology*, 76.

could become flesh and suffer. Their soteriology demanded such a conclusion.

THE APOSTOLIC FATHERS

SPIRIT-CHRISTOLOGY

Some early Christian thinkers understood the birth of Jesus as a divine act through the power of the Spirit. They understood the Son of God to be a divine spirit who indwelt the man Jesus. As noted above, little refined Christology is found in the apostolic fathers, but one can find vestiges of this Spirit-Christology in the language of Hermas and Hippolytus.[19] Once again, the struggle to emphasize the divine majesty of the Word in his enfleshment brought language that needed clarification. The Holy Spirit was the conceiving agent in the incarnation without any pagan suggestion of sexual union between deity and humanity. Later the church hesitated to say that Christ was born of the Spirit because of the inherent possibility of the divine Spirit overwhelming the person of Jesus. In the Epistle of Barnabas, the author presumes that God "becomes" man. For him, the Lord "delivered up his flesh," "it behooved him to appear in flesh," and "he manifested himself to be the Son of God." Jesus Christ actually becoming man with all the implications for a full salvation of mankind is the center of the early documents on the nature of Christ.

---

19. It might even be present in the early Roman symbol. Hermas, *Similitudes*, *ANF* 2:231, 215; *Creed of Hippolytus* (c. 215) "begotten by the Holy Spirit from the Virgin Mary" or Creed of Marcellus (340) "who was begotten of the Holy Spirit and the Virgin Mary." Rufinus compares Marcellus with what was to be known as the "Old Roman Symbol" though virtually the same Rufinus' version has "born of the Holy Spirit and the Virgin Mary," in Latin, "qui natus est de Spiritu Sanctus ex Maria Virgine" (Bettenson, *Documents of the Christian Church*, 23–24).

Ignatius: A Theological Response to Gnostic Ideas

Of these earliest thinkers, Ignatius, the bishop of Antioch who became a martyr, strongly confronts the gnostic diminishment of the Savior's humanity. He writes that Jesus was "truly born, truly ate and drank, was truly persecuted under Pontius Pilate, was truly crucified and died . . . who was also truly raised from the dead."[20] Ignatius tended to focus on Jesus as both human and divine, but he never talked about how the two natures interrelated.[21] Even so, we find the outlines of later Christological orthodoxy in his thoughts.[22] In fact, he says "God" was conceived by Mary, and that "God" experienced passion and suffered upon the Cross.[23] The heresy that Jesus was a man "adopted" by God for a special task is not found in the majority of early theologians. The allure of adoptionism has always been confronted by true Christian orthodoxy. Jesus' actual historical birth, life, death, and resurrection included both flesh and spirit. On the other hand, the focus on the Father sending him to redeem and reconcile without clearer exploration of the person of the Messiah left an opening for subordinationism.[24] Without a clear conception of the personal dynamic of the divine nature in three persons, the tendency is to separate the Father from the Son. On one side, the Father is placed above the Son, and on the other the Son is a Spirit-endowed human.

---

20. Ignatius, *Trallians*, ANF 1:70. The longer version has at points different English synonyms, e.g., "really," "not merely in appearance," and "in reality." The word "truly" or "actually" is *alethos;* Leith, *Creeds of the Churches*, 17.

21. Ignatius, *Trallians*, ANF 1:70, "For indeed God and man are not the same. He truly assumed a body." *Philadelphians*, ANF 1:82–83; *Smyrnaeans*, ANF 1:87.

22. Ignatius, *Ephesians*, ANF 1:52; *Trallians*, ANF 1:68.

23. Ignatius, *Ephesians*, ANF 1:57; *Romans*, ANF 1:76.

24. Subordinationism is the heresy that posits a distinction in the absolute equality of the persons of the Trinity. Normally based upon a philosophical concept of unity or simplicity of nature which then is extrapolated into the error that the Son is somehow less than the Father due to his enfleshment. There is a continual problem with latent dualism in much of the Christological debate.

Apologists

These remarkable defenders of the faith in the second and third centuries moved toward a clearer formulation of language both to protect the church from heresy and to clarify the person of Jesus as true God and true Man worthy of worship.

Logos Christology appeared as the first major shift in the shape of the Christological discussion. Realizing that a Spirit-Christology would not serve the purpose of distinguishing the persons led to more distinctions between the Spirit and the Word both biblically and philosophically. This is mainly due to the preoccupation with the *Logos* in the philosophical structures of the day. As with every ensuing cultural shift, Christian thinkers have had to make the hard decision of remaining with biblical language alone or "plundering the Egyptians" for a more immediate identification with surrounding thought patterns. Here was a term that was both biblical (Hebrew, *dābār*; Greek, *logos*) and philosophical. The Christian striving to connect the reality of Christ with the nature of the universe had a remarkable entrée due to the mediatorial role attributed to the *Logos* by non-believing philosophers. Between the unknowable and the material cosmos stood the orchestrating principle of the *Logos*. The *Logos* language of the New Testament (John 1, 1 John 1, Rev 19:13) served as a satisfactory premise upon which to consider the claims of Christians about their Creator/Redeemer. However, there were latent difficulties. Combining extreme notions of transcendence with a biblical cosmology and soteriology created problems for Christian thinkers. Philosophy alone cannot conceive true personhood. If one places too much of a substance metaphysic upon the gospel, one soon has a God who is transcendent and a *Logos* who is viewed as a mediator. The remote, "first" God is beyond and behind the "rational" *Logos*.

The second concern is that philosophy is most often an abstract discipline. What is difficult to find is a concrete discussion of Christ in his historical context. Comparing or identifying Jesus with the rational principle that holds the universe together may seem at first to merit belief. In this critical moment of the history of Christian thought more was needed to underscore the actual humanity of the Savior, showing how that humanity related to the *Logos*.

The Apologists knew that the key to Christology lay first in distinguishing the Son from the Father. As their predecessors had believed, he was God's saving Son. This second major issue revolved around the paradox of nature, essence, and identity. Jesus' divinity and humanity had profound implications for the Godhead. The Apologists soon found that the language of revelation and that of metaphysics were not co-equal in their capacity to elucidate the mystery of the person of Christ.

Justin Martyr and Logos Christology

Justin's initial defense against the attack that Christians are "atheists" is that the *Logos* sought by philosophers, like Socrates, was actually Jesus Christ, the Word become man. But he also immediately places Jesus Christ in the middle of the Godhead. Justin lays the groundwork of triune worship when he states of God, "But both him (Father of righteousness) and the Son (who came forth from him and . . .) and the prophetic Spirit, we worship and adore."[25] The Son is pre-existent and identified with the Godhead. *Logos* Christology displaces Spirit Christology in the thought of the Apologists.

However, two areas needed further lucidity. First, it was not enough to claim the reality of two natures. The manner of their co-existence in one person had to be further explored. The only place that Justin offers a new addition to this discussion is in his use of the "germinal logos" (*logos spermatikos*).[26] In this arrangement the *Logos* serves as the "rational principle" (or ordering principle) of the flesh. With Justin's use of the *Logos*, this principle indwells or directs the flesh of Jesus, just as the *Logos* manifested himself

---

25. Justin, *First Apology, ANF* 1:164.
26. Justin, *Second Apology, ANF* 1:192–93.

in other ways in history.[27] So, with this framework one is left with a Savior who is a mysterious mix of divine and human but not a truly mutual interrelationship. When uncertain about an action or statement of Jesus, one invariably attributes it to his divine nature. At this point one can make no mistake. Justin believes the Christ and the *Logos* are one. He is not advocating any residual principle outside of Christ. If the *Logos* worked in Moses or Isaiah, it did so only in a fragmentary way; in Jesus the *Logos* works without remainder.[28]

The second area is the relation of the Father and the Son in this paradigm. When Justin pictures the absolute nature of the Father who uses the agency of the Son to create, the formulation suggests subordinationism. The use of "second place" for the Son of the impassible and unbegotten God can feed a misrepresentation of the co-equality.[29] Asserting that Jesus Christ is "begotten by God, being his Word and first-begotten" lent itself to a diminution of Christ against the backdrop of Platonic thought where the *Logos* participates in and acts on behalf of divinity. Even so, the *Logos* is not unequivocally identified with that divinity.

Irenaeus

This brilliant theologian attacked gnosticism in every conceivable form because of the potential damage it might cause for Christian faith. The "episodic" responses to heresy up to this point fell short. A systematic response was needed. Irenaeus, the first great theologian, was a unique mix of Eastern and Western emphases.[30] He fully understood the Greek philosophical theology of the various gnostic sects and responded with a Hebraic mindset. His theological formulations were so perceptive that they came close to what the

---

27. Justin, *First Apology*, ANF 1:175.
28. Justin, *Second Apology*, ANF 1:191–93.
29. Justin, *First Apology*, ANF 1:166–67.
30. Born in Smyrna, influenced by Polycarp, trained in Rome, served as presbyter and bishop of Lyons, whose sources included Justin, Theophilus of Antioch, and Ignatius among others.

church eventually subscribed to at both Nicaea and Chalcedon. The continual theme of his apologetic response is that the God of the creation and revelation is *one and the same* and that Jesus Christ is *one and the same* as God.[31] But it is also worthy of note that Irenaeus clearly places the nature of God in a personal context. The Supreme sole Creator who experiences no contrary power is the Father who reveals himself because he loves.[32] His love is shown to humanity through Jesus, the Word made flesh. The intimacy in the theology of Irenaeus not only reflects Scriptural motifs but also incorporates both the creature and creation in a celebration of the love of God.[33]

For this bishop, any dividing of the essence of the triune God, the nature of God, or the essence of the Word made flesh directly affects salvation.[34] As we have seen above, this is not an era in which Christ is yet fully dealt with ontologically. They were capable of ontological reflection, but they had different priorities. These thinkers were primarily shepherds and pastors of communities; some were under serious theological attack. One can find hints of eternal generation in Irenaeus' discussion of the relation of the Word and the Father, but the inner life of the Trinity is inscrutable.[35] He looks at Christ principally from a soteriological standpoint (in terms of salvation). He talks about Christ being God in the context of an all-encompassing plan of divine love to save humanity.

The deity of Christ is non-negotiable for Irenaeus; he is countering all the attempts to limit that divinity in the bewildering Tetrads of the gnostics. Having dispensed with the gnostic attempt to separate the Creator from the Father Almighty, Irenaeus turns to the historical fact that Jesus is the Word made flesh[36] Unlike Justin,

---

31. A recurrent theme in Irenaeus' logical flow: *Against Heresies*, ANF 1:329, 331, 396, 422, 440–41 (3 times), 466–67, 549, 554.

32. Irenaeus, *Against Heresies*, ANF 1:449–50, 447–48, 487.

33. Irenaeus, *Against Heresies*, ANF 1:468, 475.

34. Irenaeus, *Against Heresies*, ANF 1:424.

35. Note the same confession with ontological reservation in Irenaeus, *On the Apostolic Preaching*, 68–69.

36. Irenaeus, *Against Heresies*, ANF 1:331, 392, 422–23, 426–27 (this is a notable reference where Irenaeus clarifies that none of the heretics can claim that

Irenaeus did not emphasize the *Logos*.[37] His defense and use of the four Gospels as revelation from God form the basis of his Christological defense.

His positive comments come mainly as interpretations of the text of Scripture. The flesh of Christ did not differ from that of Adam's race. Only a complete and living humanity, the *Logos* who became a human being by the taking up of humanity, could offer a true redemption. In terms of the relationship of the Word and the flesh, Irenaeus used the word "quiescent":

> For as He became man in order to undergo temptation, so also was He the Word that He might be glorified; the Word *remaining quiescent* [author's emphasis], that He might be capable of being tempted, dishonoured, crucified, and of suffering death, but the human nature being swallowed up in it (the divine), when it conquered, and endured [without yielding], and performed acts of kindness, and rose again, and was received up [into heaven]. He therefore, the Son of God, our Lord, being the Word of the Father, and the Son of man, since He had a generation as to His human nature from Mary—who was descended from mankind, and who was herself a human being—was made the Son of man.[38]

Irenaeus does not deny the totality of the divinity of Jesus Christ. "He united man with God and wrought a communion of God and man."[39] Christ "took up man into himself."[40] In this way, he dealt with the relation of the two natures in Christ. Instead of advocating subordinationism, Irenaeus is simply employing an analogical

---

the Word became flesh), 432–33 (of God and of Mary), 440–41, 443, 448, 454, 488, 526–27.

37. The abuse of the *Logos* as one of the elements of the Ogdoad from which the Aeons emanated in the miasma of Valentinian and Basilidean, Saturninan, and Carpocratian Gnosticism kept Irenaeus from offering a countering philosophy. His first clear response to these various heresies regarding the place of the *Logos* occurs in *Against Heresies, ANF* 1:400–401.

38. Irenaeus, *Against Heresies, ANF* 1:449. Bousset does not mention this in his assessment of the relationship of natures, which he feels is summarized mainly by "the Word made Flesh" and the repetition of *verbum homo* (*Kyrios Christos*, 433–34).

39. Irenaeus, *On the Apostolic Preaching*, 60.

40. Irenaeus, *Against Heresies, ANF* 1:443.

device to describe God's direct triune action in the world. The Son is the Word, and the Holy Spirit is God's Wisdom in all creation and in salvation.[41] Irenaeus consistently emphasizes the immediate work of God in his creation. He is battling the "mediacy" of the gnostics. Here again are traces of a Hebraic mindset with the "hand" and "finger" of God involved in all that occurs. In all of this, creation plays an important role. The denial of gnosticism reaches its climax in the Word made flesh who "recapitulates" all that has been defiled by sin.[42]

> For as by the disobedience of the one man who was originally moulded from virgin soil, the many were made sinners, and forfeited life; so was it necessary that, by the obedience of one man, who was originally born from a virgin, many should be justified and receive salvation. Thus, then, was the Word of God made man, as also Moses says: "God, true are His works." But if, not having been made flesh, He did appear as if flesh, His work was not a true one. But what He did appear, that He also was: God recapitulated in himself the ancient formation of man, that He might kill sin, deprive death of its power, and vivify man; and therefore His works are true.[43]

Irenaeus is firm in his conviction that in Christ all things are recapitulated, united, conjoined or "summed up."[44] The connection between the spiritual and the physical is made complete in the embodiment (*sarkosis*) of the Word.[45] All that was undone by the Fall in the physical and spiritual definitions of "flesh" had to be fully restored by the enfleshment of the Son of God. Jesus Christ sums up all of Adam and his race; "God again took dust" by his birth from

---

41. For one example see *Against Heresies*, ANF 1:488.

42. Besides the gnostics, the schools that "cut off that creation with which we are connected from the Father," like those of Marcion, and Simon, and Meander, Irenaeus also confronted (*Against Heresies*, ANF 1:407).

43. Irenaeus, *Against Heresies*, ANF 1:448.

44. Eph 1:10 term from *anakephalaioo*, other similar synonyms include: renovate, restore, recall.

45. Irenaeus, *On the Apostolic Preaching*, 60–61.

the Virgin Mary.[46] He takes all the disobedience of the first "head" of the race, and by becoming the truly obedient, truly righteous, truly suffering and dying Second Adam, he turns rebellious humanity and the atrophying universe right side up once again, in what Mathetes called "a sweet exchange."[47] Where there was death, the one who is life revivifies; where there was corruptibility, he brought incorruptibility; where the image of God was destroyed, he alone restored it.[48]

For Irenaeus, this divine Son who became flesh redirected the entire Ebionite agenda by advocating a monotheism that included the "two hands" of the Father. In his theology both Jesus Christ and the Spirit are divine.[49] No modalism appears in Irenaeus' project; nor by implication is subordination possible. The three divine persons work in concert on the same recapitulatory plan.[50] The Docetists simply disregarded the plain message of inspired Scripture that Jesus had not simply "appeared in mere seeming."[51] The Spirit is referred to as "celestial" and as "prophetic" in a much more functional mode than the Son. The person of the Spirit will not be clearly described until later centuries.[52]

Irenaeus' confronted the potentially devastating gnostic encroachments on the faith. Irenaeus bridged the divide between spirit and matter by emphasizing the triune God revealed most completely in Jesus Christ. This God has both created and entered creation out of love. Cosmologically considered, creation is not the work of a demiurge and thus unredeemable, but now through the God-Man and by the Spirit's renovating power is becoming what

---

46. Irenaeus, *Against Heresies*, ANF 1:454. He had to "receive the substance of the flesh" just as every person to reform his own handiwork.

47. Irenaeus, *Against Heresies*, ANF 1:442, 448, 450, 456, 523–24, 541, 548, *On the Apostolic Preaching*, 61; Mathetes, *Epistle to Diognetus*, ANF 1:28.

48. Irenaeus, *Against Heresies*, ANF 1:450, 538, 549.

49. Irenaeus, *Against Heresies*, ANF 1:546.

50. Irenaeus, *Against Heresies*, ANF 1:489.

51. Irenaeus, *Against Heresies*, ANF 1:527.

52. Irenaeus, *Against Heresies*, ANF 1:439–44, 507; *Of the Spirit*, ANF 1:414, 418–19, 423, 428, 521–22, esp. §3.

God intended even though the Fall has wrought incredible damage. Again, it is Jesus the son of Mary, incarnate in time and space, filled with the Spirit, who defines the nature and meaning of the cosmos. Anthropologically then, humanity is restored to the apex of creation rather than being trapped in gnosticism's dehumanizing polarities. The True Human, Jesus Christ, restored humanity by recapitulating human existence in every part of his life and passion, death and resurrection, and ascension.[53] Body and spirit are to be conjoined eternally in Christ and in those who believe in him. Irenaeus offers a completely new Christology in the face of many detractors. He clarifies areas his predecessors had left vague. There is only one Word and that is the Word who created and who became Mary's son. He "holds all things together." Here is a Savior who redeems actual fallen flesh. He does not abhor the womb of a woman or the existence of a Jewish man in history.

> Since the Lord thus has redeemed us through His own blood, giving His soul for our souls, and His flesh for our flesh, and has also poured out the Spirit of the Father for the union and communion of God and man, imparting indeed God to men by means of the Spirit, and, on the other hand, attaching man to God by His own incarnation, and bestowing upon us at His coming immortality durably and truly, by means of communion with God—all the doctrines of the heretics fall to ruin.[54]

Irenaeus re-enthrones a Christ whom gnosticism had threatened to replace with a fantasy of spiritual realms. The great "I Am" is the triune God whose being is not dissociated from humanity but is perfectly conjoined with it in the Lord Jesus Christ. He brings coherence to all that is because all that exists is through him and by him and for him. As Douglas Farrow puts it, Irenaeus "refused to allow cosmology to control Christology."[55] For this episcopal apolo-

---

53. Irenaeus, *Against Heresies*, ANF 1:388.
54. Irenaeus, *Against Heresies*, ANF 1:527.
55. Farrow, *Ascension and Ecclesia*, 53. I cannot recommend highly enough Farrow's excellent treatment of Irenaeus. More than any other commentator, he

gist, Irenaeus, Christology controls all true Christian epistemology, cosmology, anthropology, ecclesiology, and eschatology. If we start with Jesus, he must pervade the entire framework. Nothing makes sense without Jesus. We find nothing but sterility, servility, and rationality if the Son of God did not recapitulate, or re-unify, in himself the totality of creation beginning with humanity. He has incorporated human history within himself forever. By that communion what was divorced by sin can be brought back into its intended relationality. The redemption begun in him must and will conclude in him. He has descended and ascended as Son of Man and gives his Spirit to perfect what he brought together.

WESTERN CONTRIBUTIONS

HIPPOLYTUS

Hippolytus, the most important Western theologian in the third century Roman Church, was close enough to Irenaeus' thinking to have been called his disciple.[56] Bousset argues that Hippolytus was concerned with Basilidean Gnosticism.[57] He focused on the Johannine phrase "the Word became flesh." Hippolytus said that the *Logos* became flesh (*Logos-sarx*). He had a firmer grasp than anyone before him on the duality of the two natures, divine and human. He did not talk about *logos* in terms of unity, probably because he was aware of the tendency to over-philosophize. Hippolytus focused his attention upon the duality of natures in Christ. The "unfleshed" (*asarkos*) Word became flesh (*ensarkos*), mixing or mingling the corruptible and the incorruptible.[58] Like Justin Martyr's distinction between the immanent (*endiathetos) eternal*

---

has helped me to see Irenaeus' larger "systematic" viewpoints.

56. Photius began this idea concerning their relationship, which has been rigorously debated. It now seems quite unlikely. Too little of Hippolytus' background is known to be sure.

57. Bousset, *Kyrios Christos*, 262.

58. Hippolytus, *Treatise on Christ and AntiChrist*, ANF 5:205. The idea of "mixing" became clearer to the fathers as they approached Chalcedon. The commingling of natures was not a confusion of natures; it emphasized, rather, their inseparability and eternal mutuality. He is very clear on this in a Fragment,

Word and external (*prophorikos*) historical Word, the emphasis is primarily on salvation. With the onslaught of gnostic schools and sects, it was imperative that Jesus' complete, historical, physical, and real humanity be clearly emphasized but not at the expense of his deity.[59] Hippolytus certainly stresses the temporal nature of the Son. While critiquing Noetus' heresy, he states in an extreme form the importance of the incarnation for the atonement:

> What Son of His own, then, did God send through the flesh but the Word, whom He addressed as Son because He was to become such (or be begotten in the future? . . . For neither was the Word, prior to the incarnation and when by himself, yet perfect Son, although He was perfect Word, only-begotten. Nor could the flesh subsist by itself apart from the Word, because it has its subsistence in the Word. Thus, then, one perfect Son of God was manifested.[60]

Not only does this overstatement of sonship need further clarification but also the language of the unity of natures is not further defined, though it is reaffirmed as the basic claim of the church at this point. Hippolytus contends that "assumed" flesh,[61] sent by the Father was the Word made manifest.[62] In a "manner known to himself alone,"[63] he "took flesh" from Mary, "assuming a human soul," "taking to himself the flesh of the old Adam . . . manifested now God in a body."[64] It should also be noted that a term that Hippoly-

---

"was born of her (Mary) at once God and man without confusion of the one in the other" (175).

59. On the other theological battlefront of the Trinity engaged with Noetus of Smyrna, who was most likely the originator of the Patripassian heresy, a form of modalism that advocated that it was the Father who became incarnate and died, Hippolytus demonstrated the distinction between the persons while confirming their eternal unity. See Hippolytus, *Against the Heresy of One Noetus,* *ANF* 5:227. Note though the continued reservation regarding the personhood of the Spirit (a third economy or disposition) with regard to the other two persons (228).

60. Hippolytus, *Against the Heresy of One Noetus, ANF* 5:229.

61. Hippolytus, *The Refutation of All Heresies, ANF* 5:147.

62. Hippolytus, *Against the Heresy of One Noetus, ANF* 5:228.

63. Hippolytus, *Against Beron and Helix, ANF* 5:232.

64. Hippolytus, *Against the Heresy of One Noetus, ANF* 5:230. For a graphic use of Old Testament typology with the incarnation in view, see his *Treatise*

tus uses, "subsistence" (*hupistanai*), becomes a crucial term in later Christology. Still, the debate surrounding its anachronistic usage in this one place has raised some questions as to its authenticity.[65]

Equally as interesting is the use of *personae* in a comment on the meaning of John 10:30: "I and the Father are one."[66] Though giving no more than an indication that the word may help in distinguishing the Father from the Son, we have a usage that apparently precedes Tertullian's more complex discussion. Hippolytus is not a weak link in either Trinitarian or Christological development, but on the issue of the actual relation between the two natures of Christ, he does not offer theological innovation but rather a strong confirmation of this central Christological concern.

Hippolytus carries the tradition forward that without the full assumption of every aspect of humanity and the results of its fallenness, there is no salvation. His lists of the descent of the Son incorporate the same theme of total identification that we have seen others emphasize. Jesus' assumption of flesh began a thorough "remodeling" of the old man by the new creation.[67] The healing begun in Christ is telic in orientation. He says that we are destined to "become God." Deification is the purpose of the incarnation. If the image of God is to mean likeness to him, for Hippolytus, Jesus has made a way to impart to the human heart a regeneration that includes a gracious donation of his very nature, an infusion of love and holiness.[68]

---

on *Christ and AntiChrist*, *ANF* 5:205; *On the Song of Songs*, *ANF* 5:176; or Fragments of Discoursed or Homilies, *ANF* 5:238–39.

65. Grillmeier, *Christ in Christian Tradition*, 116–17. Although Grillmeier states this is the only place "subsistence" is used, there is very similar language found in *Against Beron and Helix*, *ANF* 5:233.

66. Hippolytus, *Against the Heresy of One Noetus*, *ANF* 5:226.

67. Hippolytus, *The Refutation of All Heresies*, *ANF* 5:152.

68. Hippolytus, *The Refutation of All Heresies*, *ANF* 5:153; *Treatise on Christ and AntiChrist*, *ANF* 5:205; *Against the Heresy of One Noetus*, *ANF* 5:230; *Against Beron and Helix Fragment*, *ANF* 5:233.

TERTULLIAN

Tertullian is a pivotal figure in Christian theology. He is one of the few early thinkers who was not a pastor or shepherd of believers. He was a brilliant lawyer who turned his amazing rhetorical and logical skills to theological ends. More than Hippolytus, Tertullian worked with the implications of the two natures of Christ. He is considered a master theologian in the Western tradition for both his Trinitarian thought and his Christology.[69] In the arduous task of defining *persona* (Greek, *prosopon*), Tertullian introduced the particular use of the term that would become the best word (*person*) available to delineate the Trinitarian reality. This term has become part of our theological and cultural vocabulary.[70] Tertullian was not the first to use the word *persona* in the second century. From the various meanings of "mask," "role" and "legal entity," *persona* became the demarcation for the three revealed names and voices for God: Father, Son, and Holy Spirit. What Tertullian did was to explain how the three persons co-existed in one substance. He saw that differences could co-exist in a unity. The *monarchy* (*monosarchos*, one-Lord) Tertullian envisioned was of the Father who had an eternal Son and the *economy* (works of the Trinity) of that divine reality included different activities by distinct persons of one shared substance.[71] In most Western thinkers the unity of the Godhead is the primary starting point for reflection. Tertullian insists on the priority of the Father so that the economy of the Godhead depends upon the unity that the Father guarantees. While not static in his

69. Tertullian refuted the monarchian modalism of Sabellius and Praxeas who claimed to be substantiated true monotheism against the encroaching gnostic emanationism. Tertullian rejected all forms of modalism with the added implication of patripassianism.

70. Tertullian, *Against Praxeas*, ANF 3:598.

71. Tertullian, *Against Praxeas*, ANF 3:617–18. So strong is Tertullian on the origin of the Son from the Father that some have accused him of ditheism, but his Montanist proclivities kept the Spirit very much in the middle of this discussion even though later Trinitarian doctrine would be clearer. Studer feels that it was Tertullian who moved the church clearly into a Trinitarian framework from a more latent binitarianism (Studer, *Trinity and Incarnation*, 72–73).

conception of God, Tertullian sometimes employs the language of functional subordination when referring to the Son and the Spirit. They proceed from the unity in the works in which they participate.[72] Tertullian, adamant that the substance of the Godhead was the reality shared by the Father and Son and by implication the Spirit, did not find it incoherent that *one person* could have two natures coinciding perfectly.[73]

Applying the same notion to the human and divine in Jesus was a theological breakthrough and watershed. Due to modalism, which he combated, Tertullian's main objective was to distinguish between the persons of the Trinity, especially the Father and the Son. The *Logos* is a person distinct from the Father. Yet that same *Logos* is a divine person who shares with the Father in the substantial unity of the Trinity. He used the word *substantia* (substance) for nature. In terms of the unity of divine substance, the Word was preexistent with the Father. Speaking of the divine nature and the economy of the Son, Tertullian asserts that Christ was distinct "in manner of existence—in position, not in nature; and He did not withdraw from the original source, but went forth"[74] when he became incarnate. He assumed a total human existence.[75]

Tertullian spoke of the unity or the conjoining of "two substances."[76] By the use of *person* and *nature*, Tertullian argues that Jesus is one reality: a person with two natures that remain distinct in their qualities but are perfectly conjoined in Jesus Christ. Though both divine and human, he is not divisible into sectors where a nature might reside by itself.

Two substances comprise the unity of the person of Christ. They are not mixed to produce a third substance, or as others had put it, Jesus is not some "third thing." Tertullian, in his closing critique of

---

72. Grillmeier supports this thesis in *Christ in Christian Tradition*, 120.
73. Tertullian, *Against Praxeas*, ANF 3:608.
74. Tertullian, *Apology*, ANF 3:34.
75. Tertullian, *On the Flesh of Christ*, ANF 3:524.
76. Tertullian, *On the Flesh of Christ*, ANF 3:525; *Against Praxeas*, ANF 3:623–24.

Praxeas, says, "We see plainly the twofold state (*duplicum statum*), which is not confounded, but conjoined in one person—Jesus, God and man."[77]

Though these arguments were to form the outline of all further orthodox thought, they were so closely tied to the *being* of the Father and the *economy* of the other two persons of the Trinity that Tertullian could be read by later thinkers as suggesting subordinationism. Given the time in which he wrote and the lack of consensual interaction on these issues, more theological development was necessary. Another point needing clarification was the language explaining the relationship of Word and flesh.

It is one thing to conclude that the Word was "clothed" in flesh but quite another to stress the unaltered state of the natures so as to keep them from sharing their qualities.[78] Each thinker has a particular battlefield upon which to stand that determines in large manner what issues occupy one's primary thought-world. Tertullian would correct any form of ontological subordinationism, and his doctrine of salvation was so complete that it sounds virtually Irenaen in its beauty. Because he really became a man, Christ, who came in two natures, has redeemed, restored, cleansed, renewed, and reanimated all of creation.[79] The ruminations of Tertullian were to play a large role in the ensuing debates that led ultimately to Chalcedon, but one will not find in him the nuances required to produce a full exploration of the relation of person to substance in the God-Man.[80] Tertullian's insights on the unity of the person of

---

77. Tertullian, *Against Praxeas*, ANF 3:624. In other places he uses "*duae naturae*" (two natures).

78. Tertullian, *On the Flesh of Christ*, ANF 3:523.

79. Tertullian, *On the Flesh of Christ*, ANF 3:524.

80. Another Western theologian, Novatian, whose work on the Trinity included the use of the word "person," arises around the time of Tertullian. Though he also stresses the distinction between the persons of the Trinity (Novatian, *Treatise Concerning the Trinity*, ANF 5:637), he turns to the delineation of this "one person" in describing the Son of God who became the Son of Man and uses terms like "connection," "mingling," "taking up into himself," "associated," "joined," "both sides woven in and grown together," "both substances, by the binding to

Christ did not become central to the Christological discussion for nearly two centuries, but he did pave the way for what eventually would become the consensual language.[81]

EASTERN CONTRIBUTIONS: THE ALEXANDRIAN SCHOOL

In the East, one finds a different mindset from the unitary focus of a legally trained thinker like Tertullian. Aristotelian tendencies in the West confront the more Platonic ideals and concepts. The latter permits consideration of the important themes of participation, interpenetration, and mutuality. The best of Hellenism's orientation concerning ideals and forms, symbols and realities were now to be seen as helpful counterparts in exegeting Christological texts and viewing their implications for an orthodox understanding of Jesus. Against those who have diminished this portion of Christian theology as a "Hellenization," the adoption of this cultural paradigm enabled the church to speak creatively in a way it had not found possible before. The inability of the Aristotelian/Stoic mind to move beyond the restraint of immanentism met another mind dominated by a transcendentalism. Though neither perspective is able to explain the mystery of the incarnation without the correction of the other, Greek thinking did expand Christology in spite of some of its presuppositions.[82]

CLEMENT OF ALEXANDRIA

Around the same time (late second century) as Hippolytus and Tertullian were ruminating on the nature of Christ, Clement was applying his philosophical background to this same topic.[83]

---

one another of a mutual alliance," in his attempts to deal with the Theandric Union (635).

81. Grillmeier, *Christ in Christian Tradition*, 131.

82. Note Clement's survey of pagan philosophy and the preparatory training, as a child must be taught by an elder, it provided for the gospel (*Stromata*, *ANF* 2:312–24).

83. In an interesting survey of various inadequate conceptions of truth in the Christian tradition, Zizioulas states that Clement more than Origen approached

Due both to proximity with Israel and connections with Judaism, Alexandria became a key center of Christian theology. While the West was still a mission field, a longstanding catechetical tradition existed in this important city of the Eastern Church. But thought about the Son of God had to encounter and include the major philosophical school that had attained prominence there.

The *Logos,* as the systematic principle at the center of all true being, orients the school of North African Christology. The Son of the Father is, for Clement, wisdom and knowledge. He is the Truth because he is the eternal pre-existent Word.[84] According to Clement in his defense of the reality of the incarnation, Christ is both God and man.[85] While there is not sustained argument in Clement regarding the natures of Christ, without a doubt he understood Scripture clearly to reveal God in the flesh.[86] Normally the Alexandrian school is castigated for being overly philosophical. The Alexandrians were aware of the distinct tendency to give pride of place to the *Logos* as a sort of "inner man" when referring to the person of Jesus, but wherever Clement speaks of the Son he brings the *Wisdom of God* down to practical application. He sees that salvation means that the image of God can produce his image in humanity. His wisdom can become ours because he is able to transform people into his very likeness. The ontology of the Son is, for Clement, inseparable from the personhood of humans.

ORIGEN

A systematic thinker and biblical scholar, Origen made an important addition to Christology with his emphasis on the "eter-

---

his calling as a philosopher. Origen, Zizioulas argues, attempted to stay self-consciously within the confines of tradition (*Being as Communion,* 72–74).

84. Clement, *Exhortation to the Heathen, ANF* 2:173; *Stromata, ANF* 2:438.

85. "God the Word—who became man for our sakes, and who wished in all points to be made like us" (Clement, *The Instructor, ANF* 2:215). Clement applies a preliminary Trinitarian reading of Isaiah's prophesied perfect Child: "The Son in the Father and the Father in the Son."

86. Clement, *Stromata, ANF* 2:524–25.

nal generation of the Son."[87] Origen's encyclopedic knowledge and analytic brilliance have left an indelible mark on Christology to this day. The tendency to start with a notion of being and then to include Jesus of Nazareth is all too common in theological history. Such an approach never fully answers the questions about the actual nature of the human Jesus. One cannot begin with the impersonal and move to the personal. The *logos* of early Neo-Platonism was a grand concept but an abstract one. Unable to distinguish this origin from the monistic implications of his Platonic background, Origen went too far in relating the Word and creation. This led to a belief in eternal creation, implying the "eternal pre-existence of souls."[88] Origen viewed Christ as a pre-existent soul who was eternally generated from God. Christ then joined himself with the human Jesus.[89] This is essentially adoptionism. Whatever Jesus was, he was the form of this idea from eternity. Origen never fully escaped from his insistence on the duality of natures. Each nature retained its own characteristics from eternity and never ceased to be. Origen, then, could never establish the concept of a real unity of the natures. Because of his philosophical bent, Origen tended to deny the full meaning of the incarnation. He lost the power and impact of the incarnate Word, which is a problem always found in philosophically oriented theology—the loss of the historical Jesus. If left unchecked, this Christology turns into a sort of gnosticism. Origen's conceptual roots were both philosophical and biblical/traditional; thus, both heretical and orthodox elements can be found in the massive corpus of his writings.

EAST AFTER ORIGEN: PAUL OF SAMOSATA AND MODALISM

Origen was so innovative in his explorations that some of the most tenacious heresies continue due to his strong philosophical

---

87. Origen, *De Principiis, ANF* 4:240, 245–47.
88. Origen, *De Principiis, ANF* 4:262–64.
89. Origen, *De Prinicpiis, ANF* 4:282–83.

interpretations. Origen's disciples were similarly distorted in their thinking, as exemplified by Paul of Samosata—the most famous modalist.[90] Remembering that heresy arose when individuals chose to offer concepts that were somewhat easier to comprehend than the consensual thought of the larger church, it is important to see that the Samosatenes were attempting to stay committed to a high view of the sovereignty of God while making sense of Jesus. Paul began a strain of thought called "dynamic monarchianism." He presupposed one ruler (*monos-archon*). What was needed was the corrective analysis of richer Trinitarian and Christological thought.[91] His view was another version of the triune life in which three "modes" of God formed one single "hypostasis" or person. According to his critics, this incorrigible bishop denied any personality to the *Logos* or the Holy Spirit. They were merely powers of God similar to the reason or mind in a human being. With a view of deity that did not allow personal distinction, he found that the only recourse for making sense of Scripture was to speak of three "modes" of revelation: Father, Word, and Wisdom.

The inadequate and destructive view of the relationship of the word and the flesh of Jesus found in Origen was also found in Paul of Samosata. He kept the *logos* and flesh distinct enough to have radical implications for the nature of the revelation of the Word of God. For him the Word was the most important focus, and the flesh was far less crucial. Jesus, then, was merely a human endowed with the Spirit in a manner like the prophets, only higher in degree of empowerment. The Alexandrian emphasis combined with a partic-

---

90. Paul came from the West bank of the Euphrates in what became Samosat, Turkey, but he served in Antioch and is thus an example, even though eventually condemned as a heretic, of the more literalistic interpretations of the Antiochene school, which formulated much Christology in its formative period. Sabellius, Noetus, and Praxeas were all Monarchians who had to be rejected in the early third century.

91. Paul originated from Samosata and ca. AD 260 became the bishop of Antioch. Several synods were held there in conflict with his unique views on the "monarchy" of the divine Trinity and of his proto-Nestorian (two distinct persons in the Son/Jesus) Christology. He was condemned and deposed in AD 268.

ular reading of Origen produced what has been called Samosatene Adoptionism.[92] The separation that these thinkers were compelled to maintain between divine being and humanity forced interpretations of crucial Christian terms that had to be strongly corrected by the community of faith. The word *homoousion*, which was to be a central term for Christological orthodoxy, was interpreted by Paul of Samosata in an overly materialistic way. The *Logos* did join himself with Jesus in a moral way. The nature that Jesus retained was secondary to the nature of the Word. The historical could not, in Paul's reading, be taken fully into the ineffable, unchangeable Word. Thus, Jesus was "adopted," a man merely "attached" to God. This borrowing of a human nature began at the baptism and ended before actual death on the cross. Paul would even go so far as to accept a form of "generation" of Jesus by the Holy Spirit. Paul of Samosata spoke of "two sons." One divine Son conjoined himself with a human "son" to serve the purposes of God. One was the eternal Son, and the other was a temporal Son, who expressed divinity for the extent of his earthly life.[93] Jesus, the man, was for Paul a merely ancillary figure in the modes of God's self-revelation. The humanity of Christ was deprived of ontological content. The only relationship between the Word and Jesus was one of inspiration. No matter how supremely inspired this Jesus might have been to this misguided teacher, he could not be truly worshiped nor be in himself the Savior of the world.

---

92. Here Paul is distinctive from other modalists. He is able to combine a Unitarian view of God with an adoptionistic Christology that, at points, sounds reasonable. Eusebius says he reproduced the heresy of Artemon (or Artemos to some). See *Ecclesiastical History*, NPNF2 1:246–48, 312–16. Our point that Origen was used both for good and for ill is seen in that Paul's Origenist leanings were condemned by Origenist bishops in AD 268.

93. Outler says that Paul was committed to "traditional" Christology and, in that Antiochian perspective, took *homoousion* as an actual material expression of divine power (*Christology*, 88–89).

THE FOURTH CENTURY AND
NICENE CHRISTOLOGY

Two major schools of thought began to form in light of the necessity to distinguish true doctrine regarding Christ from mere philosophical discussion and faulty Scriptural exegesis.[94] This discussion and exegesis served to diminish the mystery of Christ as the Son of Man by representing itself as either a simple gospel or a viable ontology of the Savior.

The first school of thought was the Alexandrian school, which developed a compound explanation of the Son as Word/Flesh. The presuppositions of a Platonic view of reality inform much of what these thinkers say about Jesus Christ. Without this school of thought, little theological progress in either Trinitarian or Christological thinking would have been made.

The second was the Antiochian school, which was suspicious of the "flesh" as being too detached from the actual history of Jesus. For these thinkers, Word/Man was the continual emphasis. This school took a more Aristotelian perspective, in contrast with the more Platonic Alexandrian viewpoint. Suspicious of Idealism and coupled with an emphasis on the earthly life of Jesus, this Christological camp proved to be a healthy balance to the esoteric leanings of the Alexandrian thinkers.

A comparison of the two perspectives will clarify what might otherwise be an overly confusing enterprise.

AN OVERVIEW OF THE TWO MAJOR "SCHOOLS" OF CHRISTOLOGY

ALEXANDRIA	ANTIOCH
Neo-Platonic	Aristotelian
Philosophical	Biblical/historical
Eastern	Western
Multiplicity prior to Unity	Unity prior to Multiplicity

---

94. Rome as a formulator of theology becomes less influential in the period just before the Council of Nicaea.

ALEXANDRIA	ANTIOCH
Christology: *Logos-Sarx* (Word/Flesh)	Christology: *Logos-Anthropos* (Word/Man)
Word: inner man	Word: human indwelt
Language: made flesh (fusing)	Language: made human (conjunction)
Stress: deity	Stress: humanity
History: not taken seriously	History: taken seriously
Athanasius	Eustathius
Heresies due to an emphasis on the humanity of Christ	Heresies due to an emphasis on the deity of Christ
Monarchian Adoptionism	gnosticism
Adopted at birth or at baptism	Not a real human, an aeon, phantom, intermediary
Arianism (early fourth century AD)	Apollinariasnism (mid fourth century AD)
First created being	No human spirit
Condemned at Nicaea	Condemned at Constantinople
Nestorianism (mid fifth century AD)	Eutychianism (mid fifth century AD)
Logos indwells Jesus	*Logos* absorbs humanity
Condemned at Ephesus	Condemned at Chalcedon
Monophysitism (one nature; sixth century AD)	Monothelitism (one will; seventh century AD)
Condemned at Constantinople II	Condemned at Constantinople III

The struggle for a consensual agreement on the natures of Christ reached a crisis in the fourth century. The state the church found itself in by AD 312/313 due to the Edict of Milan and the new experience of being viewed as a legitimate religion produced a situation in which a consensual statement could be made in the defense of orthodoxy. No real markers had yet been established to draw the boundaries for an orthodox Christology. Both schools of thought had important areas of emphasis: the Antiochene interest in the historical person and the Alexandrine on the divinity of the *Logos*. The bringing of those two necessary elements together would occupy the church for the next century and a half.

Arius was the primary antagonist in the period that led to the Council at Nicaea (AD 325). Arius' worldview was formed by the

Alexandrian Platonism of Origen. The strong monotheistic ontology of this charismatic preacher/theologian accented an essential difference between the eternal Father and the "Son." Jesus was understood as a unique intermediary between the divine essence and humanity, between the impassible God and the finite world. The Son, according to Arius, had to be considered as a "third thing" (*tertium quid*). The chasm between divinity and humanity had to be bridged but not by God's condescension. Therefore, Jesus had to be a being whose origin in God was inscrutable but still "created."

ARIANS: WORD/FLESH

The radical separation of the Word from Jesus seen in the Origenism of Paul of Samosata is now taken by Arius further into the very essence of God. The subtle genius of Arius was at first hard to distinguish as heresy from the fumbling theology of his colleagues. His oratory and his rhetoric were unsurpassed. As in much Christian history, emotion overtook good theology and Arius' deficient Christology almost won the day. The key phrase for Arius was that there was a time when "He [the Son] was not."[95]

Arius' monotheism was fundamentally a radical deism. The chasm is so great between Arius' god and the created order that only one of a different essence from the Father could form a connection between the two realities. When stripped down to its core, his monotheism was little more than a lightly-veneered monism. Ultimately there is no reason for creation, so all its meaning is ultimately bound up in the divine. Alexandrian Neo-Platonism served once again to form the systematic principle that forced Arius to interpret Scripture in a hyper-dualistic manner. The tension between the divine and creation is never eased or solved by philosophy in itself.[96] But God's remoteness has another pagan implication for Arius' Christology having to do with an intermedi-

---

95. For an example of the kinds of phrases used by the Arians in this regard, see Athanasius, *Defence of the Nicene Definition NPNF*2 4:160.

96. E. L. Mascall spins out the implications of a non-biblical worldview and its resultant nihilism in *Via Media*, 17–31. He states in the same work that

ary world of devils and angels. If, as Arius posited, the uncreated is fundamentally at odds with creation, then the only possible connection between the two realities must come with a divinely-initiated mediator.[97] In the end gnosticism and Deism are indistinguishable from Arius' account, and they are ultimately pagan views of reality. Sovereignty without personhood always concludes the same way.

The conflict was exacerbated by the fact that Arius used Scripture continually in his arguments but with his own presuppositional interpretive grid. Terms we have seen above were taken in their most literal and physical sense. For Arius, Jesus is "begotten" as the first born of creation. God the Father is the only God. Thus, Jesus *began to be* at a point in "eternity" that need not concern us (according to Arius). Early on, the challengers to Arius saw that in essence he was leading the church into a form of polytheism. As we shall see, Nicene orthodoxy (AD 325) was required to underscore the divinity of Jesus. His humanity was to be clarified by the Nicene counterpart, Chalcedon (AD 451).

EUSTATHIUS' REACTION TO ARIUS: WORD/MAN

Eustathius of Antioch was the first to detect the Arian drift toward a fundamental dualism (spirit opposed to flesh). He reacts to what Arius had done to Scriptural terms like "begotten," "first-born," or "only Son." Approaching the other extreme, Eustathius posited a concept of the Son as a human indwelt by the divine. At issue for him was the passibility (suffering) of God. Eustathius

---

all notions of intermediaries between divine and physical reality are "pagan notions" (55).

97. Space will not allow a full investigation of this ultra-theism, but any student of Christology must know the implications of what at first seems a refutation of paganism. In the end it is merely another form of it with Christological garb. In this camp, along with Paul of Samosata, is Theodotus of Byzantium, Photinus of Sirmium, Marcellus of Sirmium, and eventually Nestorius. On the other end of the spectrum are those who identify the Father and the Son as one being, with the humanity of Christ being a mere instrument. For them the Son has no personal identity, no true human soul. These thinkers include Noetus, Praxeas, Cleomenes, Sabellius, and most detrimentally Apollinarius.

argued that Arius (Word/Flesh) denied a rational soul to Christ so that the *Logos* could suffer. He wanted to leave the divine essence untouched by passion. In response, the Antiochene thinkers spoke in Word/Man categories. Without the longer vision of the church, Eustathius overstated the assumption of the manhood of Jesus.

The human soul of Jesus was the actual subject of Christ's passion. Though a deep mystery, the end result of this distinctive focus on the humanity disallowed a "real" unity between the natures. Some have referred to this discussion as "diophysite" or *two natures conjoined in an external rather than an internal or personal union.* He understood the *Logos* as using the human body in an instrumental way. Such an understanding precluded an awareness of the nuances of true personal unity that would follow the Nicene statement of faith.

ATHANASIUS: WORD/FLESH

Athanasius, the bishop of Alexandria, wrote one of the most profound reflections regarding Christ in *On the Incarnation*.[98] He is a classic representative of Alexandrian Christology, the thinker who cut the Arian arguments to the quick. Athanasius corrected the Origenism of Arius by actually emphasizing Origen's statements about the eternal generation of the Son. He goes back to the word "begotten" from John 1:14, 1:18, 3:16 and 1 John 4:9 to argue that the word does not mean "made." His position is that the Son is not a creature. The Father eternally wills the Son, but that will does not necessitate a beginning point. The Son is without beginning in time. The Father is the Father by his eternal giving, and the Son is the Son by his eternal receiving. The incarnation occurred in time, but the Word/Son was never created or made.

In his prologue Athanasius begins with creation because the entire argument with the Arians has profound soteriological impli-

---

98. A good translation is found in Hardy, *Christology of the Later Fathers.* References will be made to this edition unless otherwise noted. This marvelous work was originally written as an apologetic letter to a friend (Macarius) sometime in his youth.

cations. The one who made us is the one alone who can save us. Salvation must have an ontological solution. Athanasius argues that a pagan "artificer" could not redeem due to a necessary dependence on primordial existence. This salvation is based upon the God who is Life in himself. The nature of God is overflowing goodness. This self-giving and sharing of life originates in the life of God.[99] Only the Life can give life and Jesus is nothing less than "the very Life."[100] The Creator invests in his creation at a great cost to himself. In order for sin as non-being to be redeemed, true being had to be intimately involved. The Word who came in the flesh was pre-existent in full being and life.[101]

The humanity of Christ is affirmed in Athanasius' discussion as well. With the typical rational understanding of personhood present in Alexandrian thought the image of God defiled by the fall is seen often in noetic (rational) terms. Therefore, repentance is not enough to provide a full salvation. The image needs a recreation. Thus, the Word, as Savior, takes a body no different than ours, born of a virgin.[102] For a complete restoration of the image, the Word "disguised" himself in order to transfer men to himself.[103] Only the Image of God can restore what is created in the image of God.[104]

When Athanasius comes to deal with the *Logos'* relationship to the body there is a touch of Word/Flesh in a *Logos* who is impassible, the Word dwelling with humanity.[105] Though absolutely uncircumscribable in his divinity, the Word who was eternally in his Father is now "in his man's nature."[106] The two natures are not merged but act in accordance with their individual and untainted essence. The *Logos* is not affected by Christ's humanness. Even

---

99. Hardy, *Christology of the Later Fathers*, 58. Goodness tied to the essence of God is a recurrent theme (63c-64a, 65).
100. Hardy, *Christology of the Later Fathers*, 74, 90–91.
101. Hardy, *Christology of the Later Fathers*, 103.
102. Hardy, *Christology of the Later Fathers*, 62–62, 72.
103. Hardy, *Christology of the Later Fathers*, 70.
104. Hardy, *Christology of the Later Fathers*, 74.
105. Hardy, *Christology of the Later Fathers*, 63, 108.
106. Hardy, *Christology of the Later Fathers*, 70.

with his background he is able to escape Arius' fundamental problem. He knows that dualism obscures the incarnation. The inherent "reductionism" in *logos* doctrine of Greek philosophy is countered in a full rendering of the incarnation. Humanity as part of the whole is the part he chose in which to reveal himself the most clearly. He asks why it is that the universal *Logos* who dynamizes all things could not also unite himself with humanity. If that is offensive the whole idea is objectionable of a Creator ordering, uniting with the universe. The part is no less offensive than the whole.[107] Being alone can offer to contingent being, sustaining power and a full cure to that which is threatened by non-being.

Athanasius knows that both ultra-divinity and super-humanity do not offer a real salvation. Why did the Savior not act on a grander scale? This preacher argues it was because our sinful situation is not grand. The Word who is the Son of Man did not seek to bedazzle or overpower. He came as a servant to be recognizable.[108] What he came to do was historical not mythic. The incarnation outdid all the myths and magic of Greece. In his self-emptying love, he is the truth that outsmarts the philosophers. In his physical resurrected body, he makes created reality what it was meant to be. And his end was to make us like himself.[109]

Athanasius' reply to Arius is both highly soteriological and deeply ontological. Only God can save. He saw the full implications of Arianism left unchecked. Usually, Arius is attacked for diminishing the divinity of the Son, but he also impacted the humanity of Christ. It is due to Athanasius' tenacity that at Nicaea the terms "true God of true God," "very God of very God," and "begotten, not made" were used to refute the Arian heresy. Athanasius, or "the black dwarf" as he was also known, was the theologian of the eter-

---

107. Hardy, *Christology of the Later Fathers*, 96–97. He points out that even Plato sought a human form of light when facing the prospect of non-being.

108. Hardy, *Christology of the Later Fathers*, 97–98.

109. Hardy, *Christology of the Later Fathers*, 102, 104–5, 107. Athanasius often calls the end of the Incarnate One's purpose "divinization."

nal Son. He met the most decisive challenge among the earliest attacks on the person of Jesus Christ. Though misunderstood, vilified, and exiled a handful of times, this theological giant paved the way for all successive Christological orthodoxy. His arguments are still the best in confronting Arianism whenever and wherever the church finds it.

THE NICENE CREED

The content of this creed was originally written in AD 325.[110] It was necessary to add some material for further clarification in AD 381 (often distinguished by the name Niceno-Constantinopolitan Creed) due to the Arianism that doggedly hung on even after its refutation at the earlier council. The Nicene Creed was used for confirmation and preparation for baptism. It was an instructive and exclusivistic paradigm laid down for those who repudiated their former paganism. It offered a biblical worldview that could not be produced by any philosophy. Once a Christian could intelligently affirm this creed, nothing could be the same again in that one's life. Those who castigate creedal development as extra-biblical have spent little time reading about how the councils came to their conclusions. While not claiming equality with Scripture, they did express the major theological issues that distinguished and defined Christianity in relation to all other belief systems.[111] The fact that the creeds were pastorally motivated underscores the importance of understanding each theological phrase for the newly catechized and baptized Christians. They were enjoined to know who the Son was

---

110. See the creed in *NPNF2* 4:75. A fuller rendition of the entire council can be found in *NPNF2* 14:1–55.

111. The editor of the *NPNF* edition of the creed puts it this way in his introduction, "they [the fathers] understood their position to be that of witnesses, not that of exegetes" (*NPNF2* 14:1). The consistent refrain from all the ecumenical councils is not personal insight, or bringing *a priori* presuppositions, or trying to be novel or innovative. Rather the focus was to share what had been received from witnesses to the very Son of God who was also the son of Mary.

in his two natures when they were preparing for baptism. Apparently, ontology was important to early discipleship. Who Jesus was in his divinity and in his humanity set the context for all salvation and its implications in a believer's life.

Luther says all heresies disregard the second article, which deals with the "Son" in the Nicene Creed. Note the structure of the first section and its agreement with the outline of the Christology derived from the above discussion of the kerygma:

We believe in one God, the Father Almighty. . .

*And in one Lord Jesus Christ, the Son
of God, the only-begotten . . .*

*and was incarnate by the Holy Spirit of the
Virgin Mary and became man.*

And He was crucified . . .

and was buried. . . .

And ascended into heaven,

and sits at the right hand of the Father;

and He shall come again . . .

The "ands" all connect to the basic point that this is a statement of personal trust, an individual commitment that is made and maintained in the community. There is no one saying, "I believe in Jesus," outside the church's theological care. It is believing in Jesus in the community. To say, "I believe" or, "I confess his name," is to do so with the church. Faith in Christ and all this is not only a voluntary commitment but also the realization that we do not do theology outside of visible church. All heresy arose when theologians chose, volitionally and defiantly, to step outside the parameters of hard-fought and won orthodoxy. To believe in the fully deity of Jesus was no easy thing.

The logic of the creed is that there is no salvation without Christology. We must know what he does because of who he is. We must know who it is that died. Creeds did not settle everything immediately. The church must always carefully assess and maintain a proper view of their authority. The common experience of reserve about their place in the church is best responded to by repeating the outlines of the Christology proffered by heretics like Apollinarius. It is then that a true believer will see that these are not impositions on the truth about Jesus. They are signposts of reality that protect and provide a context for a complete understanding of a Savior who is the Son of God and the Son of Man.

There is little doubt due to the threat of Arianism that the creed had to tackle the divinity of Jesus, the Son of God, first and foremost. The essence of God in saving humanity was a non-negotiable argument for those who followed Athanasius' lead. If a real salvation was instituted by Christ, he must be of the same nature as the Father. In order to clarify the meaning of revealed truth found in Scripture, the church chose a summative theological term that was to share all ensuing theology. *Homoousion* was chosen at Nicaea as the most adequate term to state what was clear in the Gospels. Jesus claimed to be "one" with the Father, not in a moral unity or a spiritual unity but in a real, substantial, personal, and eternal unity. The son of Mary was the eternal Son of God who was incarnated by the power of the Holy Spirit. Any Arian notion of partial divinity, secondary transcendence, or godlikeness was rejected outright.[112]

The creed offered a Christian way of viewing reality.[113] The triune God who created all that is was first Father, Son, and Holy Spirit in an eternal relationship of mutual love. That Life was independent of all else but Itself. The only Creator chose to reveal himself completely in the incarnation. The purpose of revelation was not just to show us his nature but to invite us to share, to participate in his nature. Salvation from sin was the offer of a restored humanity inaugurated by the self-abasing descent of the Second Person of the

---

112. Athanasius, *Statement of Faith*, NPNF2 4:84–85.
113. A refreshing discussion of this is found in Willis, *Clues to the Nicene Creed*, 60–72.

Trinity. He is the clue, the key to all that we know about God and about being a human. He is the reason for creation and redemption. Nicaea stated without reservation that Jesus was not partly God but fully God. He was not, as Arius blasphemously proposed, a physically "generated" being.

In successive eras Arianism has taken on other forms but is based on the same narrow view of reality, and the church has had to clearly reject every dalliance in that diminishment of Christ's deity. He is not an effluence, an angelic being, an avatar, an aeon, a semi-divine intermediary, or one in a series of divine revelations. The church, both East and West, has stated since that Nicene era that Jesus Christ of Nazareth was of the same essential reality as the Father Almighty. The word "begotten" was never to be interpreted in any way but "ineffably and incomprehensibly."[114] That meant that the godhood of the Son was not altered in any way by the incarnation of the Word. No division or separation occurred within the triune life when Jesus came to earth. The deity of the Father was shared with the Son, "without flow or division."[115] Jesus was not unique in an ontologically subordinate way to the transcendent Father. The *Logos* became a human being, or better, took a human nature and the only expression of that nature, a body and soul, into himself and became "enmanned" or "he was made flesh" and "he took on himself a body" on our behalf. The Nicene Creed is the signpost against all heresies.[116] It provides the lynchpin for all further Christological reflection. And even though it offered a strong foundation for increasingly clear Christology, it was not fully convincing to some as subsequent reactions to it show.

---

114. Athanasius, *Statement of Faith*, NPNF2 4:84.

115. Athanasius, *Statement of Faith*, NPNF2 4:85.

116. Outler says of Nicaea, "The first half of the Christological compound was nailed to the mast, never to come down. From that day to this, the stablest motif in the Christian mind has been the essential identity of the Creator and the Savior. Monotheism *and* [original emphasis] redemption-in-history are affirmed and maintained together!" (*Christology*, 99).

POST-NICENE CHRISTOLOGY: APOLLINARIUS

The context for Nicaea arose in the midst of a challenge to the deity of Christ. Though it was not emphatic on the incarnation, some have argued that it actually lessened the humanity of Jesus. The philosophy of Alexandrian Christology (Word/Flesh) continued to need correction. The language of the incarnation that was adequate for explaining what Jesus had done in himself for humankind was in constant need of careful perusal and formulation.

One figure arose after Nicaea that shows the same difficulty we have seen above, and he did so as a reaction to the Word/Man emphasis in Eustathius. The Alexandrian desire for a "real" unity between the natures did not sit easily with strong talk about a human being. The inherent dualism that denied such discussion is seen in Apollinarius, who affirmed that Jesus is fully God but stated that he is only partially human. Though wanting to affirm the Nicene gift of *homoousion*, this extreme Word/Flesh analysis revolved around the central notion of personhood as located in the mind. The *Logos* replaced the fleshly mind (the *nous*) of Jesus. The problem again was the inability to conceive of a full human person in complete and unreserved relationship with the Word. In a comparison between the soul of a man where the will gives distinctive life, here the *Logos* carries life-giving power to the flesh—of Christ. For Apollinarius, "the Word contributes a special energy to whole [incarnate flesh]."[117] But that "special energy" was really the actual life of the God-Man. There was such an emphasis on the absolutely undiminishable divine nature that to retain a unity, the rational soul of Jesus is fused into the *hypostasis* of the Word. As we continue to see, any diminishment of either nature in Jesus produces an unreal Savior, an incomplete person. When any theologian dis-

---

117. Apollinarius, *On the Union in Christ of the Body with the Godhead*, 104.

connects the union of the two natures in their completeness trouble soon results. The "clumsy contradictions" of having to discuss the relationship between the natures in Christ give way to more reasonable definitions, and, normally, one nature wins out, and the result is a very sophisticated but inadequate reading of the nature of the Savior and his saving personhood. Arius diminished the divinity of the *Logos,* and Apollinarius diminished the humanity of Jesus. The Antiochene Word/Man school of thought heard latent in Apollinarian (Word/Flesh) discussions of the *physis* or nature of Jesus a radical convergence that confused the natures.

ORTHODOX RESPONSES

Gregory of Nazianzus (Word/Flesh) saw this immediately in his rejection of Apollinarius' fusion of natures and displacement of the human mind of Jesus as a "monstrous" folly.[118] One of the best places to enter into the thought-life of Nazianzus is in his *Orations.*[119] There he states that the full humanity of Christ cannot be denied. Along the lines that Tertullian had begun in the West, Gregory also developed the concept of the divine Father/Son relationship being a "substantial unity." This is the substance of a personal relationship, not a material construct. He would speak of the real unity between the Father and Son. Subsequently, the language of

---

118. Gregory, "To Cledonius against Apollinarius: Letter 101" in Hardy, *Christology of the Later Fathers,* 221.

119. The Orations are five sermons normally numbered in his works as Orations 27–31. Originally set against two radical forms of Arianism in the late fourth century, the Eunomians or Anomeans, there is also some clear response to the Apollinarian controversy (Hardy, *Christology of the Later Fathers,* 215–32). Eunomius, a Cappadocian, trained in Alexandria and was a participant in the Council of Antioch on the Arian Contro. Basil and both Gregories addressed his ideas. Anomean means, literally, a single supreme Substance whose simplicity is opposed to all distinction. The incorruptible nature of the divine was the only description of God that was acceptable. Gregory says that the words "unbegotten and unoriginate" are the key elements of this Arian off-shoot. This ungenerated Being did not beget the Son but immediately produced him and whom received the power from God to create. Among the first things the Son created was the Holy Spirit.

the Trinity would come to be used in the service of understanding the relation of the natures in Christ.

Concerning the methodology of the heretics whom he called the "inventors of new theology," he says that they all attempt to simplify the gospel by offering "elementary treatises" that are a diminishment of language into exactitudes that are limited by human conception.[120] But he states that their florid dialectics are insufficient to comprehend the mystery of God in his revelation. All too often elegance of language makes void the cross. In the end he calls those who move away from the mystery of God's nature as revealed through Scripture and the creeds as "sacrilegious robbers of the Bible and thieves of the sense of its contents."[121]

The *via negativa* of the apophatically-inclined Eastern mindset shows in his discussion of the "mysteries." On certain ontological speculations it is best, according to Gregory, to speak with "honor by silence."[122] He states that the divine nature can never be completely apprehended by human reason. It is undefinable, incomprehensible, illimitable, and uncircumscribed because that nature exists outside of the universe.[123] The divine mysteries are unapprehendable by human reason due to the "darkness of the human body" that exists between humanity and God.[124] According to Gregory Scripture verifies this ontological distinction. The human mind cannot pursue knowledge of the self-existent.[125]

Yet, in Alexandrian fashion, he goes on to state that we are made with a rational nature, which was made for God and his being. Creation speaks of a Creator and that existence behind all that we can see, which either begins or sustains the order of the universe. We

---

120. Hardy, *Christology*, 167, 160, 179, 175.

121. Hardy, *Christology*, 175, 177.

122. Hardy, *Christology*, 165.

123. Hardy, *Christology*, 143, 138–39, 142–43.

124. Hardy, *Christology*, 144.

125. Hardy, *Christology*, 150. If even the secondary natures of the material boggles the mind, Nazianzus argues, how much more so the immaterial or the primary or first natures (159).

must seek to intuit reality, "to grasp him," not with the heretical perversions of this God-given capacity, which is idolatry.[126]

Gregory is convinced that fundamentally all orthodoxy is an attempt to demythologize "carnal arguments" about the nature of divine reality.[127] Any Christological discussion that diminishes the transcendence of God might claim to be Christian but in reality is a mere gloss over old forms of pagan thought. This is made quite clear when the use of analogical language comes to the forefront. He states that in discussing Scripture and theology many too quickly import substance, time, place, and emotion into analogies used in describing the Godhead. He finds that theologians can become so focused on the term "Father" and by that tend to import natural fatherhood in a heretical fashion into the discussion.[128]

The third oration concerns the Son. Here he explores the meaning of the divine nature and the specific scriptural references to the Son. The only option he allows for comprehending the Father in relation to the Son is the ancient commitment to the *monarchia*, the discussion of the Trinity in which there is a personal origin to begin speaking of the divine nature first in the Father of the Son. To speak otherwise is to offer that which heretics do, which is either *anarchia* or *polyarchia*.[129] Gregory feels both lead to total theological dissolution. He posits that triune diversity does not disrupt essence because that ineffable unity is beyond all human philosophical expression. Paganism begins with and ends in necessitarian concepts. Only the triune life offers freedom and love.[130] The divine nature is uncompounded, but it is a personal reality based upon the Son's relation to the Father.[131]

---

126. Hardy, *Christology*, 147, 145.
127. Hardy, *Christology*, 165.
128. Hardy, *Christology*, 162, 171.
129. Hardy, *Christology*, 160–61.
130. Hardy, *Christology*, 161.
131. Hardy, *Christology*, 173.

Then he moves to the meaning of the "generation" of the Son. He speaks of the Word of the mind of Father.[132] Using sets of analogies he states that the Father is the "Emitter" while the Son is "Begotten," and the Holy Spirit is "Emission."[133] But every analogy breaks down if it does not point to the voluntary nature of the inter-Trinitarian life. The revealed nature of God goes beyond any human concept of cause. Both will and action are in God perfectly conjoined, not separable as they are in us.[134] Begotten does not equal cause from our understanding. But the Father as "cause" of the begotten Son is not necessarily greater than the Son. When Jesus refers to the Father as "greater than I" (John 14:28), greater is a conditioned term by the unique essence of God in relation to salvation.[135] There is no ontological subordination in being either begotten or sent by the Father. "Greater" refers to the Son's origination while always being equal, or identical, in essence with the Father. He receives life eternally. But as the Incarnate Son the terms he uses that indicate any form of inability or obedience refer to the Father's sovereign will in relation to the Son in their mutual work to offer redemption to the world.

Eternality of the divine persons is underscored as beyond our concept of time. In that essence, "was" begotten is the same as "is" begotten eternally, for generation is not a temporal distinction. Begotten is the divine way of being.[136] Even human generation is a mystery. The "how" of begottenness is beyond our ken. Christian faith affirms that the Father and Son are not of different natures or essences. The Son is not God in some ambiguous sense; thus, generation is an essence issue, not an accidence.[137]

---

132. Hardy, *Christology*, 191.

133. Hardy, *Christology*, 195.

134. Hardy, *Christology*, 164.

135. Hardy, *Christology*, 170, 173.

136. Hardy, *Christology*, 165.

137. *Accidence* is a philosophical conception that refers to all qualities of an essence that do not directly equate with the essence itself. A man may be black or white (accidence) but both are still essentially men (Hardy, *Christology*, 167).

In sum, Gregory states that to understand Scripture we must have a Trinity. There must be a Creator apart from time and space for Jesus to be truly God. *Homoousion* is a statement regarding the identity of nature and the "names" Father and Son indicate eternal relations.[138] The affirmation of a unity of essence is immediately qualified by the personal reality that everything else is a distinction within that eternal unity.[139] Essence does not admit a fundamental superiority within itself. We are presented with the Absolute Father and the Absolute Son. This means they are not mere relations but eternal persons.[140]

It is here that we find the clearest description of union of natures in Christ by Nazianzus. In the incarnation, man became God because that being was united to God. He did not become two but one person. The higher and the lower nature were unified. The distinctiveness of the begottenness and virgin-born Jesus and the Son of the Father is that both are of God.[141]

Gregory does use the term "mingled" natures, which proved to be an unfortunate analogy in the history of Christology wherever it appeared.[142] Gregory affirms that in the life of Jesus we find the joining of the names "God" and "Father" at a human level, and no one else claims or can share in the divine essence in the way that Jesus does.[143] If he is not the eternal Son, Jesus becomes an "equivocal and intruded god."[144]

When Gregory refers to the Holy Spirit in *Oration Five,* he goes farther than anyone before him to state without qualification that he is God.[145] The Christological implications in relation to the deity

---

138. Hardy, *Christology*, 171. Gregory includes an encyclopedic list of biblical terms for Christ's co-equality as well as those that pertain to his distinction from the Father (172–73).

139. Hardy, *Christology*, 169.

140. Hardy, *Christology*, 162–63.

141. Hardy, *Christology*, 174.

142. Hardy, *Christology*, 178.

143. Hardy, *Christology*, 182.

144. Hardy, *Christology*, 173.

145. Hardy, *Christology*, 199.

of the Spirit become clear. Orthodoxy must be vigilant in its anti-Sabellian (the confusion of the divine persons) and in its anti-Arian (the division of the natures of the persons) commitments. The derivation of the Son from the essence of the Father eternally has comparative essential implications for the Spirit. There is, Gregory explores, a possible "mean" between the unbegotten and the begotten. Procession is equal in meaning to both unbegotten and begotten.[146] The argumentation indirectly applies to both the Son and the Spirit. Divine nature is perfect, and that which relates to it in the unique way that the Son and Spirit do must be co-equal.[147] Both persons are self-existent and neither "accidents" to the divine nature (*ousia*) nor mere activities of God but divine actors.[148] Christian thinking moves where no pagan philosophy could in that "essence" could admit consubstantiality.[149] There is no need to return to a pagan physicality or delimitation of the consubstantial Trinity by advocating a "two sons" idea to make Scripture fit our perceptions. The Spirit and the Son are equal yet distinct.[150]

Gregory's systematic explanation of the nature of the Son formed the context for the deepest and clearest rendition of the incorporated wisdom of the church for four centuries. Like Origen, the foundation he laid not only dealt with the destructive nature of heresies like Apollinarianism but more positively paved the way to speak of Christ with more thorough theological comprehension than had been advanced before.

A systematic Christology attempts to draw together the major strands of exegesis of the revelation of God over the centuries, which have become the central life-giving and life-changing ideas that have arisen in "all places, everywhere and at all times." The preceding discussion of Gregory of Nazianzus is an example of a

---

146. Hardy, *Christology*, 198.
147. Hardy, *Christology*, 196.
148. Hardy, *Christology*, 197.
149. Hardy, *Christology*, 204.
150. Hardy, *Christology*, 197–98.

HOLY LOVE: A WESLEYAN THEOLOGY

pivotal point in Christian theology. We have seen the relationship between the maturing of Trinitarian thought and its gifts to the Christological framework of the early church. Nicaea was a foundation for the unequivocal theological commitment to the Son being of the same essence as the Father (*homoousion to patri*).

The battles over nuances may seem at first to be debates over nonsensical issues, but the Christian faith has always found that reserve on the details results in a diminishment of personhood. When divine persons are obscured, the nature of reality is threatened. When human personhood is disconnected from the essence of God's own personal life, then humanity loses its very meaning. The Cappadocians were a generation of theologians between Nicaea and Chalcedon who incorporated the best of the preceding Christological discussions and envisioned deeper thinking about the ontological substratum of a full salvation. In part eight, *Soteriology*, in volume four of this series, we will see more of the fruit of this remarkable period of thinking on the person of Jesus Christ.[151]

Gregory of Nyssa (Word/Flesh) also took great care to connect Trinitarian and Christological issues. His methodology is exemplified in *On Not Three Gods*. Like others who stood within the protection of the Holy Spirit's relation to ideas, in time he viewed all of his work as an attempt to guard the tradition. He knew what could result from heretical leanings. With the balance of humility and creativity, he affirmed the incomprehensible nature of God, the unchangeable faith received from his predecessors.[152]

---

151. Nazianzus was most helpful in his preaching at the Church of the Anastasis in Constantinople from which the *Orations* came and, in his writings, as seen above, which were deeply influential at the AD 381 affirmation of Nicaea. Nyssa was a strong voice at the same Niceno-Constantinopolitan Council. He continued to confront Arians, like Eunomius, the Apollinarians as Nazianzus did, and the resurgence of tritheistic ruminations led by Abladius to whom *On Not Three Gods* is addressed. His *Cathechetical Orations* like his predecessor are a goldmine of Eastern apophaticism, mysticism, Christian Neo-platonic philosophy, and practical faith based upon a deep Trinitarian orthodoxy.

152. Gregory, *On Not Three Gods* in Hardy, *Christology*, 257, 264. See also *NPNF2* 5:331–36.

Gregory led the discussion into its most difficult arena, the definition of nature (*ousia*). What the church means when it says "one Lord" and names Jesus as Lord is altogether important. If only viewed as a substance, in the typical sense, then the three who are called Lord in Scripture leave us with numeric essence and thus, tritheism. But Gregory makes the crucial distinction of all Christian theology. What is common to all misunderstandings about the person of Jesus is to equate person and nature; Gregory advocates a clear distinction between person and nature. A man is not the same as mankind. One can be distinguished from the common nature and be both unique while at the same time sharing with others a general nature. Christians are not pagan or polytheist. The Godhead refers to a common nature or "operation."[153] There are not three different realities in God because "nature" is not a plural term. To advocate a division in the nature of God is to posit something Scripture never affirms.

What the church has seen, Gregory affirms. In the discussion of triune action, different actions "require" individuated persons, but that does not necessitate a division in who God is. Gregory confirms Nicene insight in confrontation with any misunderstanding of divine nature. What revelation shows is a co-operative operation in concert, not a separate action of the Son but three who give life, three in one being "independent of time" who act as one.[154]

Philosophy is normally incapable of distinguishing modes from substances, but the paradigm offered by Gregory carries the discussion into the radical place of a more comprehensive view of substance or essence as personal. As Nazianzus did, he emphasized the Father as "Cause." The eternal self-giving of the Father, which is received by the Son, is an expression of different persons in relation.

---

153. Hardy, *Christology*, 261–65. In essence, Nyssa summarizes the main points he makes on the ineffable eternal generation of the Son, which he labors consistently on in his voluminous engagement with Eunomius. The argument is the same, although the ubiquity of Nyssa's comprehension on the matter is nothing short of astounding (*NPNF2* 5:33–314).

154. Hardy, *Christology*, 264

The Only-begotten or the Cause are not equal to nature. Within the divine nature generation is a "mode of existence."[155]

The basic divine nature is absolute goodness. This is a consistent theme in the Cappadocians in general and seen clearly in Nyssa's *Cathechetical Oration*.[156] The attributes revealed from the unity of God's nature are expressed in wisdom, power, and justice. That divine goodness is distinguished by *hypostaseis* (persons).[157] The self-giving of God in the eternal Son is missed by both Judaism and Greek philosophy. Thus, the goodness of the triune life is not expressed in naked power or will in order to save us. The "weakness" of the incarnation was not a Docetic divine "deceit" but the showing of the real and good nature of a self-dispensing triune Creator.[158]

God the Son assumed our nature. But Gregory goes farther. He says that the Son "was transfused throughout our nature in order that our nature might by this transfusion of the Divine become itself divine."[159] Here we find soteriology inseparable from the being of the Son of the Father. He was born in our nature not merely to pronounce judgment on sin and a redemption from it but also to produce an intimate and mutual union between himself and his creatures. His cleansing power enters all of that nature touched by sin. It is not humanity that is alien to God, only evil is, and in redeeming goodness, Jesus entered our state.

In graphic terms, Gregory states the "from the lump of our humanity came the manhood which received the Divine."[160] Reflecting his Alexandrian Word/Flesh Christology but also advocating

---

155. Hardy, *Christology*, 268.

156. Different names have been given to this Bishop's theological training text. *Address on Religious Instruction* or *The Great Catechism* are other ways the material is entitled. See the theme of divine goodness in *NPNF2* 5:474–509; "abounding goodness" (489), "before all things the indications of his goodness" (491).

157. See an immediate example in the transition of the Prologue to the *Catechism* and chapter one in *NPNF2* 5:474.

158. See a good translation of the *Catechism* in Hardy, *Christology*, 294, 303.

159. *NPNF2* 5:495.

160. Hardy, *Christology*, 310

a real unity of natures, Gregory emphasizes a whole life that was the divine nature in our nature. Jesus unites all things divine and human. His birth, life, death, and resurrection unite the human with the needed nature of salvation, divinity. Triune grace is only saving grace. And it is that grace found in Christ that can bring non-being to being saved. Without the divine-human Son of God, all we have is our nature, which is helpless in and of itself.[161] Jesus Christ alone can bring a separation from evil and a changed nature.

In the discussion of the natures of Christ, the East, as seen in both Nazianzus and Gregory of Nyssa, tends to hold the natures apart because of the implication of the divine nature suffering in the God-Man. Essence (*ousia*) must always be handled carefully. It must never be physicalized but treated as a necessary discussion couched in mystery. Always suspect as both unbiblical and philosophical, it remained the only concept whereby the two crucial natures of the Savior could be explored. The difficulty present in its usage was compounded by the differences of meaning and interpretation of the terms in both Latin, *substantia,* and Greek, *ousia.* Whatever could be said about Jesus had to be distinguished from a mere notion of abstract being. The Alexandrian school at its best was courageous enough to wade into the correction of former usages of the terminology and to connect Scripture with ideas that could protect against all forms of simplified theology, which ended up destroying the gospel.

ANTIOCHENE CHRISTOLOGY PRIOR TO CHALCEDON

Theodore (Word/Man) reacted to the Cappadocian/Alexandrian emphasis on Word/Flesh. In an attempt to correct what he saw as Apollinarian strands of the Greek Christian, he (and his pre-

---

161. Hardy, *Christology,* 309, 322–23.

vious colleague, Diodore) demanded a closer look be taken to the actual life of Jesus. He felt Alexandria limited the historical Jesus by looking at the reasons for hunger, thirst, and infirmities in the son of Mary. He felt that Diodore's idea of "two sons," one of God and one of David, was wrong-headed. To advocate a distinction of natures and affirm a unity at the same time, he chose the word "indwelling." The *Logos*, he felt, did not invade the human Jesus but "conjoined" his nature with Jesus. His defense of the humanity of Christ has been viewed as a form of "proto-Nestorianism."[162] But in recent scholarship that charge has been mollified. Nevertheless, by focusing too much attention on the humanity of Jesus by using "conjunction" terminology, he comes near a form of adoptionism. Maintaining a strong distinction between the Word and the man may have sounded more historically acceptable, but the actual real union of the Word enfleshed is muted, and an unacceptable form of imbalance is reasserted at a time when both natures were being discussed in equal measure by those who knew the problems of any over-weighting in either the divine or human direction.

THE CHRISTOLOGICAL
SETTLEMENT AT CHALCEDON

Nestorius (Word/Man) was another of the Antiochene camp who went beyond either Diodore or Theodore. It was his Christology that brought the Word/Flesh and the Word/Man Christologies to a critical mass. His Antiochene focus on the distinction of natures without nuance led to a lessening of the deity of Christ. This garnered him the accusation that he was advocating "two Sons," and others viewed him as a Samostene adoptionist. Cyril of Alexandria called Nestorius a heretic who advocated two persons in one body. The issue came back to the rigid interpretation of *homoou-*

---

162. See the Fifth Ecumenical Council of Constantinople's (AD 553) statements regarding Theodore.

sion by Nestorius, the Patriarch of Constantinople. The two distinct natures and the earthly life of Christ were of crucial importance to him. He could not accept the "hypostatic union" advocated by Cyril and others of the Alexandrian school because he felt that it confused the natures. He chose "conjunction" as a better term than "union," and he made Jesus not the eternal Word but the *prosopon* of the union. When it came to the virgin birth, Nestorius would claim that Mary was the "Christ-bearer" (*christotokos*) and not the orthodox rendering, *theotokos*, or "God-bearer." Thus, Jesus Christ was a man indwelt by God. He believed a unity of wills was much more adequate than a unity of essence when talking about the Father's relationship to Jesus Christ.

Cyril of Alexandria (Word/Flesh) responded vehemently to what he understood Nestorius to be advocating. Besides undermining redemption, he rejected the patriarch's Christology as a division of the Incarnate God. For this Word/Flesh theologian the *Logos* was always the same person both before and after the incarnation. The one who had existed in eternity outside flesh had now become embodied. There was only one Christ, only one Son. The *Logos* united his *prosopon* with the *prosopon* of Jesus in a hypostatic union. This he strongly proposed against his view of Nestorius, who had merely "put on one nature like a garment."[163]

COUNCIL OF EPHESUS (AD 431)

The immediate result of Cyril's interpretation was the condemnation of Nestorius' view—even though recent scholarship of the *Book (or Bazaar) of Heracleides* has questioned whether Cyril had accurately read Nestorius' views—at the Council of Ephesus in AD 431. Cyril's assessment and response to the ideas coming from the north are found in the *Second Letter to Nestorius*, which was confirmed by that council as the authoritative reading of the

---

163. Cyril in Norris, *Christological Controversy*, 128.

Antiochene's theology. This council was insufficient to quell the differences of perspective. A more ecumenical and thorough appropriation was necessary, especially with the arrival of one more heretical perspective on the person of Christ.

Eutyches (Word/Flesh), the Bishop of Rome, proposed the exact opposite of the Nestorian camp. He opposed the Word/Man school so much that he allowed the humanity to be thoroughly swallowed up in the divine. Rather than two persons he conflated the natures into one person. Attempting to sidestep the difficulty of nature-person (*substantia-prosopon*) deliberation, he stated that Jesus was a mixture of both human and divine components; thus, he was in reality a *tertium quid* (a third thing), neither fully God nor fully man in that both natures had changed into one theanthropic collusion. This is yet again another form of Docetism fed by a philosophical dualism that resulted in a lunatic monophysitism.

Leo I is another Western theologian who, like his forebear Tertullian, actually added something to a predominantly Eastern affair with regard to the person of Christ. Although he was not an original thinker, he was an encyclopedic scribe who accessed and collated the best of the Christological thought, both East and West, since Nicaea. He included the insights that Tertullian had offered early in the third century regarding *prosopon, persona,* and *substantia.* In what became known as Leo's *Tome,* he affirmed that the incarnate Christ and the divine Word were the identical person, that the natures existed in Christ without being altered in any way, and that they worked as distinct natures in perfect concert with one another. He also affirmed what had been more Alexandrian than Antiochene concerning the communication of the idioms (*communication idiomatum*). This was a doctrine that would see further clarification, but it pertained to the distinctive yet mutually permeative qualities of the natures in Christ so that there was no split in his personality or division of sectors of characteristics in his person.

He was always one person with two perfect natures and their inter-relationship did not alter either in any way.

COUNCIL OF CHALCEDON (AD 451)

With Leo's *Tome*, whose author had died in AD 449, as resource material and over a century of debate and exclusion, excommunication, and clarification, the ecumenical Council of Chalcedon was to become one of the most formative meetings in the history of theology. Both the unity and the duality of the natures of the God-Man, the incarnate lord and Savior Jesus Christ were affirmed. In essence, it was a middle-ground approach in its refusal of the excesses that had preceded its deliberations. It was a unique mixture of the insights worked on incessantly by Alexandrian, Antiochene, and even a bit of Roman and Carthaginian (Western) notions. It reaffirmed the full divinity of the Incarnate Christ that had been evoked at Nicaea (AD 325). It clearly drew the lines of demarcation between orthodox Christology and all the major heresies that had arisen before its statements regarding Christ.

The importance of Chalcedon cannot be overestimated. It was the summation of over four hundred years of intense theology centering on the person of Jesus. It was strongly opposed then and has been in modernity as well because all opponents know the power latent in its proclamations if believed. We also see a new perspective on the past. It took some time for Christians to be able to look to their forebears as guides for the future. At Chalcedon there was a consistent reference to past deliberations and the acceptance of the fought-for ideas from both Eastern and Western mindsets. Some have critiqued its pronouncements as insufficient, as primarily negative, or as not as constructive as needed. But since Nicaea and now for fifteen hundred years, no single statement has been as foundational for orthodox theology and primarily Christology.

While belief in a creed is not necessary for salvation, it is readily apparent to anyone who holds to the worldview of a self-revealing God though Israel and ultimately in Jesus that the entire tenor of revelation rings resonantly with the truths that the Chalcedonian summarizes. It affirms without reservation that Jesus Christ is in himself the revelation of ultimate reality. It points to the central framework on true being; that is, the Father and the Son and the Holy Spirit in co-equal and majestic love. That being is not abstract or dispassionate but is revealed to us in the flesh by one person of that glorious life. He who has come has not condescended out of a form of disdain to our humanness but has brought our humanity into himself through one physical body and that of a virgin from Judea. He is of one essence with God and with us.

The text of the Chalcedonian Creed ought to be accessible to any Christian:

> We, then, following the holy fathers, all with one consent
> teach men to confess one and the same Son, our Lord
> Jesus Christ, the same perfect in Godhead and also per-
> fect in manhood; truly God and truly man, of a rational
> soul and body; coessential with the Father according to
> the Godhead, and consubstantial with us according to the
> manhood; in all things like unto us, without sin; begotten
> before all ages of the Father according to the Godhead, and
> in these latter days, for us and for our salvation, born of the
> Virgin Mary, the mother of God, according to the man-
> hood; one and the same Christ, Son, Lord, Only-begotten,
> to be acknowledged in two natures, without confusion,
> without change, without division, without separation; the
> distinction of natures being by no means taken away by
> the union, but rather the property of each nature being
> preserved, and concurring in one person and one sub-
> sistence, not parted or divided into two persons, but one
> and the same Son, and only begotten, God the Word, the
> Lord Jesus Christ; as the prophets from the beginning
> have declared concerning Him, and the Lord Jesus Christ
> Himself has taught us, and the creed of the holy fathers has
> handed down to us.

Each of its terms is carefully chosen to both defend the faith and offer encouragement for more reflection on the mystery of Christ. As with all accepted creeds, Nicene orthodoxy is presumed before any other statements are made. "Following the holy fathers" is a testimony to the Holy Spirit's working in and through the church in time to assure that what we believe is true truth and living reality.

"One and the same" or "identical" Son is an immediate statement on the full undiluted personhood of Jesus. He is forever the Son of God who forever will be the son of Mary, and the two natures are united in him personally and dynamically. More than a prophet or a mere man as Ebionism had claimed, he is "the same Person who is perfect in Godhead." And he is a real, flesh and blood man who is God incarnate against all gnostic attempts to diminish his flesh. Since he is "truly God and truly man" it is important to reaffirm that he is "*homoousion*" (consubstantial, of the same essence) with the Father.

This allows no distinction between Jesus and the *Logos* as separate persons like the Monarchians inaccurately purported. His personhood is reaffirmed repeatedly, as eternal and divine and forever identical with the divine personhood of the Father. He was never simply a mode as Sabellianism stated. His co-eternality, "begotten before all ages" meant that he has always existed against the infamy of Arian distinction between the Absolute God and the *Logos*. He is truly, perfectly God. Against Apollinarius it stated the he was "truly man, of a reasonable soul." Jesus was completely human in every way, except that he did not sin. His mind is as human as ours. Nothing overwhelmed his ability to identify with every aspect of our humanness, individually and corporately.

Most unique in this creed was the section that spun out four negative adverbs. Each of them was carefully chosen to confront a heretical disposition that lay dangerously covered by verbiage but in the end denied both the Christ and his saving life.[164] Opposed to Nestorius' radical division between the natures, his dual natures were related "indivisibly, inseparably" and they are related in Christ in a perfect personal union. Rejecting Eutychian monophysitism, the creed used two more privative adverbs to declare that his divinity and humanity were in concert "inconfusedly, unchangeably," the "property of each nature being preserved." There was no loss in either nature whatsoever in the union.

This is, the church stated, what the all the prophets and the apostles proclaimed. God in his personal holy love gave himself in an act of self-donation that did not coerce any person to believe. He came and revealed the Father to us through an incarnate life filled with the Holy Spirit. Mutual dependence and love, which had existed forever, was now offered to humanity forever in the incarnation.

Chalcedon's strong distinction of natures in the real, vital, and personal union in the one person was the most profound gift to the church in its continued attempt to make Christ clear to the world but most of all understandable to the believers who up till that point did not have a consensual statement that covered all the salient issues pertaining to an orthodox reading of Scripture about the revelation of God in Christ. One person—true God, true man—*homoousion* was applied brilliantly in both directions. The being of Jesus Christ was of one substance with the Father and now without equivocation *homoousion* with human beings. His Lordship hung on that Christological compound.

Perhaps a concise overview of the four crucial councils of the early Christological discussions will help to situate the major points of discussion regarding the personhood of Jesus in response to its major antagonists:[165]

---

164. An excellent short translation and discussion of these adverbs can be found in Outler, *Christology*, 126. Also see Oden, *The Word of Life*, 186.

165. Paulos Mar Gregorios refers to Konidaris' suggestion that of the seven ecumenical creeds, Nicaea and Constantinople I achieved the basic structure

COUNCIL OF	WHEN	DISCUSSION	ANTAGONIST
Nicaea	325	full divinity *homoousion*	Arius
Constantinople	381	full humanity	Apollinarius
Ephesus	431	natures not separated	Nestorius
Chalcedon	451	natures not merged	Eutyches

The importance of the formula must be seen in the brilliance of the distinction between nature and person. When faced with describing ultimate reality, a Christocentric perspective takes a different tack than any other worldview. What is real is not an independent principle, being—the nature of what truly is—in and of itself. The only being for one who has believed in Jesus Christ is a personal reality. God is love and that means that holiness and love define every aspect of the Christian belief about being. All that is draws its life from that triune reality. All of the centuries of debate and exile and poring over Scripture resulted in answering a crucial question, "Who is God?" The person of Jesus Christ was the answer from which every other divine person and human person derives their definition. God is self-explanatory, but he is also self-revealing, and that is why Chalcedon is so crucial. We have seen God in the face of Jesus Christ. We are not dealing with eternal matter, rational principles, or esoteric substances; we are met by Love enfleshed, enmanned, inhominated, humanized by his own perfect self-giving. His person is not reducible to a substratum of divine nature. His nature is his sonship in the Father by the Spirit. He has eternally given himself to the other persons of the Trinity, and now for us, and for our salvation he has given us himself.

Chalcedon was not a meaningless foray into abstractions; it was the clearing out of all that threatened a fully-revealed enlight-

---

of Trinitarian and Christological framework. The five succeeding councils: Ephesus, Chalcedon, Constantinople II, Constantinople III, and Nicaea II took the first two symbols as their benchmark. The "positive achievement" of the first two were then elucidated where necessary by the following five. See Gregorios, "Ecclesiological Issues," 35.

HOLY LOVE: A WESLEYAN THEOLOGY

enment of God's own nature.[166] Here we see Christology as it was meant to be: involved in divine self-dispensing and inextricably conjoined in humanity's ultimate purpose—to become like God. That is where heresy is first exposed. Divinity is inexplicable without soteriology. Salvation is only possible through real self-bestowal and mutual real receptivity. Any diminishment of either nature in Jesus has to be rejected. Otherwise, we are left with just another myth, and human life is a hellish charade. Jesus reveals who God is (*ousia* or *natura*), what God is (*prosopa* or *personae*), and that one is three, whose mission is self-giving love.

Chalcedon goes far enough for us to begin to think about the very essence of all true personhood. To be is to give and receive. To have a relationship is foundational to all true Christianity because it is the Christian God. No ancient or modern philosophy or religion that has not been touched by Chalcedon can offer that radical insight into reality. In the consubstantial God-Man, eternity and history conjoin, and in that union, an exchange takes place that offers holy love and loving holiness.

From Chalcedon on all thought about God and humanity, grace and salvation, ecclesiology and ethics is able to distinguish between the unique freedom of personhood and its profound intimacy with nature without conflating the two. The "substance" that is God is personal, and thus the "substance" of humanity is only a true image of God when full personhood is restored. Chalcedon's Creator is the only redeemer, and he is the restorer of full humanity.

As the Cappadocians had said before Chalcedon, and what others in their train would remind the church of repeatedly, is affirmed in the phrases of the creed. There is no being that is not "*ek-static,*" or other-oriented. Jesus is both the divine Son in his

---

166. For recent reflections on the implications of the Christology of Nicaea and Chalcedon both implicitly and explicitly, see Kinlaw, *Let's Start with Jesus*; Oden, *The Living God, The Word of Life*; Torrance, *The Incarnation: Ecumenical Studies in the Nicene-Constantinopolitan Creed A.D. 381* and *Incarnation: The Person and Life of Christ*; Galot, *Who Is Christ?* and *The Person of Christ: A Theological Insight*.

being and fully human in his being. There is no anterior essence that he draws his life from. He is always completely the Word, but he does not take over a body in some monophysitic manner. The human nature is completely without mixture or confusion with the divine. This symbol discounts any form of spiritual being apart from a full humanity. Christ was not an elite human. He became one with us perfectly. His personal essence is not reduced to mere existence. It is in his mutual self-giving that he is God and man and the one in whom the two natures meet so that the triune persons and human persons can mutually participate in love. What Christology in the Chalcedonian vein offers is a Christocentric definition of all that is. Paul attempts to say it when he states, "in him all things exist." It is by the person and through the person and for the person that all things consist and subsist.

It is here that the confusions between former usages of *hypostasis* and *ousia* (Greek terms) and their counterparts *persona* and *substantia* are corrected and both East and West, for the most part, find agreement so as to deal with the mutual suspicions of modalism or tritheism. *Homoousion* and *consubstantia* are found to state the same mysterious revelation of triune personhood in which the Son dwells eternally and becomes man to invite humanity in its full essence into his co-inherent life with the Father and the Spirit.[167] The character proper to the divine and human nature was secured by the real, dynamic, personal union in the one person (Latin, *prosopon*; Greek, *hypostasis*) of the Son. The place of the concept of "person" was yet to be seen for its importance. The East gave it a relational basis from the very beginning of Trinitarian and Christological discussion. The West, it will be seen, took more of a rational

---

167. Every creed that was accepted by the general church builds upon previous articulations. At the Council of Alexandria (AD 362), *hypostases* and *homoousion* had been affirmed and distinguished from each other in a manner that allowed Chalcedon to further explore the implications of that distinction in Christ's human nature in relation to us. The *Quicunque Creed* (AD 440) also spelled out some of the nuances that Chalcedon affirmed and clarified.

orientation, and the difference caused remarkably distinctive tacks on Christ, anthropology, and soteriology.

In the modern and post-modern theological world, there are recurrent typical reservations about Chalcedon, or all major creeds for that matter. The normal trajectory of the arguments against creedal formulation is that they instantiate a static metaphysics, are attempts to objectify God and thus, diminish encounter, and most often that they do us the disservice of "hellenizing" biblical language. It is claimed that they spoil the simple gospel that one can find by a single reading of the New Testament.

Nothing could be farther from the truth. Creeds are only ever witnesses to what has been received from the apostles, who were themselves witnesses to the resurrection. The creeds are human reflections upon the kerygma and were accepted as valid because they were in alignment with scriptural revelation.[168]

The church's response has been that merely because terminology is extra-biblical, it is not necessarily un-biblical. The church accepted the Nicean Creed as the correct interpretation of New Testament scriptures. The church, through the Nicean Creed, corrected the influence of Hellenistic philosophy on biblical theology.

The Nicean Creed centers on who Jesus was and is—the eternal Second Person of the Trinity, who became incarnate to be our savior and redeemer. Those who challenge the veracity of the creeds need to offer something in their stead. A list of proof-texts will soon find another contradictory list, and both will end up having to explain the reason for the choices. That very move is theologizing, and the statements made are in essence a creed. What may sound orthodox when pushed will soon have to either align itself with the essence of Chalcedon or it will take on the shading of the heresies that it precluded.

---

168. Outler refers to creedal orthodoxy as "valid coordinate with the history and *kerygma* of Scripture" (*Christology*, 128).

The present theological milieu has been riddled with modernistic rationalism and post-modern nihilism. So, the creeds are often set aside as dusty old trophies. The reservations of the enlightenment were repristinated in modernity when the brilliantly wrong Schleiermacher claimed that the two natures of Christ were incoherent. Schleiermacher was sharply critical of the Chalcedon formula. He claimed that the two natures cannot be conjoined. He argued that it was a vacuous attempt at ontology that would offend the modern mind. He claimed it would make Christ a different kind of being, a monstrosity if you will. But what he missed was the massive delineation of Chalcedon that set it apart from the misunderstandings regarding Christ's natures and person. Schleiermacher could only envisage the concept of nature as a fixed universal essence, a concrete entity, which is a non-Chalcedonian view of the divine nature. The two natures, he said, cannot fit together. They are abstractions as divorced from each other as reality and unreality might be seen in contrast. Chalcedon had responded to this much earlier. Essence does allow differentiation. In fact, essence is differentiated. The essence of God is three distinct and co-inherent persons. God can ordain the union of two different essences without either one being defaced. Because both natures are defined most completely in their receptivity and self-giving, it is not only possible that they co-exist but that to explain the claims of Jesus, they must. As stated above, the radical importance of a distinction between person and nature is necessary to respond to all wrong views of nature. Philosophy demands a fixed universal essence, but Jesus of Nazareth embodies two natures.

Because so few today are willing to take the thought time necessary to delve into ontological issues, more common is the criticism of Chalcedon as being a part of a dead tradition that is obtuse and impersonal and thus does not minister to anyone. The second criticism began with Albrect Ritschl, the German reductionist, and also Rudolph Bultmann. They both claimed that Nicaea and Chalcedon represented an abstract tradition that is nonpastoral and, therefore, unusable. It is not focused on what Ritschl called value judgments. This is a very modern approach again, the approach that says truth is only truth if it has a value that can be described as true or good from a ethical perspective.

An immediate response to this reserve is that "value-judgments" presuppose a certain status or being of entity to that which they ascribe value. If there is no real truth, then it is no use talking about truth. What is claimed about Christ only has value if his being has value. So, the critics of the creeds themselves presuppose something ontological, something about the status or being of the entity, of course, in this case, Christ, to whom they ascribe value. Chalcedon mutes their arguments by placing all ethics and encounters in the very nature of the Godhead before, during, and after the incarnation. He is who he said he is. He is who the New Testament says he is. Otherwise, all Christian values are simply idols we have made to ourselves.

Another common attack is that the creeds are an historical attempt to produce something that is really not in the text of Scripture. These critics state that the church advocated a "high" Christology when really all the Gospels did was to show us a deeply spirit-filled sage or miracle worker. By "high" what is normally meant is that the "supernaturalness" of the incarnation is imposed from without the Jesus event. A false ceiling of modern reductionism is imposed to dictate what cannot be present in certain favored texts. This false dichotomy, between "high" and "low," has become so common that we tend to accept it without reflection. But the highest Christology already exists in the New Testament.[169] Chalcedon, and the other ecumenical councils, affirmed that the ontological statements about the being of Jesus as the divine pre-existent Son of God were present early in the formulation of the canon. Chalcedon is only an explanation, an amplification of what is already there

169. Moule, *The Origins of Christology*, 136–37.

in the New Testament. Bultmann and his disciples, of course, would excise this material from the New Testament in the interest of his demythologizing.

A third criticism says that the tradition instituted by the creeds is philosophized dogma. This was the consistent refrain from Adolph Harnack.[170] He claimed that all writings like Chalcedon's was an obfuscation of the gospel. Like Bultmann after him, they claimed there was a kernel of ethical truth that could be mined from the corrupted theological trappings of the New Testament writing communities.

What Nicaea and Chalcedon do is exactly the opposite of the "de-hellenizers." Rather than the church simply imbibing the philosophical milieu, it was actually militantly confronting the surrounding culture in which theology grew. It did borrow and adopt terms to use in Christian discourse. *Homoousion* and *ousia* were taken and applied to the exegetical discussions of the church. The church gave these terms new meanings and often meanings that were directly opposite from the original usage in light of the reality of God becoming a man. Instead of being Hellenized, the gospel actually confronted Greek thought.

Since the beginning of Christian thought there has been a careful borrowing. The "plundering of the Egyptians" produced some of Christianity's most brilliant insights. But beyond the terminological issues, it is intriguing to note what gets lost in the "de-hellenizers." The very things that tradition warned against happens in every critique who claims to desire to get back behind Chalcedon to a pristine gospel. The first thing lost is a straightforward reading of Scripture. With the unbridled reductionism applied to prophecy about Jesus, the claims in the Gospels by him and others, and the deepening Christology of the epistles, it is clear that one thing is not allowed: a divine Son who becomes the son of Mary. De-hellenizers

---

170. Harnack called Chalcedon a "synod of robbers and traitors"—he was an adoptionist.

HOLY LOVE: A WESLEYAN THEOLOGY

have one major agenda, and that is to deny that the Messiah has come in the person of Jesus of Nazareth.

Second, these liberalizing tendencies leave us with nothing. If there is no incarnation, no Trinity, no blood atonement and, therefore, no salvation, then what is the reason for any Christology? These claims to undo philosophy's grasp on truth are regressive, not progressive. In comparison to the paradigm shift that occurred at Nicaea, Chalcedon was the dawning of a new era. It established a radical new trajectory founded on the personhood of Jesus that no previous ontological framework could support. The major councils were not perfect definitions. Mystery cannot be reduced to terms. But the shift in theological perspective had taken place. At Nicaea the shift had moved from a focus on what God has done for us in Christ to the nature of the one who was equal to the Father. Theology *ad nos* (for us) moved to a discussion of God *in se* (in himself). At Chalcedon the shift from "what is it" (nature) that saves to "who is it" (person) that saves. The actual personhood of the Savior, in both divinity and humanity, is stated clearly and concisely. It is not speculative as the critics claim. By reading the creed one will see immediately that it is not concerned with defining everything, or explaining. It did not attempt to be exhaustive. It did claim to offer a reasonable explanation of Jesus Christ in two fundamental realities: his person and his natures. It is an invitation to continue to explore the incarnation. The critics of tradition often miss the sense of mystery, the humble approach to Scripture, and the rigorous desire to offer no empty propositions but rather pointers to ultimate reality. Notice also that Nicaea and Chalcedon replace the *Logos* concept with the Son. They do not attempt to define the *Logos* but use instead the Father/Son model, which is primarily a biblical relational category, not a philosophical one. Thus, the councils were deliberately trying to avoid being too philosophical on every point.

The creeds give to us the freedom to move beyond a functional Christology to a fuller orbed ontology that, in the end, opens up every other aspect of Christian thought. We see that piety is not enough to clearly present Jesus in the church or the world. There are important questions that may not be exhausted but can be cogently approached. Chalcedon did not convince everyone even in its own day. The Monophysites (those who believed in only one nature) and then the Monothelites (those who believed in only one will, the divine will) both disagreed with its premises. But it did produce a grand framework of the Christian belief that there is no salvation without the Trinity and the incarnation.

CHAPTER FIVE

Other Christological Nexus Points in History

THE CHALCEDONIAN DEFINITION HAD set the parameters for the most complete stance on the consubstantiality of the Son of God and Son of Man, the Lord Jesus Christ. Though all the battles were not over, it can be said that the fundamental conflict had produced a victory that has offered freedom to successive generations of Christians.[1]

The Monophysites, primarily from North Africa, could not accept the redefinition of *phusis* (nature) that the councils had hammered out.[2] It was suggested Chalcedon be put aside and the church return simply to Nicaea. Divinity is somehow easier to deal with than the humanity of Christ. They could not comprehend "nature" meaning anything other than a particular entity. That would mean then that there were always two in number in Christ thus dividing the person. So, the Monophysites returned to a unity of nature in which the divine was secured as being the motivating principle of the life of Jesus.[3] Alexandrian thought always leaves an indel-

---

1. Fries and Nersoyan, *Christ in East and West*.

2. Intuiting a political move over a theological one, Dioscorus of Alexandrian led the rejection of the Chalcedonian use of *phusis*. Political intrigue never is very far from theological discussion, which sometimes makes it hard to discern what is of the Holy Spirit and what is not. Again, the best response is the belief that what is true is what is believed by all, in all times, in all places.

3. An extreme form of this predilection to the divine came from Julian of Halicarnassus who advocated *aphthartodocetism* (*aphtharto*, impassible), which stated that when the Word took on a human body, its nature was incorruptible.

ible neoplatonic impression. This perspective was challenged and met although agreement could not be found in Constantinople II (AD 553). The Monophysites position was never a heretical one, but it did cause a split in the church, which is still not healed.

The Monothelites (one-will) were another group that was unable to see the two natures in complete union. This time it was not the actual nature of the human Christ but his will that was subordinated to the divine *Logos*. Though, as with the monophysites, there seems to be no overt attempt to diminish the full humanity of Christ at the level of his being, it nevertheless came across to the typical onlooker that that was exactly the result. The Incarnate One had a will that was absorbed by the Almighty God in some way. Constantinople III (AD 680/681) was called to respond and affirmed not only two natures in Christ but two wills that were co-inherently related without damaging the integrity of either.[4] The concern was that the "one-will" camp was really a return to Apollinarian perspectives. The methodology of this last critical council regarding the person of Jesus shows the cumulative effect of the conciliar agreements since Nicaea in AD 325. Now three and a half centuries later, the church is not creating new thought but clarifying past pronouncements and applying that interpretation to "novel" ideas the theologians of Constantinople affirmed they were.

> Following the five holy and universal synods and the holy and accepted fathers, and defining in unison, *it professes*

This was felt to protect the divinity of the Word from suffering, although they did say he could accept suffering and death by his own will. It was rejected because it was deemed to not affirm Christ's full consubstantiality with humanity.

4. The language is strong due to the concern that this schismatic proclivity might be allowed to go too far, so a portion of the correction at Constantinople reads that Honorius and others were sowing with novel speech among the orthodox people the heresy of a single will and a single principle of action in the two natures of the one member of the holy Trinity, Christ our true God, a heresy in harmony with the evil belief, ruinous to the mind, of the impious Apollinarius, Severus, and Themistius, and one intent on removing the perfection of the becoming man of the same one Lord Jesus Christ our God, through a certain guileful device, leading from there to the blasphemous conclusion that his rationally animate flesh is without a will and a principle of action.

our Lord Jesus Christ our true God, one of the holy Trinity, which is of one same being and is the source of life, to be perfect in divinity and perfect in humanity, the same truly God and truly man, of a rational soul and a body; consubstantial with the Father as regards his divinity, and the same consubstantial with us as regards his humanity, like us in all respects except for sin; begotten before the ages from the Father as regards his divinity, and in the last days the same for us and for our salvation from the holy Spirit and the virgin Mary, who is properly and truly called mother of God, as regards his humanity; one and the same Christ, Son, Lord, only-begotten, acknowledged in two natures *which undergo no confusion, no change, no separation, no division; at no point was the difference between the natures taken away through the union, but rather the property of both natures is preserved and comes together into* a single subsistent being; he is not parted or divided into two persons, but is one and the same only-begotten Son, Word of God, Lord Jesus Christ, just as the prophets taught from the beginning about him, and as Jesus the Christ himself instructed us, and as the creed of the holy fathers handed it down to us.[5]

The importance of the full humanity of Jesus after the incarnation was expressed here as his having "two natures (*naturas*) shining forth in his one subsistence (*subsistentia*)." Salvation was at stake if the "natural" wills and principles of action of the Word and Jesus of Nazareth were not in full, real, and proper communion. Nestorius' separation was rejected and so was the Eutychian blending of the natures. A personal salvation that met the needs of every human being must come from a human being who was truly connected to us in every way. Salvation never occurs by power alone, not even the holiest of powers.

Nicaea II in AD 787 was an intriguing implicational synod.[6] If the enfleshment of the Word of God was acceptable as a non-dualistic means of revelation, then the place of representational art, as a part

---

5. Constantinople III; *NPNF2* 14:345.
6. Outler calls this synod, Nicaea II, an "epilogue" to the six major councils beforehand (*Christology*, 197).

of the created order, was affirmed as a proper avenue of "imaging" the incarnate Christ. Some had called Christian art idolatry, and there is little doubt that it was abused as such, but this statement retained an openness to images that would assist the mind and heart to reflect on what God had done in Christ, in the flesh. Art held the possibility of being a continual reminder that the Word did become flesh, and that flesh was not ultra-mundane but was as vibrant as actual colors and forms that surrounded the worshiping community and assisted in pointing to Christ.

Nicaea II became a sort of ecclesiastical watershed in Christological discussion. The movement from one nature and one will to incarnation and its symbols marked the move into a growing understanding of the mysteries of Christ as his divine-human nature came to be seen in every facet of life. The full text of any of the councils normally make the modern Evangelical believer blanch. There is language that is extremely strong and tied into a Catholic (both Eastern and Western) conception of authority. The Protestant tradition would have no foundation for orthodox theology without the councils. One need only look at some of the recent proposals regarding Christ to see that a rejection of tradition has not given any fundamental progress on the person of Christ. Without the guiding and the guarding of the creeds, even the most committed Bible students will soon find themselves in the midst of interpretations that have been met by the church before and have needed to be excised.

The importance of Nicaea I to Nicaea II is seen in the broadening realization that the uniqueness of Christ was not an addendum to theology but the very center of all that is Christian. The Father, Son, and Holy Spirit are the only God there is, and at the center of that life is Jesus of Nazareth, the glorified eternal Son now enfleshed. Nothing makes ultimate sense without him. The church, in its best moments, has continued to bring the fullness of the God-Man into every aspect of human existence.[7]

The Western Church was deeply affected by Augustine's theology. It is intriguing that in all that the Bishop of Hippo stated about Christ, he wrote only one treatise given specifically to the issue of the natures in Christ. He is clear that the Word assumed a human nature, not a human person, as he states:

> Wherefore the Word of God, who is also the Son of God, co-eternal with the FATHER, the Power and the Wisdom of GOD, 1 Corinthians 1:24 mightily pervading and harmoniously ordering all things, from the highest limit of the intelligent to the lowest limit of the material creation, WISDOM 8:1 revealed and concealed, nowhere confined, nowhere divided, nowhere distended, but without dimensions, everywhere present in His entirety—this WORD OF GOD, I say, took to himself, in a manner entirely different from that in which he is present to other creatures, the SOUL and body of a MAN, and made, by the union of himself therewith, the one person JESUS CHRIST, Mediator between God and men.[8]

There are some scattered comments amidst his voluminous writings that did raise particular concerns, but by and large, there is an affirmation in Augustine of the hypostatic union while rejecting any form of mixing or diluting of the natures.[9]

---

7. One of the most insightful readings of the creeds in terms of the core of Christology as "ultimate reality has been produced in a monography by Tibor Horvath entitled *Jesus Christ as Ultimate Reality: A Contribution to the Hermeneutics of Conciliar Theology.* He has been able to discern, quite accurately, beneath the mountains of other important and no-so important issues the Christological center in each of the successive Western theological statements. An overview of this short piece shows the possibilities of reading Christian thought in the West since AD 681 as a continuing dialogue, whether cognizant of it or not, on the person of Christ. He has imposed a paradigm that reflects the divinity and humanity of Jesus in an apophatic way (uncircumscribability) and cataphatic (self-limiting revelation) in each.

8. Augustine, Letter 137 to Volusanius, *NPNF*1 1:477.

9. Hilary of Poitiers did offer some helpful counterbalance to the Augustinian framework. On Christology, see his *On the Trinity, NPNF*2 9:158–59, 168–70, 187–88. He does more with the nature of God as love and emphasizes the Father as love.

The medieval period, some say, was ushered in by the philosophy of Boethius (AD 480–524). It is here that some of the crucial distinctions of the Alexandrian and subsequently the Cappadocian school come into conflict with the West. Where the councils had set the parameters for the horizons of orthodox Christology, there still loomed the necessity of particular definitions. One that was to produce large differences was that of "person." Boethius cast a long shadow of influence over medieval theology. Some place him only second to Augustine.

As he confronted the Nestorian division of Christ's natures and the Eutychian mingling of the same, he realized that the central problems were, as we have seen, the meaning of the terms "nature" and "person." He created a definition of "person" that still predominates in the West. As an Aristotelian philosopher who was attempting to make sense of the conundrum of how a "person" could be comprised of more than a single "nature," he presented the statement that a person is "an individual substance of a rational nature."[10] To define personhood as a being possessing reason (noetic) turned the discussion away from relationality and placed it firmly in a rationalistic understanding. From a primarily orthodox perspective, Boethius' focus on the mind that individuates a person moved away from the Eastern insight that to be a person was not necessarily defined by mind or will but by love. That trajectory may be one of the turning points in all of the history of ideas. It was definitely a direction that the Western theological tradition has been dealing with ever since. More specifically, where Christology took center stage, this "psychological" or "noetic" orientation shifted the

---

10. Boethius, *Against Eutyches and Nestorius*, ch. 3. It should be remembered that the majority of Christological controversy was written in Greek. Boethius was the first to use Latin in this metaphysical vein. His determinations must be held in account as anyone looks into the medieval discussions. Along with another whose philosophy actually fed into Augustine's psychological analogies for the Trinity, Marius Victorinus, Boethius set the framework for most of the Latin translations and definitions of the Greek terms pertaining to major theological issues for the next millennium in the West.

discussion significantly. The difference can be distilled in the way the word "hypostasis" is used in its unique Greek usage by the Cappadocians and the use of the Latin "persona" by Boethius.[11]

To start a definition of person from a discrete or distinct substance in intellectual nature (*distinctum subsistens in natura intellectuali*) is to determine a person by a concrete being (*ens physicum concretum*).[12] The tendency to describe the person by their characteristics—mind, will, energy, and actions—quickly take center stage. While it is imperative in both Trinitology and Christology to ascertain that which distinguishes the person, it is also vitally important to define the person in the only way that ultimately gives personhood meaning in another. Characteristics, qualities, and traits are secondary elements to personhood when we speak of being personal. Distinctive personhood in the Medieval period starting with Boethius moved Western philosophy and theology, in the main, toward an independent and self-contained understanding of person. The insights of Nicaea and Chalcedon were not built upon. Individualism is a hallmark of the Western tradition. With all that has brought in terms of deeper implications for ethics and experience and self-understanding, it has likewise brought a loss of the gifts of a profoundly personal triune reality and more so a Christology that became a side issue to individual preoccupation and a deepening narcissism.

---

11. The distinction between *hypostasis* and *physis* (sometimes transliterated as *phusis*) did not originate with Chalcedon. Proclus of Constantinople offered the first reading of the terms as distinguishable. Nazianzus' "three *hypostaseis* and one *ousia*," since *ousia* and *phusis*, were seen as synonyms, which necessitated a similar distinction. The move from Trinitarian distinction to Christological became more clear in Gregory of Nyssa's discussion of *hypostasis* in Letter 38. Even though still leaving huge questions about how to specifically distinguish *hypostasis* from *phusis*, he did define *hypostasis* as an individual reality. And that, Grillmeier says, was the basic meaning at the Chalcedonian Council (*Christ in East and West*, 74–82). The phrase "one *hypostasis* in two *ousia*" made it imperative that *phusis* and *hypostasis* were undeniably defined as different concepts.

12. Gilson, *The Spirit of Mediaeval Philosophy*, 189–208.

There is no gauge sufficient to measure the influence of the Boethian-Thomistic lineage of person as a "subsistent relation." Thomas Aquinas, whose brilliance embodies the grandeur of the medieval synthesis, in his *Summa* and other major works, defines person in similar noetic fashion. A single rational nature: a person signifies a mode of substance; a person is a subsistent relation; all are very common definitions of person in the West as a result of the influence of Thomas. Positively, there is a need in theology and anthropology to delineate the incommunicable (unique) nature of every person. However, with that gift came another problem, which was how to describe love, a God who is love, and his desire to enable human persons to share in that love. Communion, participation, indwelling are the foundations wherein a discrete person finds the true self. No mind or will or person is ever complete in themselves.

There was another line of thought in the medieval period that countered the rational. Bonaventure, the Franciscans and Richard of St. Victor all offered a concept of being that was fundamentally relational. Richard was castigated by Thomas, in much the same way in which the Cappadocians were dispensed with by Augustine, for their forays into personhood as defined by relationships with other persons. We shall see the influence of both lines of thought in the rest of this theology. Very little that could be counted as progress of dogma transpired Christologically along either line.

Protestant Christology offered no remarkable addition to the Christological discussion. Mainly due to the inherent nominalism of William of Ockham and the rejection of Catholic scholasticism, the major Reformers rejected a form of speculative Christology. While the Chalcedonian definition continued to be affirmed in each of the magisterial Reformers, there were nuances that bear mentioning.

The debate between Luther and Zwingli on ubiquity of Christ based upon Luther's understanding of Cyril of Alexandria's gift long before concerning the *communicatio idiomatum* is one example. Luther's aversion to metaphysics did not deter him from reading

Chalcedon's emphasis on the passibility of God in the incarnation. And he clearly rejected any form of monophysitism. If the preceding Scholastics had allowed the natures of Christ to devolve into philosophy, Luther's perspective was immediately tempered by his strong soteriology. The suffering of Christ was a true suffering in God's very being. That was a move that Chalcedon was not willing to make. Nor were Zwingli or Calvin convinced that this description of the union was fully adequate. The reserve goes back to the ancient concern to keep both natures distinct. The divine and the human can never be merged or mingled.

Luther rejected any form of abstract essence in Christ. He saw the need to explore the reciprocal nature within the one person of both the divine and human essences. The human flesh assumed did affect the eternal Son without altering his nature. He argued that it was in the mutual communication of the qualities of the natures that our salvation was confirmed. An exchange in the person of Christ assured the exchange of life for us by grace.

The ubiquity of Christ was also a Lutheran concern. If Christ is the God-Man then his omnipresence is a necessary corollary. This was hotly debated even among Lutherans because it implied a deification of the human nature that went beyond "assumption." Some argued that this ubiquity began in Christ's infancy while others called that a "monstrosity."

Though thoroughly orthodox there is the typical Protestant aversion to any ontological discussion in early Calvinist thought. The anti-speculative nature of Calvinism is seen especially on the hypostatic union. At points he seems to use the Antiochene language of the divine nature "dwelling" in the man, Jesus. But he also shared interest in Alexandrian emphases. Calvin was very sensitive to Eutychianism—the merging of the natures. Thus, his aversion to Luther's passible Christ. Calvin was always uneasy with what he saw as the implications of an overly interpreted *communicatio idiomatum*.

THE IMPORTANCE OF
CHRISTOLOGICAL DOGMA

Why is this discussion necessary? The typical Christian in post-modernity has either little interest or has been lulled into the lie that theology is not important for life. C. S. Lewis would respond to that by asking if theology is not of interest, then pray tell what is interesting? As Dorothy Sayers rightfully discerned, dogma is the drama. It is vitally necessary for the well-being of the church to know its essential thought. There is no more fundamental issue to Christianity than the person of Jesus Christ. Anyone who believes in him or wants to believe ought to be aware not only of what the New Testament says about him but also what subsequent generations debated and decided based upon revelation concerning his person. They believed everything that was saving hung on a right understanding on what was appropriated. They also show us how important the battle for orthodox Christology is in every generation.

CRUCIAL SYSTEMATIC ISSUES
CONCERNING THE PERSON OF CHRIST

Christology from "below" and "above" are delineations that are used often in modern discussions about Christ. In many ways this recent language is reflective of the concerns Alexandrian thought (above) had with the Antiochene school (below). But the similarities soon cease because modernity has so shaken orthodox Christology that there is virtually no ontological discussion of any depth within this framework. It primarily focuses on how we come to know that Christ is God (epistemology).

If one advocates a Christology from "above," that is normally viewed as primacy given to the kerygma. This view of Christ, as Pannenberg critiques, is a claim that discernment regarding Christ is exclusively from a revelatory stance. This is to presuppose his divinity. In effect, it is to say that we know Jesus is God even before a close analysis of the history of Jesus is performed. It presupposes that the claims of the epistles regarding the universal Lordship of Christ that was the early proclamation of the church is the starting point for the kerygma.

This is intriguing given the tenor of all of the New Testament. Neither the Apostles nor anyone else who wrote a canonical text ever presupposed his deity. They saw history and revelation as inseparable. They always started with history. The early church councils were always based on biblical data pointing to the historical Jesus.

The second criticism of Pannenberg is that it tends to neglect the real significance of Jesus as a real historical man. Therefore, it becomes focused on faith, or maybe better, a presumed creedal system, and not on an encounter with real history. In other words, belief that starts with the presupposed is fideistic. A short review of historical systematic statements about Jesus reveals that none of the fathers were fideistic nor encouraged it. Athanasius, Ambrose, Augustine, and their counterparts in this endeavor to explore the mystery of Christ always placed Jesus in his historical context, even though by modern standards they may not have focused on history in the same way we experience in our time due to the transformation of the philosophy of history brought on by the Enlightenment.

The third of Pannenberg's criticisms is that it presupposes a knowledge of what God is about; that is, putting oneself in the position of God himself. It diminishes mystery by beginning with certain theological commitments. While each of these criticisms have merit in that there are tendencies in Christian theology to presume or to forget rigorous historical analysis and to place our concept of God above the true self-revealing God, it is good to take the early fathers as examples of humility, receptivity, and correctability. No exegete should ever make any pronouncement about God in presumption.

But those who understand and believe God has spoken through his word believe also that he has spoken through his historical word.

Whatever value the criticism of "Christology from above" bears to us, it must not be allowed to limit the divine self-donation that has occurred in all forms of revelation, specifically in the incarnation and in the inspiration of Scripture. Too much has been lost in the so-called historical quests for Jesus. Many of those who began with their own predisposition against the possibility of propositional revelation ended up with a spirit-filled man along the lines of the Ebionites. There is a crucial element in Christology that understands the personal, Trinitarian nature of God. Revelation is not first our words about God but God inspiring the writers and text of Scripture to give to us interpretive truths. The "Word made flesh" bears the implications of an orthodox perspective on what Christ has done to show us the nature of God in himself.

Christology from "above" is focused on the reality of Christian belief. In an era of nihilism, it is imperative to know that the belief is based upon the one who walked by the Sea of Galilee, healed the sick, and died to ransom us. If the position is taken that our minds are so fallen that we cannot know any history about the Son of God for sure and so God has had to break through to our minds, the result is a diminishment of the need for history. If historical skepticism is given ascendancy in how we come to know, then the foundations of all that is true about "Christology from above" is lost. This view removes history from value. History, according to this view, distorts. The value, therefore, only comes because God has put it there.

But what about "below"? One of the strongest points of this school of thought is its emphasis on the historical Jesus. This view recognizes that the kerygma alone is not enough. It starts with what happened in Judea in the first century with the rabbi named Jesus of Nazareth and uses the historical method to test both the words of Jesus and what was claimed about him.

It places strong emphasis on a fully human Jesus living on earth with us. The problem is that they drive a wedge between his humanity and his divinity. The claims regarding his divinity and his human history are placed on separate tracks. On this view, his divinity gets de-emphasized and ends up being obliterated altogether. This view already presupposes that the divine cannot permeate the human in an ontological way but possibly in a moral or ethical union.

In evaluating "Christology from below" it may be helpful to see that in reality it cannot deliver what it promises on its own. If we only have "history," which normally means occurrences defined by the standards of modern historicism, then how is the divinity of Christ established? It must be a complete history, a revealed historical account, if all the aspects of what the early Christians encountered in Christ are allowed. Christology from below depends upon objectivity for its success, but its practitioners end up being subjective, ruled by a modern kerygma.[13]

Christology from below has trouble even locating Jesus in history. This view is selective in what it claims to be truth. How are we to deal with the attributions of deity in the New Testament? They cannot be written off as being simply unhistorical because they do not fit in the framework of repeatable verifiability. As one reads Christologians from below, more often than not what is offered are feeble, uncertain affirmations about the divinity of Christ.

---

13. In his *Systematic Theology*, Vol 2, it seems that Pannenberg has moved to a more balanced position over the years when it comes to this question. He sees the early confessions as explications of the history of Jesus (283). He critiques the "from-below" schools for focusing on the claims of Christ while ignoring the reaction they caused in those who recognized what Jesus was saying. He recognizes that if one ejects the creeds, the only authority for discerning Christ is subjective, faith alone (286). He says the two approaches should be complementary to enable a distinction between primary Christological elements and "secondary features or distortions" (289). He defends himself against Kasper's criticism of his view of the resurrection in Kasper, *Jesus the Christ* (287), along the same line. But Kasper does have the sense we do that Pannenberg has not adequately perceived the resurrection in its fullest meaning. Whatever is said Pannenberg is a far cry closer to reality than most of his scholarly predecessors from the continent, centering as he does on the Resurrection as the fulcrum of Christian faith.

In his remarkable work on Christology, Thomas Oden offers the same response as his forebears. The answer on where to start with Jesus is first to be able and willing to meet Christ personally. He is unique in his personhood. He is the God-Man. Faith and history must be kept together. The historical data of scripture and the interpretive data give us a complete picture of Christ's person.

CHAPTER SIX

Conclusion

IN THE CONTINUING EFFORT to express the subtleties of Christological dogma to all believers, there is a pastoral analogy found first in Origen which arises often over the centuries, and that is the figure of heated iron. Iron still remains iron even when heated till it is so hot that it becomes impossible to discern metal from fire. Fire doesn't cease to be fire. That's an analogy of this mutual indwelling. One can't tell when one or the other starts. With a red hot knife, you have a cut burn or a burned cut, but it's just a single action. This is just one attempt to come up with an analogy for this interpenetration of the two natures. It's important that we look at the total witness of Scripture to the person of Christ. We should not isolate this or that quality. The New Testament witnesses to Christ's full humanity as well as his full divinity. The two natures are in one person. The natures are distinct but inseparable. Our redemption depends upon the unity of his person and the interpenetration of the two natures. It is absolutely vital that he become human and that he continues to be human as well as divine.

In 1979, during one of the now famous debates on whether or not the notion of Jesus was a myth or the true incarnation of God, John Stott asked a theologian from the opposing viewpoint: "Do you ever worship Jesus?" The response was shockingly stark, "No, I don't." Upon later reflection Stott responded:

> This is a simple test which the most theologically illiterate person in the pew can understand and apply. What is at stake is not the Chalcedonian definition, nor the question of myth or metaphor, but whether we bow the knee to Jesus, call upon him for salvation, and worship him as Lord. Can those who refuse to do this be Christian? I think not.

Stott makes three concluding points, which can be found from the New Testament and from two thousand years of reflection upon the incarnation:

> (1) Jesus was conscious of himself as God. He said in his Sermon on the Mount, "You have heard it said, but I say to you," as one of many affirmations that he was speaking authoritatively as God. This also comes out in the way that he addressed his Father in heaven and in his power to bestow the Holy Spirit.

> (2) This divinity was also his enemies' consciousness. They claimed he was a blasphemer, and not because Christology was added later in the third century, but because Christ's divinity is found throughout. It is found in the titles that Jesus claimed for himself, his prayers, and his actions to which his enemies objected. They knew exactly what he was claiming, and for that he was crucified.

> (3) It was the universal faith of the primitive church to ascribe to Jesus an unrivaled cosmic lordship. He is the cosmic Lord. His is the name that is above every name.[1]

---

1. Stott, "The Mythmakers' Myth," 56–57.

Bibliography

Aune, David Edward. "Son of Man." *ISBE* 4:574–81.

Baillie, D. M. *God Was in Christ*. New York: Charles Scribner's Sons, 1955.

Bainton, Roland. *Martin Luther's Christmas Book*. Minneapolis: Augsburg Publishing House, 1948.

Barth, Karl. *Church Dogmatics*. 13 vols. Geoffrey Bromiley and Thomas F. Torrance, eds. Edinburgh: T&T Clark, 1956–1975.

_____. *Dogmatics in Outline*. Translated by G. T. Thomson. London: SCM Press, 1957.

Beasley-Murray, George. *Baptism on the New Testament*. Grand Rapids, Eerdmans: 1961.

_____. *The Gospel of John: Word Bible Commentary*. Waco: Word, 1987.

_____. "Baptism." *NIDNTT* 1:144–50.

Bernard of Clairvaux. *The Nativity*. Translated by Leo Hickey in *Proclaiming the Christmas Gospel*. Edited by John D. Witvliet and David Vroge. Grand Rapids: Baker Books, 2004.

Bettenson, Henry Scowcraft. *Documents of the Early Church*. 3rd ed. Chris Maunder, ed. New York: Oxford University Press, 1999.

Bornkamm, Günther. *Jesus of Nazareth*. New York: Harper and Row, 1960.

Bousset, Wilhelm. *Kyrios Christos: A History of the Belief in Christ from the Beginnings of Christianity to Irenaeus*. Nashville: Abingdon, 1969.

Bouyer, Louis. *Liturgical Piety*. Notre Dame: University of Notre Dame Press, 1955.

Braumann, Georg. "Child," *NIDNTT* 1:280–91.

Brown, Raymond. *The Birth of the Messiah*. Garden City, NY: Doubleday, 1977.

Bruce, F. F. *New Testament History*. New York: Doubleday, 1980.

Brummer, Vincent. *The Model of Love: A Study in Philosophical Theology*. New York: Cambridge University Press, 1993.

Bultmann, Rudolf. *Theology of the New Testament*. New York: Charles Scribner's Sons, 1951.

_____. *Jesus Christ and Mythology*. New York: Charles Scribners' Sons, 1958.

_____. *The Johannine Epistles*. Philadelphia: Fortress, 1973.

Calvin, John. *Institutes of the Christian Religion*. 2 vols. J. T. McNeill, ed. Philadelphia: Westminster. 1960.

Campbell, J. Macleod. *The Nature of the Atonement*. London: James Clarke, 1959.

Carter, Craig A. *Contemplating God with the Great Tradition: Recovering Trinitarian Classical Theism*. Grand Rapids: Baker, 2021.

Cochrane, Charles. *Christianity and Classical Culture*. New York: Oxford University Press, 1957.

Coppedge, Allan. *Portraits of God: A Biblical Theology of Holiness*. Downers Grove, IL: InterVarsity Press, 2001.

Cross, Richard. *The Metaphysics of the Incarnation: Thomas Aquinas to Duns Scotus*. Oxford: Oxford University Press, 2005.

Cullmann, Oscar. *The Christology of the New Testament*. Translated by Guthrie and Hall. Philadelphia: Westminster, 1963.

_____. *Christ and Time.* London: SCM Press, 1962.

Dawe, Donald. *The Form of a Servant.* Philadelphia: Westminster, 1963.

Dix, Gregory. *The Shape of the Liturgy.* London: Dacre Press, 1945.

Dodd, C. H. *The Apostolic Preaching and Its Developments.* New York: Willett, Clark, & Co, 1937.

_____. *The Johnannine Epistles.* London: Hodder and Stoughton, 1961.

Dunn, James D. G. *Christology in the Making.* 2nd ed. Grand Rapids: Eerdmans, 1996.

Eckman, Edward. "The Identification of Christ with *Yahweh* by New Testament Writers." *Gordon Review* 7:4 (1964): 145–53.

Eichrodt, Walther. *Theology of the Old Testament.* 2 vols. Philadelphia: Westminster Press, 1961.

Farrer, Austin. *Saving Belief: A Discussion of Essentials.* New York: Morehouse-Barlow Co., 1964.

Farrow, Douglas. *Ascension and Ecclesia: On the Significance of the Doctrine of the Ascension for Ecclesiology and Christian Cosmology.* Grand Rapids: Eerdmans, 1999.

Forsyth, P. T. *The Work of Christ.* London: Independent Press, 1948.

Frei, Hans. *The Identity of Jesus Christ.* Philadelphia: Fortress, 1975.

Galot, Jean. *Who Is Christ?: A Theology of the Incarnation.* Chicago: Franciscan Herald Press, 1981.

_____. *The Person of Christ: A Theological Insight.* Chicago: Franciscan Herald Press, 1984.

Geisler, Norman. *The Battle for the Resurrection.* Nashville: Thomas Nelson, 1989.

Gilson, Etienne. *The Spirit of Mediaeval Philosophy.* New York: Charles Scribner's Sons, 1936.

Gregorios, Paulos Mar. "Ecclesiological Issues Concerning the Relation of Eastern Orthodox and Oriental Orthodox Churches." In *Christ in East and West*, edited by Paul Fries and Tiran Nersoyan. Macon, GA: Mercer Univ. Press, 1987.

Grenz, Stanley. *Theology for the Community of God*. Nashville: Broadman and Holman, 1994.

Grillmeier, Aloys. *Christ in Christian Tradition*. 2 vols. Translated by John Bowden. Atlanta: John Knox Press, 1965.

Grudem, Wayne. *Systematic Theology*. Grand Rapids: Zondervan, 1994.

Gruenler, Royce. *The Trinity in the Gospel of John: A Thematic Commentary on the Fourth Gospel*. Grand Rapids: Baker, 1986.

Gunton, Colin. *Act and Being*. Grand Rapids: Eerdmans, 2002.

_____. *Enlightenment and Alienation*. Grand Rapids: Eerdmans, 1985.

_____. *The One, the Three and the Many*. Cambridge: Cambridge University Press, 1993.

_____. *Yesterday and Today: A Study of Continuities in Christology*. Grand Rapids: Eerdmans, 1983.

Hardy, Edward, ed. *Christology of the Later Fathers*. Philadelphia: Westminster Press, 1954.

Harris, Murray. *Raised Immortal*. Grand Rapids: Eerdmans, 1985.

_____. *From Grave to Glory*. Grand Rapids: Zondervan, 1990.

Harrison, R. K. "Leprosy." *NIDNTT* 2:463–64.

Heidelberg Catechism with Commentary. 1563. Reprint, New York: Pilgrim Press, 1979.

Hengstenberg, E. W. *The Christology of the Old Testament*. 1847. Reprint, Grand Rapids, Kregel, 1970.

Hicks, John, ed. *The Myth of God Incarnate*. Philadelphia: Westminster, 1977.

Holmes, Stephen R. "Response to Thomas H. McCall." *Two Views on the Doctrine of the Trinity*. Edited by Jason S. Sexton. Grand Rapids: Zondervan, 2014. 138–43.

Horvath, Tibor. *Jesus Christ as Ultimate Reality: A Contribution to the Hermeneutics of Conciliar Theology*. Toronto: University of Toronto Press, 1984.

Irenaeus. *On the Apostolic Preaching*. Crestwood, NY: SVS Press, 1997.

Jacob, Edmund. *Theology of the Old Testament*. Translated by Heathcote and Allcock. London: Hodder and Stoughton, 1958.

Jenkins, Philip. *Hidden Gospels*. Oxford: Oxford University Press, 2001.

Jenson, Robert W. *Systematic Theology: Volume One, The Triune God*. New York: Oxford University Press, 2001.

Johnson, Elizabeth. *She Who Is*. New York: Crossroad, 1994.

Kaiser, Christopher. *The Doctrine of God: An Historical Survey*. Westchester, IL: Crossway Books, 1982.

Käsemann, Ernst. *Essays on New Testament Themes*. Translated by W. J. Montague. Philadelphia: Fortress, 1982.

Kasper, Walter. *The God of Jesus Christ*. New York: Crossroad, 1986.

_____. *Jesus the Christ*. New York: Paulist Press, 1977.

Keener, Craig S. *The Gospel of John: A Commentary*. 2 vols. Peabody, MA: Hendrickson, 2003.

Kinlaw, Dennis F. *Let's Start with Jesus*. Grand Rapids: Zondervan, 2005.

Köstenberger, Andreas J. *John: Baker Exegetical Commentary on the New Testament*. Grand Rapids: Baker, 2004.

Kruse, Colin G. *The Letters of John: The Pillar New Testament Commentary*. Grand Rapids: Eerdmans, 2000.

Leith, John, ed. *Creeds of the Churches*. 3rd ed. Atlanta: John Knox Press, 1982.

Lenski, R. C. H. *The Gospel Selections of the Ancient Church.* Columbus, OH: Lutheran Book Concern, 1936.

Lewis, C. S. *Mere Christianity.* New York: Macmillan, 1952.

_____. *Miracles.* New York: MacMillan, 1960.

_____, ed. *George MacDonald: An Anthology.* New York: Macmillan, 1978.

_____. *Letters to Malcolm: Chiefly on Prayer.* Orlando: Harcourt Brace Jovanovich, 1964.

Lindars, Barnabas. *Jesus Son of Man.* Grand Rapids: Eerdmans, 1983.

Marshall, I. Howard. *The Epistles of John. NICNT.* Grand Rapids: Eerdmans, 1981.

Mascall, E. L. *Via Media: An Essay in Theological Synthesis.* Greenwich, CT: Seabury Press, 1957.

McCall, Thomas H. *Analytic Christology and the Theological Interpretation of the New Testament.* Oxford: Oxford University Press, 2021.

_____. "What's Not to Love? Rethinking Appeals to Tradition in Contemporary Debates in Trinitarian Theology." *International Journal of Systematic Theology* 25:4 (Oct 2023): 610–30.

McCall, Thomas and Michael C. Rea, eds., *Philosophical and Theological Essays on the Trinity.* Oxford: Oxford University Press, 2009.

Michel, Otto. "Son." *NIDNTT* 3:607–34.

Morris, Leon. *The Gospel According to John. NICNT.* Grand Rapids: Eerdmans, 1971.

Moule, C. F. D. *The Origin of Christology.* New York: Cambridge University Press, 1977.

Nellas, Panayiotis. *Deification in Christ.* Crestwood, NY: St. Vladimir's Seminary Press, 1987.

Nersoyan, Tiran. *Problems of Consensus in Christology: The Function of Councils.* In *Christ in East and West.* Edited by

Paul Fries and Tiran Nersoyan. Macon, GA: Mercer University Press, 1987.

Oden, Thomas C. *The Living God: Systematic Theology: Volume One*. San Francisco: Harper & Row, 1987.

_____. *The Word of Life: Systematic Theology: Volume Two*. San Francisco: HarperSanFrancisco, 1989.

Oden, Thomas C. and Christopher A. Hall, *Mark. ACCS* New Testament Vol 2.

O'Collins, Gerald. *Christology*. New York, Oxford, 1995.

_____. "Criteria for Interpreting the Traditions." In *Problems and Perspectives of Fundamental Theology*. Edited by René Latourelle and Gerald O'Collins. New York: Paulist, 1980.

O'Keefe, J. J. and R. R. Reno. *Sanctified Vision: An Introduction to Early Interpretation of the Bible*. Baltimore: Johns Hopkins, 2005.

Otto, Rudolf. *The Idea of the Holy*. Translated by John W. Harvey. 1923. Reprint, New York: Oxford University Press, 1958.

Outler, Albert C. *Christology*. Coral Springs, FL: Bristol House, 1996.

Pannenberg, Wolfhart. *Jesus-God and Man*. 2nd ed. Translated by Wilkins and Priebe. Philadelphia: Westminster, 1977.

_____. *Systematic Theology*. Vol. 2. Translated by Geoffrey W. Bromiley. Grand Rapids: Eerdmans, 1994.

Perrin, Norman. *Rediscovering the Teaching of Jesus*. New York: Harper & Row, 1967.

Pelikan, Jaroslav. *Credo*. New Haven: Yale University Press, 2003.

Pinnock, Clark and Delwin Brown. *Theological Crossfire*. Grand Rapids: Zondervan, 1990.

Quasten, Johannes. *Patrology*. 4 vols. Utrecht: Spectrum, 1950.

Radner, Ephriam. *Hope Among the Fragments: The Broken Church and Its Engagement with Scripture*. Grand Rapids: Brazos, 2004.

Rahner, Karl. *Sacramentum Mundi: An Encyclopedia of Theology.* 6 vols. New York: Herder and Herder, 1969.

Richard of St. Victor. *De Trinitate* in *Trinity and Creation: A Selection of Works of Hugh, Richard, and Adam of St Victor.* Edited by Boyd Taylor Coolman and Dale M. Coulter. Turnhout: Brepols Publishers, 2010.

Ridderbos, Herman N. *Paul: An Outline of His Theology.* Grand Rapids: Eerdmans, 1975.

Sanday, William. *Christologies Ancient and Modern.* Oxford: Clarendon Press, 1910.

Sayers, Dorothy. *The Man Who Would Be King.* Harper and Row: New York, 1943.

Schleiermacher, Friedrich. *The Christian Faith: A New Translation and Critical Edition.* 2 vols. Edited by Terrence N. Tice and Catherine L. Kelsey. Louisville: Westminster John Knox, 2016.

Schweitzer, Albert. *The Quest for the Historical Jesus.* New York: Macmillan, 1948.

Schweizer, Eduard. "υἱός." *TDNT* 8:334–57.

The Scots Confession:1560. In *The Book of Confessions.* Louisville: Office of the General Assembly of the Presbyterian Church (USA), 1967.

The Shorter Catechism: The Constitution of the United Presbyterian Church. Philadelphia: Office of the General Assembly of the United Presbyterian Church in the United States of America, 1967.

Sonderegger, Katherine. *Systematic Theology.* Vol. 1. *The Doctrine of God.* Minneapolis: Fortress Press, 2015.

Stauffer, Ethelbert. *New Testament Theology.* London: SCM Press, 1963.

Strecker, George. *The Johannine Letters.* Minneapolis: Fortress, 1996.

Stott, John R. W. "The Mythmakers' Myth." *Christianity Today* (7 Dec 1979): 56–57.

Studer, Basil. *Trinity and Incarnation: The Faith of the Early Church.* Collegeville: Liturgical Press, 1993.

Svigel, Michael J. "Power in Unity, Diversity in Rank: Subordination and the Trinity in the Fathers of the Early Church." Southwest Region Evangelical Theological Society (13 Mar 2004). Dallas, TX.

Taft, Robert. *The Liturgy of the Hours in East and West: The Origins of the Divine Office and Its Meaning for Today.* Collegeville, MN: Liturgical Press, 1986.

Thomasius, Gottfried. *Christi Person und Werk.* Erlangen: Theodor Bläsing, 1853.

Thompson, Marianne Meye. *God in the Gospel of John.* Grand Rapids: Eerdmans, 2001.

Torrance, Thomas F. *Divine Meaning: Studies in Patristic Hermeneutics.* Edinburgh: T&T Clark, 1995.

_____. *The Mediation of Christ.* Colorado Springs: Helmers and Howard, 1992.

_____. *Reality and Evangelical Theology: The Realism of Christian Revelation.* Philadelphia: Westminster Press, 1982.

_____. *The Trinitarian Faith.* Edinburgh: T&T Clark, 1997.

_____. ed., *The Incarnation: Ecumenical Studies in the Nicene-Constantinopolitan Creed A.D. 381.* Edinburgh: Handsel Press, 1981.

_____. *Incarnation: The Person and Life of Christ.* Downers Grove, IL: InterVarsity, 2008.

Volf, Miroslav. *After Our Likeness: The Church as the Image of the Trinity.* Grand Rapids: Eerdmans, 1998.

von Balthasar, Hans Urs. *The Scandal of the Incarnation: Irenaeus Against the Heresies.* San Francisco: Ignatius Press, 1990.

von Rad, Gerhard. *Old Testament Theology*. 2 vols. New York: Harper & Row, 1962.

Wainwright, Geoffrey. *Doxology: The Praise of God in Worship, Doctrine and Life: A Systematic Theology*. New York: Oxford University Press, 1984.

Wells, David. *The Person of Christ*. Westchester, IL: Crossway Books, 1984.

Wesley, John. *The Bicentennial Edition of the Works of John Wesley*. 24 vols. to date. Nashville: Abingdon, 1976–.

_____. *Explanatory Notes Upon the New Testament*. 1754. Reprint, Salem, OH: Schmul, 1976.

_____. *Explanatory Notes Upon the Old Testament*. 3 vols. 1765. Reprint, Salem, OH: Schmul, 1975.

Wilken, Robert Louis. *The Spirit of Early Christian Thought: Seeking the Face of God*. New Haven: Yale University Press, 2003.

Willis, David. *Clues to the Nicene Creed: A Brief Outline of the Faith*. Grand Rapids: Eerdmans, 2005.

Witherington, Ben, III. *The Indelible Image: The Theological and Ethical Thought World of the New Testament*. Vol. 1. *The Individual Witnesses*. Downers Grove, IL: InterVarsity Press, 2010.

Wright, N. T. *The Climax of the Covenant*. Minneapolis: Fortress, 1993.

_____. *Jesus and the Victory of God*. Minneapolis: Fortress Press, 1996.

_____. *New Testament and the People of God*. Minneapolis: Fortress, 1992.

Wright, N. T. and Marcus J. Borg. *The Meaning of Jesus: Two Visions*. San Francisco: Harper Collins, 1999.

Zimmerli, Walther. *Ezekiel: A Commentary on the Book of the Prophet Ezekiel*. 2 vols. Philadelphia: Fortress, 1979.

Zizioulas, John D. *Being as Communion: Studies in Person-hood and the Church.* Crestwood, NY: St. Vladimirs Seminary Press, 1997.

Ancient Sources

Anselm. *Cur Deus Homo?* 1094–1098. Reprint, London: Religious Tract Society, 1800.

Apollinarius of Laodicea. *On the Union in Christ of the Body with the Godhead.* In *The Christological Controversy.* Edited and translated by Richard A. Norris, Jr. Philadelphia: Fortress, 1980.

Aquinas, Thomas. *Summa Theologica.* AD 1265–1273. Edited by Thomas Gilby. 18 vols. Reprint, Garden City, NY: Image, 1969.

Athanasius. *Against the Arians. NPNF* Second Series. Vol 4.

_____. *Defence of the Nicene Definition. NPNF* Second series. Vol 4.

_____. *Four Discourses Against the Arians. NPNF* Second series. Vol 4.

_____. *Letters. NPNF* Second series. Vol 4.

_____. *On the Incarnation. NPNF* Second series. Vol 4.

_____. *On the Incarnation of the Word. NPNF* Second series. Vol 4.

_____. *On the Opinion of Dionysius. NPNF* Second series. Vol 4.

_____. *Statement of Faith. NPNF* Second Series. Vol 4.

Aristides. *Apology of Aristides. ANF* Vol 10.

Augustine. *De Trinitate. NPNF* First Series. Vol 3.

_____. *Lectures on the Gospel of John. NPNF* First Series. Vol 7.

_____. *On the Creed. NPNF* First Series. Vol 3.

_____. *On the Trinity. NPNF* First Series. Vol 3.

_____. *Ten Homilies on the Epistle of St. John. NPNF* First Series. Vol 7.

Barnabas. *Epistle. ANF* Vol 1.

Boethius. *Against Eutyches and Nestorius.* AD 513. In *The Theological Tractates.* Translated by H. F. Stewart and E. K. Rand. Cambridge: Harvard University Press, 1918.

Clement of Alexandria. *Exhortation to the Heathen. ANF* Vol 2.

_____. *The Instructor. ANF* Vol 2.

_____. *Stromateis. ANF* Vol 2.

Chrysostom, *Homilies on Colossians. NPNF* First Series. Vol 13.

_____. *Homilies on Philippians. NPNF* First series. Vol 13.

Cyril of Jerusalem, *Catechetical Lectures. NPNF* Second Series. Vol 7.

The Didache. ANF Vol 7.

Eusebius of Caeasarea. *Ecclesiastical History. NPNF* Second Series. Vol 1.

Gregory of Nyssa. *Against Eunomius. NPNF* Second Series. Vol 5.

Gregory Nazianzen. *Second Theological Oration. NPNF* Second series. Vol 7.

Hilary of Poitiers. *On the Trinity. NPNF* Second series. Vol 9.

_____. *On the Trinity.* Washington, D.C.: Catholic University Press, 1954.

Hippolytus. *Against Beron and Helix. ANF* Vol 5.

_____. *Against the Heresy of One Noetus. ANF* Vol 5.

_____. *Ephesians. ANF* Vol 1.

_____. *Epistle to the Romans. ANF* Vol 1.

_____. *Fragments of Discoursed or Homilies. ANF* Vol 5.

_____. *On the Song of Songs. ANF* Vol 5.

_____. *Treatise on Christ and Antichrist. ANF* Vol 5.

Ignatius. *Trallians. ANF* Vol 1.

Irenaeus. *Against Heresies. ANF* Vol 1.

_____. *On the Apostolic Preaching.* New York: SVS, 1997.

John of Damascus. *Exposition of the Orthodox Faith. NPNF* Second Series. Vol 9.

Justin Martyr. *Dialogue with Trypho. ANF* Vol 1.

_____. *First Apology. ANF* Vol 1.

_____. *On the Resurrection. ANF* Vol 1.

Lactantius. *Divine Institutes. ANF* Vol 7.

Leo the Great. Sermons. *NPNF* Second Series. Vol 12.

Mathetes. *Epistle to Diognetus. ANF* Vol 1.

Melito of Sardis. *On Pascha with the Fragments of Melito and Other Material Related to the Quartodecimans.* Translated by Alistair Steward-Sykes. Crestwood, NY: St. Vladimir's Seminary Press, 2001.

Novatian. *Treatise Concerning the Trinity. ANF* Vol 5.

Origen. *Against Celsus. ANF* Vol 4.

_____. *Commentary on John. ANF* Vol 10.

_____. *De Principiis. ANF* Vol 4.

Peter of Alexandria. *On the Godhead. ANF* Vol 6.

Tertullian. *Against All Heresies. ANF* Vol 3.

_____. *Against Hermogenes. ANF* Vol 3.

_____. *Against Marcion. ANF* Vol 3.

_____. *Against Praxeas. ANF* Vol 3.

_____. *Apology. ANF* Vol 3.

_____. *On the Flesh of Christ. ANF* Vol 3.

_____. *On the Resurrection of the Flesh. ANF* Vol 3.

Vincent of Lérins. *Commonitory. NPNF* Second Series. Vol 11.

Let's Start with Jesus

Edited by Vic Reasoner, DMin

IN HIS GROUNDBREAKING BOOK, *Let's Start with Jesus* (2005), Dennis F. Kinlaw unpacked how Jesus defines God and humanity. Jesus Christ impacts every doctrine of systematic theology. While there are three monotheistic world religions, the most fundamental difference between Christianity and the other two, Islam and Judaism, is the centrality of Jesus Christ. Jesus separates Christian monotheism from Israel and Islam. He is the climax of God's revelation. Therefore, the whole of biblical revelation must be read and interpreted through the clearest of lenses. God is best seen in the face of Christ (2 Cor 4:6). This means that instead of beginning with God, as most theologies do, we should begin our theological studies with Jesus who has made known the one true God (John 1:18). If we get Jesus, we get God; if we miss him, we miss God. If our concept of God is wrong, the more religious we get the more dangerous we become. Because Dr. Kinlaw's thinking was so foundational for this work, we have chosen to summarize it here.

A NEW CONCEPT OF GOD

The first great intellectual revolution was the oneness of God. This separated monotheism from all pantheistic and polytheistic religions. Monotheism is rooted in history, not nature. Monotheism alone has an answer to the problem of evil because it separates that which is evil from that which is divine.

However, Islam and Judaism stop here. The second great intellectual revolution is that within the Godhead there is diversity in oneness. The world's problem with Christianity is Jesus. Yet he is the image of the invisible God (Col 1:15). Within the holy Trinity there exists both Father and Son. Neither person can be ignored nor completely separated. Jesus is one with the Father, but in that oneness is also otherness. God's self-giving love is who he is, and it is that which the three persons of the Trinity share. God the Father gives life to the Son and from the self-giving love of the Father and Son comes the third—the Spirit. The Holy Spirit is another person of the same kind.

Within the Godhead there is a reciprocal relationship bound by agape love—a love that cares more for another than for itself. There must be two for love to exist, the lover and the one loved. One needs an *other* to love. The early church theologians utilized the word *perichoresis*, which means *space around*. It came to express how one person can be open to another. It describes how the three divine persons live from, for, and in each other without coalescing or commingling. This inner-penetration describes how the Trinity lives through a giving and receiving of love that forms the basis of perfect communion. There is nothing higher than this agape love because that is what God is.

In order for us to understand God, we have no option but to use metaphors. God cannot be described without analogies. The term *father* is the best description of the character and nature of the first member of the Trinity. Other terms describe what God does; *Father* describes who he is. John's Gospel is a paraphrase of the creation account in Genesis, but through John what was implicit becomes explicit—the fatherhood of God and the eternal sonship of Jesus Christ. The difference between the first two members of the Trinity is conceived in familial terms. This relationship is not simply an analogy; it is the prototype of all human familial relations. The fatherhood of God is not simply a metaphor, but his ontological nature.

The Son is identified as *the* Word. A word is a means of interpersonal communication. Only persons, not animals or things, have words. Yet when persons speak, they must speak to another. There is communication between the persons of the Godhead. God is a speaking God because love cannot be silent, but the original dialogue is not with us. The inner life of the Trinity is dialogical. Creation began with a conversation. There is enough likeness between God and mankind that we can communicate and know each other as persons.

Understanding God as a Trinity of free persons gives us one of the most striking differences between the monotheism of Christianity and the other monotheistic religions. In these other monotheistic religions, God reigns alone. The emphasis is on his sovereign will. If God is capricious, his capriciousness is right because he alone is God. If he loves, it is something he does. It is not who he is. Therefore, the emphasis is on obedience to God's sovereign will. Salvation is the reward for obedience. In Christianity, however, God is also free yet bound by love. He is not under external compulsion, but his will is conditioned by the interrelated love between the three persons of the Godhead. This love provides an atmosphere of trust, and salvation is a gift of grace.

God desires intimacy with his creatures. Yet God is holy, and this holiness creates a chasm between him and his fallen creatures. The creatures do not share the divine nature of the Creator nor his moral character. Although we continue to share the image of God, that image is deeply marred. As a result of all this we are alienated from God. In short, God is good, but we are not because we are separated from him.

Because God desires a personal, intimate relationship with his creatures, this separation creates tension. He is holy, but because of our sin we are not. Therefore, God designed a tabernacle so that he could dwell with his people. The architecture and ritual of the tabernacle and the subsequent temple contained graduations of access and a system of sacrificial offerings. The innermost room was the Holy of Holies where God dwelt. Yet there could be no fellowship with God apart from a sacrifice of life. God did not interject this sense of tension to deter his people from having close fellowship with him. Rather, he did it to ensure they did not miss his presence. It was to protect them from merely a religious communion with themselves.

But God's desire for intimacy is more fully evident in the incarnation of Christ. The oneness of God in both Islam and Judaism has no inner differentiation to make such a thing as the incarnation possible. For the Muslim or orthodox Jew, the very thought is blasphemy. Yet God does not simply want to dwell in the temple among his people. He takes on flesh so he can be one with us and gives us his Spirit so he can dwell within us. Through the incarnation, God crossed the chasm to us. Now we are the temple of the living God.

A NEW CONCEPT OF PERSONHOOD

Across the first four centuries after the advent of Christ, the Christian church wrestled with the nature of the triune God and the nature of Jesus Christ. It took centuries for the church to think through the implications of what they had learned in Jesus. The ecumenical creedal statements of the church were the result. However, this theological dialog needs to be followed up by a "second act" in which the church defines biblically the nature of mankind. We cannot stand without the foundation previously laid, but we should be able to see some things more clearly as a result of what has been previously understood.

Jesus connects God to his creation. The works of his hands are objects of his love because he is love. God is wed to his own creation. God's purpose for us is illustrated in three metaphors: forensic, familial, and nuptial. Our identity is defined politically, through family, and through marriage.

THE ROYAL/LEGAL METAPHOR

The court is where the sovereign reigns and where law governs. Judicial decisions are made there. God is both King and Judge, the giver of the law and the executor of it. God declares us righteous. As his servants we are subjects of his kingdom. Yet this metaphor is not intimate enough. Forgiveness and reconciliation are not enough. If we view Christ's saving work only in terms of a legal change, this handles the problem of sin's penalty but gives no answer to the problem of human sinfulness.

God wants us to participate in the communion of the Trinity. Through the incarnation God takes on flesh so that he can be one with us. He wants to close the distance. Pardon is not enough. God wants us to internalize his values and ways so that we are eternally compatible with him. We must be regenerated and reciprocate the Father's love. We must be related to the Father as Jesus was. Thus, to have a right conception of mankind, we must also start with Jesus.

THE FAMILIAL METAPHOR

As the eternal Son, the relationship between the Father and the Son is an ontological reality. It also reflects the family relationship God wants with us. We are adopted into God's family as his children. God becomes our heavenly Father and we become his children. We do not define the Fatherhood of God through human fathers, nor do we define the person of the Trinity through human personality. Jesus is the one who gives definition to personhood. He is the prototype. No person, divine or human, is complete within himself or herself. To be part of a family means a mingling of our life with that of others. Again, to have a right conception of Jesus, we must start with Jesus.

THE NUPTIAL METAPHOR

Marriage is the best image of the self-giving love within the Trinity and the best image of the church. The Father is also seeking a bride for his Son. As his bride, we are married to Christ. The covenant at Sinai was not just a legal transaction. It was a marital covenant with Israel, whom God had chosen. Human sexuality becomes Paul's key to understanding the church as the body of Christ. If history began with a wedding in Eden and closes with one in the New Jerusalem, the biblical story runs from wedding to wedding, from temporal symbol to eternal reality. When we see Jesus as groom, we gain a proper understanding both of humanity and of God.

SEVEN CHARACTERISTICS OF PERSONHOOD

In both Greek and Latin, the words for *face* were connected to the concept of personhood. In the three revelatory events of Sinai, Bethlehem, and Pentecost, we see the three faces of God: Father, Son, and Spirit. In these three faces we are enabled to see ourselves.

Jesus is the prototype for all humanity. Jesus helps us understand ourselves. God is not like us, but we are like him. Modern social science has little grasp of what it means to be a *person*. Instead, they emphasize *self.* They advocate the goal of the individual self as the center. Jesus reflected a polar opposite concept in which persons are to be understood in terms of relationship and mutuality. To be sure, as we examine the Gospels, we see that Jesus had a clear consciousness of his own unique identity. Likewise, we too must have such a consciousness. Individuals cannot give away themselves in self-giving love if they are not first of all in possession of their own selves. However, no individual can ever find their full potential in themselves alone.

1. WE ARE CONSCIOUS OF OUR IDENTITY

Jesus had a clear consciousness of his own identity as the Son. He knew his own identity, mission, and purpose. But while he is not identical with the Father and the Spirit, he insists that there is a oneness with the Father and the Spirit.

2. WE LIVE IN RELATIONSHIPS

Just as the Son cannot be explained apart from the Father and the Spirit, so we cannot be defined alone. We are not self-explanatory or autonomous. We are conscious that we are not alone.

3. WE WERE CREATED FOR RECIPROCAL RELATIONSHIPS

Jesus declared, "I am in the Father and the Father is in me" (John 14:11). While every person is unique, we are never independent. In Christ we may be participants in other-oriented, self-giving, holy love. We find ourselves in webs of relationships with others that are distinct from ourselves. We are to live for one another. Yet our relationships are not one-way.

4. WE WERE CREATED TO BE FREE

"Therefore if the Son makes you free, you shall be free indeed" (John 8:36). Jesus was free, and he longed for everyone else to experience the freedom he enjoyed. If relationships are to be meaningful, they must be rooted in personal freedom. Without this freedom, there can be neither trust nor love, evil nor holiness. This inherent human freedom ultimately forces the collapse of all political totalitarianism. Our most personal actions are not determined by any force external to ourselves. Christ did not express his freedom by doing what he pleased but in doing the will of the Father. However, that submission was voluntary. The forces of nature obey God, but they cannot reciprocate his love. External obedience is never enough to please God. He wants a relationship of loving trust from a creature who freely chooses the relationship. We cannot love unless we are free. This is a major distinction between animals and humans. Animals are not made in the image of God.

5. WE HAVE A MORAL CONSCIOUSNESS

The essential nature of the God of Scripture is holy-love. Even the demons acknowledged that Jesus is "the Holy One of God" (Mark 1:24). Holiness is not an essential part of all personhood. God alone is holy. He is ontologically distinct. Anything else that possesses holiness does so because of its association with him. No human is by nature holy. Our holiness is derived from God.

However, moral consciousness *is* a natural component in human personhood. When Rudolf Otto searched the religions of the world where Yahweh could not be found, he discovered that humans could be religious without being moral or ethical. While Adam and Eve began their lives as holy, that holiness was lost when they were separated from the presence of God. However, this change was from moral to immoral, not to amoral. They still retained an acute moral consciousness, unlike animals, which are not in the image of God. Thus, relations can be either constructive—good, or destructive—evil.

6. WE WERE CREATED TO LIVE IN OPENNESS

There was an openness in the personality of Jesus. This self-transcendence is the ability to see ourselves objectively, to stand outside ourselves. It is the consciousness of subject and object. This also produces a universal capacity for guilt. Each person is responsible for the consequences of his or her actions. We also have an inner need to relate to the world beyond the self. We are not self-subsistent. No person is complete in themselves. No person who is alone is a whole person because no person is ever supposed to be completely alone. That would be to have entered into hell.

7. We Were Created to Relate in Trusting Love

When Jesus talks about losing one's life to find it, he reflects a relationship of trusting love with the Father. If the eternal Son of God had protected himself, refused to trust himself to the will of his Father, and ceased to live for someone other than himself, he would cease to be who he is, because God by definition is self-giving love. Jesus says that the Father loves him in the same way he loves us. No one can love if that person has nothing to give and no one to give to.

A NEW CONCEPT OF SIN

Irenaeus declared, "The glory of God is man fully alive." But the old glory of humanity is gone after sin. How could a world so good fall so far? Eve believed that something could be good in itself, apart from God. In our first parents we turned our faces away from him, becoming less than he intended. Sin was a deliberate reorientation, a turning of our faces away from God and making ourselves the ultimate point of reference.

Adam and Eve centered their existence in themselves. However, to shut ourselves off from God is to diminish ourselves. To separate ourselves from our source means to implode on ourselves. And when we shut ourselves off from God, we shut ourselves off from others. Because the key to all other relationships is found in our relationship to God, if we are not open to God, we cannot properly be open to others.

Other-orientation was replaced by self-interest, which produced rivalry, suspicion, distrust, fear, and insecurity. Other people became a threat, not a source of fulfillment. After sin we became lawbreakers, prodigal children, and adulterous spouses in our relationship with God.

Because God is the source of life and good, separation from him meant the advent of evil and death. Life without God is life in the *flesh*. Flesh is not evil in itself. When we are God-centered, flesh is permeated with God's Spirit and agape love. When we are separated from our source and become centered in ourselves, however, we turn inward. Everything is approached on the basis of—what's in it for me? When sin is understood from a relational perspective, it is much easier to grasp that the way of salvation is a journey of faith. Sin began with doubt. The road back is the reverse—a journey of faith.

A NEW CONCEPT OF SALVATION

Sin is a perversion of personal relationship with God. The flesh describes human life out of the will of God. How can God be true to himself and also save us? If the problem is personal, the solution must be personal. Salvation was provided through the counterpart to Adam—a second Adam. The offended one takes the offense to himself in order to save the one who offends. The only possibility for human salvation was for God's holy love to enter into a human person. Jesus becomes the arm of the Lord. The Physician assumes the very disease of the ones he has come to heal. The eternal Judge sentences himself to bear the very judgment that should be imposed on the lawbreaker.

Only Christianity among the religions of the world is a religion of atonement. In every other religion we must save ourselves. This is because there is no other religion with a triune God and a corresponding understanding of personhood. The gospel is the road back. But the gospel is bigger and better than we have often thought. This requires metaphors besides the royal/legal metaphor. We need more than another chance; we need a radical change in our nature. We need an infusion of holy love. There is nothing higher than agape love because he offers himself to any who will receive him.

Certainly, salvation involves reconciliation. We can know the assurance of forgiveness. But we can also know that we are adopted into God's family. The new life through agape love establishes a new point of reference. The process of sanctification has begun. We now have the freedom to choose God and to obey his commands.

However, we also need the illumination of the marriage metaphor. The purpose of the Spirit in the life of the new believer is to bring the person as part of the bride of Christ to a devotion to Christ that fulfills the demands implicit within the nuptial metaphor. The relationship sought is one of total self-giving love. We can offer ourselves as living sacrifices, which restores the agape love of God without rival. Our union with Christ can be a union of total self-giving love. The result is an undivided heart. This can be a present reality through the power of the Spirit. It is a gift to be received by faith. Such a relationship does not automatically come when salvation is begun in justification and new birth because at that time we are not aware of this deeper need. The reality is that we will not trust God to do something for us if we do not feel the need. As we walk with him and expose ourselves to the Scriptures and to the constraints of the Holy Spirit, we begin to sense the inner division in the depths of our being.

The New Testament pattern for the believer is the Spirit-filled, Spirit-led, Spirit-permeated, Spirit-controlled, and thus other-oriented person. This produces freedom. Paul taught that we are free only when we can live for one beyond ourselves, and this is possible only through the Spirit. The Holy Spirit, through the blood of Christ can "perfect our hearts in love" so that we can love Christ with all of our hearts. Unbroken, unobstructed communion is the answer to the divided heart

A NEW CONCEPT OF PRAYER

If we exist in inter-dependant relationship with others, as the Son does with the Father and the Spirit, intercessory prayer must take on a new dimension. When we intercede for others, their well-being becomes more important than our own. We travail in prayer as a mother who bears a child. No one can make another's decisions, yet the key to a person's possibilities lies in someone else. This perichoretic relationship also occurs within the holy Trinity. The Holy Spirit bears our prayers to the Son, who intercedes for us to the Father.

In his 2012 book, *Prayer: Bearing the World as Jesus Did*, Dr. Kinlaw expanded this concept that Jesus is the prototype of how we should pray. He said the most staggering thing he had ever learned is that the eternal God—who is Father, Son, and Holy Spirit—has invited each of us to enter into conversation with that exclusive group. We are not called to work *for* him but *with* him. There is nothing redemptive in us. Only as God is present in us and works through us can our work count eternally. People are never individually autonomous. They come *from*, live *in*, and exist *for* and *through* others. However, sin disrupts the conversation. Most of our prayers are intended to serve ourselves. God wants us to bear the burdens of others as Jesus did.

Index

Scripture References

Genesis
  1:1–4 146
  1:3 140
  1:26 94
  3:7 82
  3:16–17 82
  6:2 110
  6:4 110
  16:7–11 139
  16:13 139
  17:1 74
  21:17 139, 149
  22:11–15 139
  31:13 139

Exodus
  3:2 139, 149
  3:14 141
  3:21–23 25
  4:22 110, 112, 144
  4:23 144
  14:19 139
  19:6 112
  20:1 140
  34:1 140

Leviticus
  12:1–15:32 90
  18:1–19:37 90

Numbers
  23:19 126

Deuteronomy
  4:10 140
  6:4 26, 132

Judges
  2:1–4 149
  6:20 139

1 Samuel
  13 111
  29:9 139

2 Samuel
  7:12–16 111
  7:14 26
  14:17–20 139

Job
  1:6 110
  2:1 110
  16:21 125
  38:7 110

Psalms
  2:7 76, 113
  8:4 125
  19:1–4 147
  29:1 110
  89:7 110
  89:26–27 26
  89:27 144
  102:5 135
  123:1–2 27

Proverbs
  8:22 141

HOLY LOVE: A WESLEYAN THEOLOGY

Topics/Persons

A

B

Bettenson, Henry Scowcraft 52, 170

Boethius 234

Bonaventure 20, 236

Borg, Marcus 47

Bornkamm, Günther 122

Bousset, Wilhelm 176, 180

Bouyer, Louis 55

Braumann, Georg 112

Brown, Delwin 159

Brown, Raymond 60

Bruce, F. F. 130

Brummer, Vincent 19

Bultmann, Rudolph 132, 143, 224

C

Calvin, John 237

Campbell, J. Macleod 91

Carter, Craig A. 18

Chalcedon Creed 165, 175, 185, 192, 194, 209, 212–213, 216–228, 229, 235, 237

Christian year 50, 54, 73, 84

christotokos 214

Chrysostom 83, 87, 89, 145

circumcision 70, 74, 77

Clement of Alexandria 54, 169, 186

Cochrane, Charles 166

consensual 42, 46, 59, 62, 109, 134, 139, 152, 162, 185, 189, 192, 219

consubstantial 208, 217, 221, 231

Coppedge, Allan 12, 109

Council of Ephesus 214

creation 24, 29, 39, 43, 56, 59, 62, 64, 66, 68, 78, 80, 83, 87, 89, 92–94, 98, 115, 121, 127, 134, 141, 144–146, 148, 152, 158, 162, 175, 177–182, 185, 188, 193, 195, 201, 204, 233

Cullmann, Oscar 108, 126, 131, 135, 149

Cyril of Alexandria 213, 236

Cyril of Jerusalem 54

D

demythologize 46

descent of Christ 38, 40, 54, 78, 93, 96, 99, 108, 124, 129, 131, 148, 153, 182, 200

Didache, The 53, 67, 100, 102

Dix, Gregory 54, 162

Docetism 62, 78, 94, 167, 169, 178, 215

Dodd, C. H. 143

dogmatic theology 47

dualism 48, 59, 62, 93, 158, 166, 169, 171, 194, 197, 202, 215

Dunn, James D. G. 151

E

Ebionites 168, 240

Eckman, Edward 136

Edict of Milan 192

Eichrodt, Walther 140

Enlightenment 47, 72, 239

Epistle of Barnabas 170

essence 15, 21, 28, 39, 52, 54, 63, 71, 84, 90, 99, 101, 103, 110, 114, 116, 117, 119, 134, 139, 142, 143, 152, 158, 160, 173, 175, 193, 195, 196, 200, 205,